CLIVEDEN

The Preservation Press— 1976
National Trust for Historic Preservation
740-748 Jackson Place, N.W.
Washington, D. C. 20006

ISBN 0-89133-049-6

Cliveden, reprinted by The Preservation Press, was first published in 1903 by the Lothrop Publishing Company, Boston.

The National Trust for Historic Preservation, chartered by Congress in 1949, is the only private, nonprofit, educational organization with the responsibility to encourage public participation in the preservation of sites, buildings and objects significant in American history and culture. Support is provided by membership dues, endowment funds, contributions and matching grants from federal agencies, including the U. S. Department of the Interior, National Park Service, under provisions of the National Historic Preservation Act of 1966. Cliveden, a property of the National Trust, is located at 6401 Germantown Avenue, Philadelphia, Pa. Visitors are welcome daily (except Christmas) from 10 a.m. until 4 p.m.

Cover: Cliveden in the 1777 Battle of Germantown. The painting by E. L. Henry (1841-1919) hangs in the entrance hall.

INTRODUCTION

In the early years of this century the story of the Battle of Germantown inspired Frances Louise Howland to write the novel *Cliveden,* published in 1903 under the pseudonym Kenyon West. *Cliveden* is the fictional account, based on historical fact, of what happened during the battle to the inhabitants of the stately Germantown country house built between 1763 and 1767 for Benjamin Chew, a distinguished Philadelphia lawyer and political leader.

In the novel, the Chew family becomes the "mythical Murrays," residents of Cliveden during its use as a stronghold by the British to ward off the advancing Americans. In fact, no member of the Chew family was living at Cliveden at the time of the battle; all were in Philadelphia except for Justice Chew who was being held under house arrest in Union Forge, N.J., because of his refusal to sign the American loyalty oath. There is no evidence that anyone was living in the house during the battle.

Kenyon West takes other liberties with historical and physical fact in the novel. For example, no tunnel or secret passageway has been found on the property. In addition, archaeological and documentary evidence to date do not substantiate existence of a lake at Cliveden in the 18th century.

By the fall of 1777 the British were in possession of Philadelphia and neighboring Germantown. By October, however, the American army had been reinforced and General George Washington planned an attack at Germantown. The Marquis de Chastellux, a French military observer, pieced together various accounts by participants in the Battle of Germantown; in 1780 he described it this way:

"General Washington . . . left his camp towards midnight [of October 3rd], marching in two columns, one of which was to turn Germantown on the eastward, the other on the west: two brigades of the right column were ordered to form the *corps de reserve,* to separate themselves from the column . . . and follow the main street of Germantown. A very thick fog came on. . . . While everything thus succeeded on the right, General Washington, at the head of the reserve, was expecting to see his left column arrive, and pursued his march through the main street. But a fire of musketry, which proceeded from a large house within pistol shot of the street, suddenly checked the van of his troops. It was resolved to attack this house [Cliveden]; but cannon were necessary, for it was known to be of stone, and could not therefore be set on fire. Unfortunately they had only six-pounders . . . this cannonade produced to effect; it penetrated the walls, but did not demolish them. The Chevalier de Mauduit . . . proposed . . . to get from a nearby barn some straw and hay which they would pile against the front door and set afire. . . . By this time the enemy began to rally . . . Cornwallis was coming with all haste from Philadelphia . . . the American army was losing their time at the stone house. . . . The contest had become too unequal; it became necessary to think of retreat. . . . General Washington retired to an excellent position four miles from Germantown. . . ."

Although Justice Chew pronounced his house "an absolute wreck" after the battle, the two-and-one-half story rectangular stone structure managed to survive the clash between British and colonial forces. Actually, young Benjamin Chew reported to his father after the battle that accounts of the damage were exaggerated; this must have been true because the house was in good enough condition to be rented out in the summer of 1778. Evidently the fighting in the Battle of Germantown was not as dramatic as it appears in E. L. Henry's 1880 painting (shown on the cover of this book) which was influenced by the changed conditions of warfare following the Revolution. Fighting during the Battle of Germantown consisted mostly of small arms fire and the use of cannons; although cannonballs were found inside Cliveden they were of a nonexploding type and caused only minor damage. However, damage to the plaster walls is still visible today at Cliveden, as are two muskets used in the battle.

The house was refurbished after the war and, except for a period of 18 years in the late 18th century, served continuously as the country house of the Chew family for almost 200 years. In June 1972, Cliveden, one of the last surviving examples of domestic architecture in Philadelphia from the late-colonial period, became a property of the National Trust for Historic Preservation. The Trust continues to maintain the house, grounds and furnishings, which represent an important collection of American decorative and fine art. Furniture, books, costumes, porcelain, paintings and prints in the house were acquired by succeeding generations of Chews who saved the family objects over the decades.

CLIVEDEN

BY

KENYON
WEST

LOTHROP PUBLISHING COMPANY
BOSTON

PREFATORY NOTE

*I*F any one expects to find in this book anything but an "action-tale," he will be disappointed. Psychological analyses, extensive descriptions, are purposely avoided. An attempt is made to catch the atmosphere of the time, and to present history accurately. But the characters reveal themselves by what they say and do; and it is not believable that the people in the every-day life of 1777 and 1778 talked in epigrams and raved about their souls any more than they do now.

The story opens two days before the battle of Germantown. The battle of the Brandywine has been fought, and the British under Cornwallis are in possession of Philadelphia.

The army of Sir William Howe occupies Germantown. Washington is not many miles away, waiting for a chance to fall upon Howe. This chance comes when he learns by means of intercepted letters of Howe's to his brother, the Admiral, that the camp at Germantown has been weakened by the withdrawal of many troops. He therefore decides to move his army and surprise the enemy.

"Germantown of that time consisted of the single street, built for a space of about two miles with houses of stone, set close to the highway, from which the farm fences, orchards, and enclosures extended

v

*back a considerable distance on each side. In an
open space in the centre was the Market House.
From the head of the village, one mile from the
Market House, the street continued northward
through Beggarstown to Mount Airy, a mile distant, and thence another mile to Chestnut Hill. . . .
On the west of the village the land rolled away to
the high bluffs of the Wissahickon near its con-
fluence with the Schuylkill; while the ground on
the east, intersected by the Wingohocken and other
remote tributaries of the Delaware was also well
disposed for defence. Howe's army was encamped
upon the general line of School House and Church
Lanes, crossing the town at its centre."*

*Between the village and Mount Airy was Clive-
den, the summer home of Benjamin Chew. It stood
back from the village street — the famous " Germantown Road " — in the midst of extensive
grounds. The British retreated past this house, and
six companies under Colonel Musgrave threw themselves into the house, barred doors and windows,
and defied the pursuing Americans. They shot
dead from the upper windows a young Virginian
who bore a flag of truce from the besiegers. The
making of this strong, stone house into an impregnable fort contributed as much to the loss of
the battle of Germantown as the mist and the fog
that frustrated Washington's daring plans.*

*Cliveden is of much interest to the tourist, the
broken statuary still adorns the beautiful grounds.
In the big hall are many traces of the destructive
work of cannon and bullets; the front doors, all
riddled with musket-balls, are still shown to visitors
fortunate enough to be admitted. The servants of*

*the house even fancy they see upon the walls phantom
soldiers, with outstretched hands. The spacious
stairway up and down which the soldiers rushed is
peopled with ghosts of the past.*

*It is hoped that the descendants of the illustrious
Chews will have patience with the mythical Murrays
who were inside this memorable house at the time
of the great battle, and endured the excitement and
stress of the conflict.*

New York, January, 1903.

CLIVEDEN

CLIVEDEN

CHAPTER I.

" Here's to the success of what is righteous, and holy, and just."

ON that unforgettable October morning, when Margaret Murray threw back the heavy bars from across the shutters of her window, little did she dream that two days later the beautiful garden would be desolate: the shrubbery and trees torn and bruised; the statuary broken; the fences and gates in ruins; — the dead and dying of both armies strewing the trampled, blood-stained lawn and paths.

Nor did she dream of the important part she herself was to play in the tragic drama of the fourth of October, seventeen hundred and seventy-seven.

Beyond the garden gate was the Main Road in broad sunlight, lost in the distance towards Chestnut Hill. Somewhere beyond that hill was the camp of Washington, the beloved leader.

Across the road, in a large field, Margaret could see the white tents and rough huts of the Fortieth Regiment of British. Further up the road, on a height, was the Second Battalion of Light Infantry, with pickets stationed as far as Mount Airy. The fences between had been used to make rude huts, covered with the grain from the fields or with the turf bordering the highway. The peacefulness, the charm of the roads were gone. There was commotion, tumult, disorder everywhere. From the distant Schuylkill on the west to the Market Square of the village, then running to the Old York Road, Margaret knew that the army of General Howe extended its camp — he himself stationed far down off the Main Road at Stenton, the Logan homestead.

"That our quiet village should have come to this!" Margaret thought, bitterly. "A refuge for these haughty British, and the city, too, given over to them!"

For days, it had seemed to Margaret that she had seen naught but red. That flashing colour was continually before her eyes. It had spoiled the beauty of the sky, changed the look of the glad, green earth. Here, at Cliveden, there had been British everywhere: in the gardens, in the vine-covered summer-house, in the kitchens and stables. The big front doors of the mansion stood open to receive them; in deference to Benjamin Chew many of these British had been entertained with lavish hospitality. Even now, as she looked from her window, Margaret could see two horsemen passing the front gate. No need to wonder if they were friend or foe: the flashing red betrayed them.

Friend or foe? How could she, in good truth, look upon these British as foes except in relation to the political interests of her native land? She had won friends in England. Even now there were hearts there beating with love for her. The gracious years spent in travelling in Europe with her brother had been enriched by many beautiful experiences, and the most beautiful of these experiences had come to her in England. Her whole soul had thrilled in welcome to the mother-land. It did not seem strange or foreign. The best that had been hers in America seemed a part of that which was best and fairest in this old England. There was a comforting sense of companionship, of kinship. It seemed as if she had been there before. It seemed as if there were scope for memory.

And yet it was not in Margaret Murray's nature to be blind to the wrongs of America. She could not welcome with joy the sight of troops in martial array, and looked with rueful eye upon Patriotism in Rags. Patriotism in Rags appealed to her imagination, touched her quick sympathies. She had been in Philadelphia when the American army, with Washington and Lafayette at its head, had marched through the streets, — the army with its motley uniforms, its pathetic striving to appear symmetrical, with sprigs of green in the men's hats. Her soul had thrilled to the sight of these brave men in warfare against a foe so formidable.

When Margaret's ear first caught the sound of the cannonading at the Brandywine, she had hoped for great things: a victory to rival the victories of Trenton and of Princeton. But as the hours passed, suspense grew almost unbearable. Bidding Jake saddle Selim in haste, she had ridden to the Market Square of Germantown, to get, perchance, some advance news. But no courier had come. The square was thronged with eager villagers, and here and there, at a tavern door, excited groups of farmers. On the result of the battle, they all knew, depended the fate of Philadelphia. In a frenzy of unrest, Margaret rode further — on — on. The roads were found to be filled with wagons, horses, men and women and children on foot. They were fleeing from the city.

Then she came to a quiet, peaceful place on the Wissahickon. The trees cast cool, refreshing shadows; the brook flowed caressingly over white, smooth pebbles; the birds were singing, the air was soft and flower-perfumed. The world seemed a joyous place, — full of light and warmth and beauty.

How could the birds sing, the sun shine, when brave men, not far away, were fighting and dying?

She reached the garden gate as a courier flung himself from his smoking horse. The news he brought spread consternation through the village, — consternation which spread quickly to the anxious, waiting city.

CHAPTER II.

"How beautiful it will be to see him again. The mere look of his calm eyes strengthens my heart."

TWO hours after that a coach had been driven hastily along Third Street. Arrived at Walnut Street, it had had scant opportunity because of the press of excited people, horses, and heavily loaded wagons; but finally it had taken its way along Front Street and come to the Germantown Road. 'Twas to prove a tedious journey: the road was cut up badly; the mud was deep, and there were vicious holes to harass coachman and horses. At the tavern of the Rising Sun, where the Old York Road runs into the Germantown Highway, there had been a long delay. The tavern was thronged with eager, anxious farmers, and a change of horses had been effected with some difficulty; but in due time the coach had reached the Market Square of Germantown, then toiled slowly up the street till it had turned into the grounds of Cliveden. It had been Margaret herself who had welcomed her brother and his wife at the portico of the big house.

"O Henry! O Annette! 'Tis glad I am, glad!"

"Of a truth I see no cause for flight, even if the Whigs are leaving the city," Henry Murray had answered, smiling, "but I feel that 'twere best not wholly to be cut off from communication with the patriot army."

"Yes," Annette had added, as she noted the anxious inquiry in Margaret's eyes. "'Tis the general opinion that Howe and Cornwallis will soon be in the city."

"In that case, then the village, too, will fall into their hands."

"Perchance not," Henry had said. "The British will probably march from the south, and the patriot army is expected here any moment. We are nearer Washington than if we had remained in the city."

"And we can return home any time we choose."

"I fear me, Annette, that would scarce be possible. Our home on Third Street will prove most attractive to the enemy."

"What mean you, Henry?"

"There, there, dear! Look not so troubled. 'Twill like be seized by British officers who will make it their headquarters. We would have scant comfort there."

'Twas of this arrival of her brother from the city and of all the events that had crowded themselves together since, that Margaret Murray was thinking, as she stood by her window this morning of October the second. Her thoughts were vivid with both anticipation and memory. How long ago the first of June seemed; and yet that was the day on which she and her father had come to live at Cliveden. "'Twould scarce be possible to describe to you my love for this beautiful place," she had written to her friend, Lady Susan Strangways. "In England I had seen many a fine country-seat, but never any that seems so to touch my heart as this summer home of Mr. Benjamin Chew. Smile, dear Susan, smile as much as it pleasures you, but of a truth 'tis so. For the first time in many years I seem to be *at home*. When I parted from you in London, my soul was on fire with a passionate longing for my native land, and yet I scarce knew where my home would be. Ever since my childhood spent in dear old Virginia, where my mother lived and died, we have been more or less wanderers. As you know, my father had been a dashing colonel in the Virginia army, concerned in many a perilous campaign. Then he and George Washington, his close friend, were both chosen members of General Braddock's staff. They were with that unfortunate general in his disastrous expedition through the wilderness; together they were at The Great Meadows when Braddock died. How often my brother Henry and I have thrilled to the stories of those old days — told in the twilight, told to the rhythmic accompaniment of our beating hearts. Then there were tales of wars under Lord Loudon, finally of the engagement with Wolfe before Quebec. Had but our brave fighter not there been so desperately wounded! In truth, I can write that of which I cannot trust myself to speak. My youth was shadowed by the great sorrow of my mother's death, and by the long illness of my father, culminating in the darkness — cruel, relentless, full of terrors and mysteries — which has finally overwhelmed him. He could never fight again, and as the years have passed, and men like him have been sorely needed, no one, except, perchance, myself, has ever known how much it has cost him not to be able to bear a part in the struggle and the stress of the time. . . .

" O Susan! Dear heart, scarce can you conceive of
the conflict of opinion that has been raging so
hotly here. How many questions I have put to
myself and tried to answer — but with little success,
I fear. We are passing through dark days, and the
agitations and perplexities in which we are placed
might daunt the bravest. Full seven years you spent
here in America, and methinks you and your husband, Mr. O'Brien, will have knowledge which will
give you sympathy with the problems and obstacles
that beset our path. Well may your cousin, Mr.
Charles Fox, and others of your friends, be concerned for the state of affairs in America. . . . But
I must keep aloof from politics, dear Susan. . . .

" You will prefer that I tell you how 'tis that I
am living in the house that Benjamin Chew built
for his own use. As you know, he and my father
and Washington were dear friends in Virginia. He
has had a most illustrious career in the law, and
has attained the highest rank. He is held in great
esteem here in Philadelphia. When we first came
to the city we were welcomed with gracious kindness
by the Chews and our many old friends. My
brother, who had lived in the city many years, was
also of much comfort. Through him we soon became familiar with that which is most worthy in
the different manifestations of the life of the town.
Whatever compensation is for my father in his grief
and desolation of spirit, that has, of a truth, been
his. Quakers, members of Christ Church, lawyers,
radical Whigs, and cautious Tories, all seem his
friends. . . .

" You may, perchance, have remembrance of the
beauty of Benjamin Chew's daughters. But I wish

you could see some one yet more beautiful, an that were possible. Some day you will see my brother's wife. They have been but recently married, and their home is not far from Mr. Chew's town house on Third Street, below Walnut. He had met her first at the famous dinner Judge Chew gave to Washington and John Adams three years ago. She was the youngest of all the guests, but her wit, even more than her beauty, delighted and gave charm. ' She truly hath bewitched your brave brother,' whispered Peggy Chew to me. 'Hast noticed how reluctant his eyes leave her, and how gladly they return to her?' I have been told by a young lawyer of the city that he once got a peep at a portion of Mr. Adams's diary. In it Mr. Adams recorded his admiration of Benjamin Chew's house, the elegance of the furniture, the ' dinner that ran from turtle to flummery, to sweetmeats and trifles.' ' I drank Madeira at a great rate,' he said, ' and found no inconvenience in it.' In truth, Susan, I have no memory of this. But the Madeira must have made him forgetful of the sensation caused by the host's daughters, and the wit of their young friend, Anne Gloucester (Annette, as Henry calls her), for strange to say, Mr. John Adams made no mention of this in his diary. . . .

"O Susan, this letter is swelled to great proportions, and if I write much more the packet that is to take it to England may perchance not be able to give it room, and I have not yet told you about Cliveden. In this year of grace, 1777, the Chews have a wish to spend little time in the country. Mr. Chew has felt reluctant about agreeing to all the rapid political changes that have taken place of late. The Whigs of the town have been, forsooth, too rash for many men who yet are true lovers of liberty. Even my father and my brother have held back in some opinions, and not gone so far as the Binghams and other friends, although they think Mr. Chew has not gone far enough. Mr. Chew wished to be in town this year; his wife and pleasure-loving daughters seem to prefer the city to the serene and quiet charm of the country, as well as to be with him. He persuaded my father and myself to come to Cliveden. Thus it is that we are here. I have brought my own servants and horses. I am practically the mistress of the beautiful place. I have learned to love every tree and shrub. Methinks I know the exact number of the blades of grass in the garden. Every stone in the big house seems a friend; the roads to the village, to the hills to the north, over which I gallop daily have grown familiar and dear. And the village! It hath a charm I could ne'er put into words. These Germans, I shall love them well. They are so simple and so sincere. There are quaint folk everywhere. There is romance, charm, interest, in the whole country roundabout. Many of our friends have their country homes here. We shall not be lonely. There are regions on the Wissahickon which I have yet to explore. A hundred years ago there dwelt there Johannes Kelpius and sundry other pious hermits. Perchance his spirit is hovering there. I must find his cave ere I die. I have two trusty grooms who bear me companionship in my rides. Ah! you remember my Jake whom I brought from Virginia. I know not how I could live without him. . . . I will write you of my discoveries as occasion may serve. . . .

"I open this packet to add that a dire misfortune has befallen our friend, Mr. Chew. He has incurred the suspicion of the Congress. He with Mr. John Penn and sundry others were arrested. Only yesterday Mr. Chew was forced to betake himself to Virginia. I know not when he will be allowed to return. I am writing under date of August the seventeenth. Your General Howe is drawing nearer. His fleet sailed from New York towards the end of July. Our General Washington's army has been encamped in Germantown, but has again departed. We know not what our future is to be. Heaven spare this quiet, beautiful village from the desolations and the griefs of war."

This letter had been written before the British general had brought the war so close, so ominously close. On the twenty-fifth of August he began to land his troops, and early in September started on his march toward the Brandywine. On the eleventh came the fateful battle.

After the battle at the Brandywine one great joy had been Margaret Murray's, — Washington had been in her home. His army had come to Germantown for a brief rest; and when the night fell, he and Alexander Hamilton, with a small escort, had ridden out to Cliveden. It was with peculiar intensity of feeling that the General and his old friend met on this memorable night of September the twelfth. The time was rich in counsel, in reminiscence, in eager looking forward. The General, Charles Murray, Alexander Hamilton, and Margaret, Henry, and Annette, had talked together by the big fire till the reluctant dawn. Dinah and Chloe had cooked marvellous things; Jake and Tom and Sam had shown lavish hospitality to the warriors' noble steeds.

Ah! it had been a memorable night! Would such a night ever come again?

CHAPTER III.

"A damned rebel fox got possession of some letters of Sir William Howe's to his brother the admiral."

HENRY MURRAY was ever on the watch to be of some service to the patriot cause. He had no thought of making this service secret, no thought nor wish to be a spy. His political opinions were well known by his friends. But these British encamped in and about Germantown knew naught of him. He might be a Tory for all they cared; or if a patriot, it mattered little. He was safe within their lines and could do no harm.

But circumstances were shaping themselves this fateful morning of October the second which were to be of great significance to Henry Murray and all his friends. An opportunity to serve the cause so dear showed itself. It brought with it great peril; but the blood of the intrepid Murrays as well as of the peace-loving Trents flowed in his veins.

He had slight wish to mingle with these gay officers that thronged the taverns or had taken possession of many of the deserted country-houses. The sorrow with which he had watched Washington's ragged, weary army depart was too recent. Contrasts appealed to his sympathy as they did to Margaret's. And yet his heart was tender to many of these British, too. The common soldier

23

interested him, the man who was doing his duty straight, who obeyed and asked no questions, who gave up his life with rough heroism or bore his wounds with fortitude. The stragglers of the camp appealed to him: those who lived from hand to mouth; the weary, reckless women, some who had come from across the sea with their Hessian husbands to share with them a compulsory exile without honour — these Hessians who were fighting for a master for whom they had no love.

Thus because camp-life interested him, and because he was too restless to stay quietly at home, he had ridden now for two mornings, to the village or beyond, with no conscious purpose but to observe, to study, to think. He had no plan to make practical use of what he saw.

Yesterday he had gone as far as the Schuylkill, had been stopped by the sentries, and had turned back along School House Lane. The Market Square was thronged, but he slowly rode down the Main Street towards Neglee's Hill. He had nearly reached the long road through the trees that led to the door of Stenton, when he bethought himself that he was right upon the headquarters of General Howe, and it were perchance wise not to venture further. On his way up the street he had seen strange sights. The taverns were full, many of the houses had been turned into hospitals for the wounded, brought in from the Brandywine or the skirmishes that had taken place since. In " Ye Roebuck Inn," in front of which was the gigantic buttonwood-tree, pride of every villager, there were several wounded Continental soldiers. But these prisoners seemed to have the attention of the surgeons, for as he stopped a

moment to look in through an open window, he
saw that a tall surgeon was bending over a rough
litter. There came a time long afterwards when
Henry Murray remembered the shape of this surgeon's shoulders, the somewhat peculiar carriage
of his head. It was one of those things, seen in
a flash, then forgotten, on occasion to spring forth
into the vividness of memory.

He had thrown the bridle on the horse's neck,
ready to dismount, that he might, if possible, obtain
permission to have speech with these poor prisoners,
when the scream of a man in agony rang out in
the clear air. "Only cutting off a poor devil's leg,"
explained a roughly dressed man standing near, as
he noticed Henry's quick start. "Any friends in
there?"

Henry Murray shook his head. Had he known
that this man had followed him for two hours,
waiting for the chance to speak, he might have
honoured him with a brief glance. But he did not
even turn, till the man took hold of the bridle he
had thrown on his horse's neck. "I will hold your
horse, sir," he said, in a loud tone, then added, in a
faint whisper, "Read this when you arrive at home,
not before. 'Tis possible we may be watched."
Henry Murray had enough quick wit not to show
surprise. He reached forward for the bridle, taking
hold at the same time of a small piece of paper which
the man had held concealed.

The next moment he was riding up to Church
Lane. Then he turned to the right, till he came
to the green banks of the Wingohocken. Here he
got free from the crowds of soldiers, the huts and
tents, for he struck directly north across the fields.

Then on through the dim and restful woods till he came to the orchards and farm-lands back of Cliveden. He rode around the " pond," past the summer-house, then through the rear gate to the stables.

He had thought he had grown old enough to have outgrown curiosity; but in truth he felt in a fever of impatience to be alone at home to read the paper that had come to him so suddenly and without warning. He might have read it in the woods, but he was too well trained not to obey the writer's command to wait.

The words were few:

"I knew you were at Cliveden, but I have not tried to see you, for I have felt it best not to mix you up in this. But to-day I feel strongly in need of companionship. I am weak and childish, you may think. I know not, but an illness may be upon me to make me so forget myself. And 'tis possible that I may repent myself too late. Henry — dear old friend — can you come to-morrow morning early to the Wissahickon Bluffs, somewhere between the cross-road leading from Mount Airy and the point where the Wissahickon flows into the Schuylkill? Follow the windings of the creek till you meet me, or receive from me some signal. I shall be where we can be secure from observation. You will see me ere you reach the redoubt near the old mill where the Hessians are so thick."

The paper was not signed. Henry Murray crushed it in his hand. His face grew grave and thoughtful. Then following the habit that had governed him for years, he went in search of his sister.

" The garden seems a part of my dreams of what

the fairies fashioned to console us poor mortals for the ugliness we have created for ourselves," Margaret had written Lady Susan Strangways. " There are long paths, moss-grown, leading underneath overhanging trees which must be remainders from the primeval forests. . . . I come upon unexpected places that cause my heart to leap. They make me pause to wish that all poor mortals might forget the stir and strife, the turmoil and unrest, the griefs and desolations of life — they are so calm, so filled with serene peace, they are such balm to the tired spirit."

It was in one of these " places " that Henry Murray had found her after an hour's hurried search.

In the rear of the house there was a gate from the garden which opened out upon a path nearly a quarter of a mile long which led past the summer-house down to an apple-orchard. The ground rose here to a hill, then sloped down again to a large lake. The Chews called it " the pond," but people of sound discrimination followed Annette's example and called it by the dignified name of lake. Beyond the lake was a beautiful woodland; meadows and fields to the right, with farm buildings scattered here and there.

Henry Murray thought he might find Margaret in the summer-house. But this was rather Annette's favourite retreat.

Margaret had gone further. The lake was dark and beautiful because of the huge trees that grew close to its borders and cast shadows from the thickly leaved branches. An Indian canoe had been tied to one of these trees. Margaret had got in and gently pushed off. It had taken her not long to paddle across to the woodland side. There was a sheltered nook here which she loved — green and fragrant, at the foot of a tree, dark and soft with moss. She sat down and wondered if in all the world there was a lovelier or more quiet place. Nothing broke the stillness around her but the low hum of insects or the rustle of the leaves that were like footfalls; though in the distance she could hear the farm-work going on. . . . She heard the hoofs of her brother's horse as he rode around the drive which skirted the lake, and took his way past the summer-house up to the rear garden gate. But she knew that no one could see or hear her in her sheltered retreat — and her mood was to be alone.

All at once she raised herself on her elbow and listened. The sound of a sob, or what seemed like a sob, came from a thicket not far away. What was it? Where was it? Who was there?

When Henry Murray found his sister an hour after that she was not alone. A young girl was seated on the moss beside her, Margaret's arm thrown across her shoulders; a violin lay on her lap.

Margaret followed her brother down to the water's edge. Then she spoke in a low tone.

" I was here alone when I heard sobbing. Searching among the bushes I came upon this young girl, lying face downward on the moss, that old violin beside her. My anxious questions won at first slight response. She was agitated and trembling, dazed with grief and terror. 'Twas difficult to understand her or to make her understand. But finally, more by intuition than aught else, I learned

that her father, a Hessian soldier, has this morning
died of his wounds. Her heart had been broken
at the thought of his coming to this terrible America
without her. They had only each other in all the
world. She sold everything except the precious
violin, and came across the sea with these rough
soldiers. She has tramped weary miles, or been
driven occasionally in rough carts; but she has kept
near her father. . . .

"He fell at the Brandywine. But she has helped
nurse him. The end came this morning. . . . She
is alone in a foreign land. She fled from camp —
away from the lawless soldiers. She knew not
where she was going. Finally she found herself in
the woods — and knew naught else till she heard
me coming to her. . . . Her tale, told in a strange
blending of broken English and incoherent German,
has touched my heart, Henry. She is a mere child.
She knows not what will be her future. . . . Would
she come to live with me? Ah! would she not!
But she must have with her the beloved violin. She
could work. Yes, she could work, and she showed
me her delicate hands. She could dig and spade,
as the women did in Germany, only she could not
play so well. The music was not so lovely. The
notes were harsh. . . . Henry, she cannot be left
to the perils of a lawless camp. She must be saved;
and if she plays well, Annette may of a truth find
comfort in this music."

If she played well! They were all to find out
that night when they heard the strings sigh and
sob under the girl's magic fingers. Once or twice
it seemed to Margaret as if she could not bear this

wondrous music.   It went down too deep into her heart.

On the morning of October the second, Henry Murray rose before daybreak.   " I know not when I shall return," he whispered softly to Annette.   " I will go out quietly and saddle for myself and not rouse Jake.   The earlier I get to the Wissahickon, the better."

" Take neither Selim nor Tempest, Henry.   Of a truth, Tempest would give you scant comfort. He fumes at the unwonted noises roundabout; and Selim, Margaret tells me, she wishes to keep ready for herself should occasion serve.   O Henry! Go not away so early.   Some misfortune may sure befall.   I like not to have you go — "

And the merry, vivacious face looked drawn and anxious.   But he quieted her.   " Of a truth I am too desperate and restless, dear, to wait longer. Margaret and I are alike in that naught but a gallop will satisfy us at certain times."

Annette smiled softly through her tears.   " What I love best is to go through the rear garden to the summer-house."

" There to read all the names of the distinguished visitors who have honoured Cliveden, whose names are writ on the inside."

" Yes, and to meditate getting writ there the names of General Howe, of my Lord Cornwallis, of General Grey, and Agnew, and Colonel Bird."

" And what of Sir Thomas Musgrave, who is camped yonder ? "

And Henry Murray pointed in the direction of

the encampment of the Fortieth Regiment. Annette laughed. " We must have his name, too."

Jake was still in his quarters when Henry Murray got out his horse and rode down the avenue to the front gate which opened on to the Germantown Road. The first faint flush of the dawn was coming in the sky to the east. The road seemed quiet and peaceful, though there were faint sounds coming from the encampment where the soldiers of the Fortieth were stationed. He could see two or three men stumbling sleepily out of their tents and huts. Then suddenly a bugle sounded in the distance. It would not be long before the whole encampment would be astir.

Henry Murray galloped up through Beggarstown till he came near the pickets at Mount Airy. Then he turned into the cross-road that ran westward. He soon struck a lane that led him to the Wissahickon. He saw here how easy it would be for any one who knew the paths through the woods, around the bluffs, through the thick tangle of bushes and shrubs, to elude pursuit, get on the other side of the Wissahickon, then strike swiftly across country. It was all strange to him; but he trusted that he soon would be enabled to find the trysting-place and meet his friend in safety.

And this unexpected summons had stirred the spirit of adventure that had been slumbering within him. He someway felt a wild longing to bear an active part in the great struggle. He almost envied the men who felt free to go and fight. And yet, had Henry Murray only realised the value of the aid he had been enabled to render the patriot cause by remaining the " mere money-maker," as he some-

what contemptuously termed it, his modest soul
might have received encouragement.

By this time the sun was already climbing up
the eastern sky. What a perfect day it was to be!
How beautiful this rugged, picturesque region of the
Wissahickon! Henry Murray's heart swelled within
him. He had turned his horse to ford the creek
at a shallow spot when his ear caught the sound of
a footstep on the soft pine-needles on the opposite
bank. He looked up. A man in quaint garb was
standing there. His broad hat shaded his face,
and Murray thought him to be a stranger; but he
waved his hand in somewhat friendlier fashion than
a stranger would affect.

"Come across as quick as you can. In good truth
I am dying to see you."

The familiar voice was not in harmony with the
strange, quaint garb. Murray smiled, and yet he
felt a good measure of surprise.

"Make haste, now, make haste. Push your horse
in. Egad! the beast has naught to fear."

The horse stepped daintily into the stream, rip-
pling the clear water and scattering in fright the
shoals of little fish. Arrived on the other bank,
Murray sprang from the saddle. The stranger
threw aside his hat. The two men grasped hands
and looked into each other's eyes. Though the
stranger was smiling, his eyes were full of tears,
and Murray himself could not speak for a moment.

"Of a truth, but for your voice I would never
have known you. What mean you by this disguise?"

"I am the hermit of the Wissahickon," the other
answered, laughingly. Then he assumed an ex-

pression solemn and grave. " Hast heard of Kelpius? He lived in truth nearly a hundred years
ago, but his spirit hath entered into mine. I dwell
not in his hermitage nor in his tabernacle of logs,
but my place of asylum is a cave. When you have
children of your own, Murray, you can make them
good by telling them I shall of a surety come and
carry them off to my cave, unless they are obe-
dient — "

" What in the heavens mean you? " exclaimed
Murray, interrupting the rapid flow of words.

The other's voice lowered itself involuntarily,
though they were entirely alone. " I mean that the
well-known patriot, Rodney Bingham, left Philadelphia the day the British arrived. He would have
had short shrift had he stayed to welcome them.
He was supposed to have gone with the Congress
to Lancaster, and letters written by him have been
actually sent from that town to friends in Philadelphia. But no one suspects that these letters were
written long before — and that a faithful sister sees
that they are despatched at the proper intervals. This
rascal Bingham, who has the effrontery to seek to
deceive these British, went to his country-seat one
dark night, and came forth from it in garb different
from that in which he entered. He was another
man, not only in garb, but in speech, in expression
of face, in gesture, in walk. For he had been a
worldly dog in Philadelphia, and in spite of Quaker
protests had oft entertained his friends at the old
Southwark Theatre by playing different parts.
'Twas not difficult for him to assume a part now,
in the hope that his country might be served. But
come, Murray, let us sit on those rocks in the shade

of those trees. Your horse can graze at will. There is no one near. There is no one within half a mile. 'Tis well you came so early. 'Tis a fit place for the telling of secrets, for the devising of plots. . . . Years ago this Bingham had become well acquaint with the Wissahickon. These bluffs, these recesses, these mysterious defiles and caves, had interested and allured him. One day the boy had discovered a cave which ran some distance under a huge mass of rocks, then deflected and took a strange course well-nigh to the river. It had an opening entirely hidden by a dense growth of tangled shrubbery and vegetation. This opening came in the rear of a cut-throat inn which fronts on the Ridge Road, not far from School House Lane. The entrance to the cave is now within the British lines — the opening some distance beyond them. If the British stay here long enough, Murray, I shall yet have chance to show to Washington this mysterious way by which he could surprise the enemy's camp."

The speaker's eyes were bright with excitement.

"I feel sure, Murray, that the keepers of that inn know naught of this mysterious cave, or if they do, they know not how far it extends, nor of the entrance to it. From boyhood it had been a beautiful mystery to Bingham, a secret which he shared with no one, not even with a friend so dear as you."

He reached over and touched Murray's hand caressingly.

"Even now I shall not tell you where this cave is situate. Bingham prefers to share this dangerous secret with no one. But during the past week he has made good use of that cave. Were he noticed, it would not matter, for he has given out in the taverns that 'tis his whim to be a hermit, — an occupation not unknown in this region, where folk quaint and curious are abundant; and memories of Johannes Kelpius and other pious hermits of the past are cherished with reverence. So, Bingham is now a hermit, but he emerges from his retreat to go to the village for food. When he is in the village he uses his eyes, he notes what Sir William Howe is doing, how the troops are stationed, how entrenched. He returns to his cave and spends hours drawing a most beautiful map. He leaves the cave one day — he is outside of the British lines. He wanders far, over rocks and rough places. He gets tired, but he walks on, till at last he reaches Washington's camp. The General is glad to get that map, for it tells him what he knew not before."

The voice sank to a whisper. Even in that quiet, sheltered spot, 'twas best, 'twas wisest to speak with hushed breath. "And now, Murray, I must tell you why I made myself known to you. 'Tis as I said — I am getting fearsome, childish. I have been alone for a full week, and for a temperament such as mine, you know well it has been torture. You know not the comfort of my having speech with you. Besides — "

Bingham's face flushed. "Besides, Murray, my money is all gone, and I am just now away from the supplies."

Murray's hand flew to his belt.

"I must have a horse. My feet are swollen from this constant tramping, and may fail me when most required."

"Say no more, no more," cried Murray. "Here,

here. I will bring you more to-morrow, and were this horse not a favourite of my sister's I would leave him here with you. Stay! You can come to Cliveden to-night — in the night, I will have a horse tied outside the stables, waiting for you to take. You will be there? "

" Ay — I will. And thank you. Pray Heaven the horse be not seized by these beggarly British. They are pressing all the horses they can find on the country-side."

" Rodney, this is too perilous, too lonely an enterprise for you. Give it up. Go to Washington. Enlist in the army. There is much need of brave men like you."

Bingham shook his head. " I spoke to the General about it, and to Alexander Hamilton. They are most anxious that a man be here within these lines, and with chance to find out the movements of the enemy that are in the city. Should the enemy move, I am to take intelligence at once, at once — that Washington may fall on his rear. No, my place is here, Murray, God help me."

" You are sure, quite sure, that you are not known in the village? "

" Quite sure, Henry. Not since my boyhood have I been in Germantown. I was too busy with my studies and my gaieties and my travels to have time to visit this quaint, humdrum place. Be not anxious, Henry. Methinks I am taking needful precautions."

An hour longer the two friends talked, and when the time came to separate, Bingham said over and over that the comfort of the talk had been like wine to him. He was made over; renewed in body and in spirit; braced to endure, to work, to hope, to plan; ready for any desperate venture; strong, full of courage.

Back the way he had come Henry Murray slowly rode. At first he had mind that when he arrived at Cliveden he would enter the grounds and ride no more that day. But a strange influence came to him suddenly. It swayed him irresistibly. He suddenly felt that he must go on into the village. Whither this strange impulse would lead him, he knew not, but into the village he must ride.

His horse was clearly of the opinion that Cliveden was a far more satisfying place than the village; and therefore he turned instinctively in at the gate. But he was disappointed when a sudden signal at the bit told him to keep to the highway.

As Henry Murray passed the field opposite the front gate, he little dreamed that two days later there would be Continental cannon planted there to send their deadly balls flying across the street to storm the stone walls of Cliveden.

Early as it was, the tavern just below the Johnson House was already filled with noisy soldiers, the yard in front crowded with horses.

By the Mennonite meeting-house the street was somewhat quiet, though a few idlers were leaning against the wall. Even the old burying-ground seemed not to awe certain audacious trespassers.

The shutters of Doctor Shippen's house were tightly closed. Henry Murray knew it would be useless to knock there, although he had a strong desire to see his friend. The beautiful garden of the Haines House was crowded thick with tents for the wounded. Had he been disposed to look through the open windows he might have seen the surgeons busy.

The Green Tree Tavern was full of memories to Henry Murray. How often he and his friends had come here on their frequent sleigh-rides from the city! Here he had often been with Peggy Chew and Annette Gloucester and Madam Gloucester, her beautiful mother, who had captivated the heart of that stern soldier, General Trescott. And now, that beautiful woman was sleeping beneath a stone in the aisle of Christ Church, and Annette, her daughter, was his own beloved wife.

Between the Haines House and the Green Tree Tavern the street was very crowded. Hastily dismounting, he threw his bridle to a round-faced, blue-eyed villager. As he entered the tavern a number of British officers jostled him rudely as they were coming from the tap-room. To avoid them he stepped into the " parlour," but 'twas scarce comfortable there to a man of his tastes. How changed everything was! Could this be the place where he had once brought his friends from the city? Why had he come? He scarce knew, unless it was in obedience to that strange influence he had been feeling so strongly since he turned into the Main Street from the cross-road of the Wissahickon.

Ah! there in the tap-room was a familiar face, — Tim Johnson, a well-known patriot. Johnson looked pale and anxious, but at sight of Murray through the open door his face brightened. Yet when Murray hastily went through the hall and entered the tap-room, he was met with no sign

of recognition. Johnson simply turned to a serving-man and called loudly for a mug of ale. Murray took his hint. He suddenly felt a strong desire
for the same comforting beverage. He paid no
attention to a tall man who was standing by the
door, his hat drawn well down over his eyes. He
did not note how sharply those eyes were watching
him. Had Johnson known that this man had followed him all the way from Stenton, he might have
shown more care. As it was, he fancied he was
more careful than was at all needful. The ale
disposed of, as all good ale in those merry days
was apt to be, Johnson slowly and carelessly saun-
tered out the door leading to the rear of the
house. The Widow Mackinnet was hanging clothes
upon a line. She returned Johnson's greeting
cordially. He seemed neither an unwelcome nor an
infrequent guest. Out through the same door came
Henry Murray. Neither noticed that the tall man
with the disguising hat had slipped behind the door
as it swung back, and that he stood within earshot.

Johnson thought he had good opportunity now.
" 'Tis glad I am I saw thee, Henry," he whispered
hoarsely, " for my heart was heavy, and I liked
not to send one message by a friend."

Murray looked his question.

" If aught happen to me, let Mary know my last
thought was of her."

" What mean you, man? " Murray whispered
back.

" There are rumours of a movement among the
troops. I have been on the watch all night. Methinks many are soon to withdraw. The camp here

will be much weakened. His Excellency must be informed."

There was a grave pause, then Johnson whispered again: " Howe is busy with his scribes at Stenton. I fancied I was watched, and to avoid suspicion came up here. But I return thither within the half-hour. 'Tis near time for Howe's messenger to leave headquarters with despatches. Perchance 'twill be my fortune to intercept him."

" 'Tis certain death," whispered Murray, gravely. " The press of people is so great, you could not get through."

" In truth, I know the danger. And thou wilt of a surety see Mary? Should I succeed, there may be news of moment to carry to his Excellency."

" Have you a pass through the lines? "

" Nay, but I know a way. This side of Mount Airy, behind the Keyser House, near the tannery, thou knowest the stone wall — there is a rift in the wall. I can get through, then strike across the fields."

Johnson's voice was husky. He felt he had scarce time for picturesque description.

" Yes, yes, I know the place well," returned Murray. " Have you a good horse? "

" Ay — the best."

The man behind the door slipped back into the tap-room. He had heard enough. Murray and Johnson moved aside hurriedly; but Murray gave Johnson a silent handshake, token of his sympathy in his perilous task.

An hour after that, as he was about to mount his horse at the tavern door, he perceived Johnson riding full speed up the village street. Then, to his horror, he heard a quick shot. Johnson reeled in his saddle, then fell headlong.

It took but a moment for Murray to reach his side.

CHAPTER IV.

"We might fare ill were we not to treat these British well."

IN the little room adjoining the big hall — called by Benjamin Chew the schoolroom — a bright fire was burning, and Annette was amusing herself at the spinning-wheel, singing a merry song. The song floated up the spacious stairway to Margaret as she stood there by her window. Annette had a "pretty wit," and oft used it in the turning of a neat rhyme. But soon the merry song changed to one soft and plaintive. And as she sang the song seemed to touch the strings of Margaret's heart in some subtle fashion, and vibrate even after the voice was silent.

"Love were not mine, and it were all unblest, —
Full of doubt and turmoil, and a wild unrest;
Were it not of Heaven, — strong, unchanging, true —
Tender, strong, unchanging: thus my heart loves you.

"Love were mine own, and life were fair and blest,
Could you trust me wholly and be thus at rest;
Think me true and faithful; — strong, unchanging, true —
Tender, strong, unchanging: thus my heart loves you."

As the last note died away into silence, Chloe appeared at the door, her arms full of wood. On the threshold she dropped a stick, and in a frantic

effort to reach it, another fell. Annette looked up
from the wheel and smiled.

"Where go you, Chloe, with that heavy load?"
she asked, kindly.

Chloe smiled radiantly in reply.

"Deed, an' I doan' know, Missus Annette. Jest
whar dese hyar logs wants ter go, I reckon."

"Leave them for Jake, or Tom, or — "

"Dat no use. Dem men ain't wuff nuffin."

Chloe became too earnest in her sarcastic scorn;
her vigilance relaxed. Down came the wood in a
heap at her feet.

"Nay, Chloe, 'tis not well to be thus burdened.
Send Clem for the remainder."

"Clem!" The increase of scorn in Chloe's tone
made Annette look at her with somewhat of surprise.

"Chloe, what has Clem done to make you thus
chary of his presence?"

"He hab gone and done nuffin! — cepp what he
can't help doin'. He's lazy, no 'count, from his
birf, missus, from his birf, but he can't help dat, he
can't, dat's shuh. Now wot you tink he done?"

The wheel revolved more slowly, then stopped.
Annette was honestly interested and amused. Chloe
gathered confidence from her look.

"'Stead o' takin' Massa Murray's brekfus' in to
him, he leff his baid and done gone to steal out to
breebe dis lubly October air, he duz. He done gone
to de cross-roads, shuh 'nuff, to watch de redcoats
pass up an' down an' show demselves off. My! an'
dey do look lubly, not much like Gen'al Washington's sojers, shuh 'nuff. But der insides — Lord!

Missus Annette, pow'ful sight diff'rence dare, shuh
'nuff."

"Difference, indeed!"

"Say, missus, how you feel to hab so many
redcoats comin' 'long four an' five times de day?
An' Massa Murray feed dem all."

"I feel not well over it, Chloe. But it has to
be borne, since the disastrous battle of the Brandywine."

There was a pause, then Annette added:

"Be constrained, good Chloe, to leave some of
that wood on the floor, and come again for it."

"No, I reckon not. Chloe will get it done dis
time."

But Chloe was again unsuccessful.

"Dare! I 'clare to goodness dat Jake done gone
an' put a bewitchment in dis wood."

"Jake?"

"He allays busy wid de horses, shuh 'nuff, he
do make 'em shine, dat's a fac', an' Missy Margaret
she do ride jest splendid. She look pow'ful fine
on Selim or Prince. Doan' she now, honey?" Chloe
was never tired of hearing the praises of her beloved
mistress.

"Yes, Chloe, but how doth Jake bewitch you?"

Chloe gave a significant smile. "Eben if I be
a widder wid a chile like Clem, I 'clare to goodness
dat Jake he a most lubly young man. Missy —
Missus, I mean — you know dat. My arms a-trem-
ble when I tink of him. I tremble an' de wood
fall."

Annette strove to hide her smiles, and said, kindly:
"Now make haste. Here is Mr. Murray."

At that moment a tall, stately man appeared at

the dining-room door. Annette hastened to go to his help, but with a smile he came across the hall to her. But his step was slow. He took hold of each chair on his way.

"Chloe! Open the front doors. 'Tis stifling here."

As Chloe did his bidding, Annette gently put him in an armchair. The doors once open, the beautiful garden was plainly revealed. Charles Murray sighed. That beauty was not for him.

"Has any news come?" he asked, as he listened to Chloe's retreating footsteps.

"Naught, but there have been many unwonted noises coming to us faintly from the village."

"We may expect intrusion to-day."

Annette's face shadowed over. "I like it not," she said, impatiently, "that Henry tarries from us so long. He rode away before daybreak."

"Henry is ever on the watch to be of some service to the Congress or to General Washington. Trust his prudence, girl."

"How close have the armies come together?" Annette asked.

"Not more than two days' march, perchance. Henry is of opinion that Washington is but fourteen miles away — at Pott's Grove, on the Skippack Creek."

"There may be another battle soon?"

"Yes, the General waits but for the chance. Let him but find a weak point in the defence of the British camp yonder, and he will fall upon Howe."

"May he consider well before he strike."

"Hark! What is that? Of a surety Margaret has not ridden forth."

Mr. Murray's quick ear had caught the sound of hoofs. He rose in agitation. Annette hastened to the window.

" No, it appears to be a horseman riding. Ah! he has stopped."

" More attacks upon our larder, I doubt not."

Annette shaded her eyes with her hand. " It pleasures me not that you so oft feed our enemies, and show hospitality to these disturbers of our peace."

Charles Murray threw back his head proudly. " Neither friend nor foe was ever turned away from The Chew House. Besides, we might fare ill were we not to treat these British well. Look! Annette! Tell me what you see."

" The horse is hidden by the shrubbery. Ah! there he is again. No — 'tis another horse. The rider dismounts. He has passed through the gate. He is a right comely and pleasing youth, father. 'Tis well Margaret is not here, for the colour of his coat were not beautiful in her eyes. The other rider remains by the gate."

The next moment, the comely and pleasing youth appeared at the doorway, dusting his uniform. His face lit up when he saw Annette coming to meet him.

" Good-morrow to you, sweet lady! " he said, bowing low.

She swept him a graceful curtsy. " Good-morrow to you."

" Your pardon, I am Lieutenant Shipton, on the staff of Lord Cornwallis, at your service. I have been riding with Captain Peyton across country from the city. We took a road that led us too far up,

and now ere we reach camp something must befall
his mare. He craves permission that he take her
to your stables."

"Certainly, sir. Lead your horse thither. One
of my servants will attend you. Will not Captain
Peyton enter and rest from his long ride from the
city?" Mr. Murray's tone was friendly. The
ready colour flushed the boy's cheeks.

"I thank you, sir, Captain Peyton wishes not
to intrude upon you."

"Of a verity, a most extraordinary captain he
must be," thought Annette.

The young lieutenant looked back into the garden.

"Egad! but you have a pretty place here. In
faith, sir, I have seen naught like it before in
this country."

Annette smiled mischievously. "You have not
travelled far then, methinks."

He smiled in return. "No, mistress. 'Tis but
three short months since I landed from England.
'Twould have been but the flip of a dice whether
I should join Burgoyne or Howe, but my friend
who is in this country on a most important mission wished me to be with him. Methinks I cared
little whether I fought these rebels or not. I wished
to see this new country. Egad, sir!" he added,
turning to Mr. Murray, "yours is a country of sur-
prises."

"You thought to find a nation of boors or Indians or pirates, whereas you find — "

"Gentlemen, sir! Gentlemen!"

There was a light step on the stairs. The youth
turned and saw Margaret. He bowed nearly to
the floor, his hand on his heart. But as she came

down the hall he seemed to feel that her greeting, courteous as it was, had little warmth in it. He turned again to Annette, his honest eyes aglow.

"A soldier, Margaret, who craves assistance for his captain's horse," said Annette, smiling.

The soldier drew himself up proudly.

"Captain, the Honourable Arthur Peyton, lady, at your service, the second son of Lord Castlereagh — cousin of Lord Carlisle, who will soon come to this country as one of the King's commissioners."

"We humble Colonists are truly honoured by visits from men of title in England," said Mr. Murray, with an impatient gesture. Annette looked at Margaret with a whimsical smile. This lieutenant's visit was proving entertainment on this dull morning.

"Far be it from me to give you the impression that my friend thinks of his rank or his estates. He is the goodliest, most modest of men, — the bravest and most honourable."

"Verily, he has a most excellent champion in you, Lieutenant," said Annette.

The Lieutenant continued to Mr. Murray: "But he is a man of moods, sir — a man of moods, I said, sir. Now he loves Brown Bess, but he has ridden so fast and furiously I could scarce keep up with him, and all for naught. No desperate venture in the teeth of the foe, no battle, naught but exercise, exercise. He wot not that Bess was tiring, but when he found it out, was he not contrite!"

Then Margaret spoke. "It were a pity that your beauteous captain, your man of moods, were not in a battle to work off his energy and show some reason for his desperate riding."

" By my troth, sweet lady, you mistake me, if I give you the impression that Captain Peyton is not brave. He has been in battles. He fought at Brandywine — like a — like an Englishman ! "

" Brandywine ! "

" He is even braver than General Grey, who did such fine work on the twentieth of September at Paoli."

" Some of the rebels in these parts call the twentieth of September a massacre, sir," said Charles Murray. " Others say that Anthony Wayne will avenge it when occasion serves."

There was an unquiet pause, then Annette said, laughingly :

" Perchance 'twill not pleasure your captain to be kept waiting."

" Yes," said Mr. Murray. " If Brown Bess needs attention, be so good, sir, as to take her to the stables."

The Lieutenant glanced out the big doorway. " He is standing in the shade of that oak. 'Tis well that so reckless a rider takes a moment's rest. We had a close thing of it but yester-eve. We were chased by Light-Horse Harry Lee."

" Ah ! hast heard of him ? Light-Horse Harry catches many British troops."

" Yes, the devil take him for it."

" Tut, tut ! Beware of how you speak of him should you chance to meet any rebels," said Mr. Murray, smiling.

" I will show you the way to the stables, Lieutenant," said Annette, going towards the dining-room. " Methinks I will take you this way through the corridor to the kitchens — for Jake is probably there. We can enlist his services and then you can go and tell your captain of your success."

Annette, though scarce older than the young lieutenant, felt quite motherly.

" I thank you," he said, fervently. " I must hasten. You are most kind, most kind."

As he passed out into the dining-room, he turned back to bow again to Margaret, but her cold and formal manner gave him the vague feeling that this house, so hospitable and with so much apparent cheer, was scarce the place for him that October morning. But he would enjoy Annette's smiles a few moments before he rode away.

Margaret marvelled afterwards at the happy impulse that led Annette to take him through the corridor to the kitchens, rather than by the more direct course through the narrow passageway with the spiral stairway to the outside door which opened on to the lawn. But why did she not return the way she went?

CHAPTER V.

"Stay behind the panel, until you hear me strike three blows."

MARGARET drew a breath of relief. "Now the air is clearer, father. Oh! I am tired of these British, so tired! Would I might never see one again. . . . That captain fought like an Englishman! How they boast! How insufferable are their arrogance and pride! Oh! the misery of that battle!"

The weariness in her tone touched her father's heart. Then he said, bitterly: "The situation of our house makes us peculiarly exposed to stragglers of both armies, and strolling troopers and chance marauders. Daughter, it is a perilous time for you. Oh! had I but my two eyes again and my strong right arm."

This was an oft-heard wish. And Margaret was always ready to administer comfort.

"Hush, hush! I shall be safe, dear father. The servants are trusty. Why, father, Jake is so strong he could knock down at one blow a man like that little lieutenant — was he?"

"Yes, Lieutenant Shipton, of the staff of Lord Cornwallis, at your service."

Margaret smiled at her father's change of tone.

A shadow darkened the big doorway! She turned

quickly to find herself face to face with a man taller
than Jake, taller even than her father. He was
dressed in brilliant uniform; but strange to say,
she seemed to be unconscious of that. His face,
the nobility of his look, his air of distinction, were
the important things about him. The fact that he
was British was quite forgotten.

"I fear me my friend is trespassing beyond your
patience. Ah! he is not here, as I thought." Captain Peyton looked around hastily. "Your pardon,
will you tell me where he is?"

Charles Murray pointed towards the dining-room.
"He has gone to the stables to get aid for your
Brown Bess."

The Captain's face grew very bright: "Ah! you
know her name already."

"A good name, in sooth!" said Charles Murray.
He could not see the Captain's face, but he could
feel the charm of his voice, and he had the wish
to keep him a moment longer than perchance were
needful. As for Margaret, she stood in silence;
but she was full conscious of the simple directness
of the eyes that were looking at her father. She
saw their kindness, their truth. There was a certain
royalty about this Englishman, a compelling dignity which won her confidence. Then as he turned
to her, she seemed to feel all at once how dear
and sweet a place this earth can be — sweeter and
more beautiful than even she had ever dreamed.

"If you wish to follow your friend, you are
welcome," Mr. Murray added. "The shorter,
quicker way is to go out the doors by which you
entered; get Brown Bess and lead her across the
lawn at the side of the house. The stables are

some distance to the right, half-hidden by the trees, I am told." Mr. Murray smiled half-sadly. " I cannot see them for myself. You will be there even before your friend."

" Thank you, thank you."

The Captain went out the big doorway, and in a moment or two Margaret could see him leading his horse across the lawn.

Near the stairway at the back of the hall there was a door which led out into the rear garden. The corridor to the kitchens was at the left of this garden. Over at the right were the servants' quarters, a large house by itself. This rear door chanced to be open. Margaret started down the hall. " This October air is chill," she said. " Methinks 'twere best to have one of these doors closed." But she was stopped by an excited exclamation from her father.

" Hark! what is that? "

" I hear naught."

" Hoofs — a horseman riding furiously."

" It must be that captain taking his — "

" No! No! 'tis on the highway yonder. Listen, Margaret."

She rushed out on the front portico. " I can see no one, father."

" 'Tis a messenger, perchance, taking the news to Howe's headquarters of some fresh disaster to our army."

" Had a battle occurred, father, we had heard the cannonading, for Washington is not many miles away."

" True, true. What see you? Look! Look! "

" Of a truth, there is naught to see from here,"

she answered, then hurried down the hall to the
rear door. "There is some one, father, there is,"
she called back in a loud whisper. "He must be
some patriot fugitive."

"Look, look, Margaret! Tell me what you see!"

"He has stopped behind those trees. There!
there! He is coming. He is hiding among the
shrubbery, as if afraid of being seen from the
stables. There! he has got beyond, he is near the
kitchens and is running upright! Father! Father!
'Tis — Yes! Yes! Father, 'tis Harry!"

She flung the door wide open, and there were a
few moments of suspense; then Henry Murray entered, breathless, without hat or coat. He closed the
door behind him, and rushed to his father. His
voice was low and husky.

"They are after me. They are tearing up the
road. I have no time to lose. I had not thought
to stop, but my horse stumbled. I climbed the
wall and got behind the shrubbery while they are
plunging on towards the front gate. Quick! Margaret! Take these letters! Hide them in your
gown."

He turned to her and thrust into her outstretched
hand a packet with broken seals.

"They are despatches of Howe's seized by one
of our patriots. I fear me he is dead. . . . If aught
happen to me they must go to Washington. His
camp is somewhere this side of Skippack Creek.
You know the way. I have read the letters, and
if happily I arrive in camp I can tell them to Washington. Of a truth, they be safer with you than
with me. My only hope is the secret panel and
the underground passage to the stables."

Margaret was too wise to waste his time by questions; though she was sorely puzzled. She seized the packet and hid it in her gown. "Yes! Yes! the secret panel!"

"If they come, give me some signal when it will be safe for me to start away. Try to keep my danger from Annette, perchance she need not know I have been here." He looked anxiously at Margaret, and she gave him a reassuring smile.

The spacious staircase at the rear of the hall just beyond the massive pillars turned at the landing to the left and ran up one story only. Two days later the British soldiers were to use this staircase in their headlong rush to fire from the upper windows. But there was another stairway at Cliveden — a narrow spiral that ran down into the basement and up to the third story. Near the entrance to the dining-room, just behind a pillar, there was a small door which opened into a narrow passageway. This had, at its end, a door set in the outer wall which led directly out on to the lawn. The servants went this way, but Margaret herself made use of it on her visits to the stables. The spiral stairs were in the centre of this passageway. In the wainscoting of the passage, near the dining-room, just behind the chimney of that room, there was set a secret panel, so cleverly contrived that it was in no whit unlike the other panels adorning the walls. If the builder of Cliveden had had in mind the "secret way" at Stenton, called "The Priest's Escape," he had shown the skill to make his own the better of the two.

A hurried grasp of his father's hand and Henry

Murray rushed to the door of the passage. Margaret followed.

"If they come, I will either seek to detain them, or I will persuade them to take the wrong road, the Limekiln Road, perchance, or the Old York," she said, breathlessly. "You will go by the Main Road to Chestnut Hill? I thought so. Stay behind the panel till you hear me strike three blows on the hearth or on the wall. If you hear naught, do not leave, remember! You understand? Leave not until you hear me."

Henry touched a hidden spring. The magic panel slowly moved. A dark space beyond was revealed. He held the panel open while Margaret continued, hurriedly: "There are Englishmen in the stables now. But I will get them away as soon as 'tis possible. When you hear my signal, you can go through the underground way. But remember to wait till you hear me. When you get to the stables, take Selim. He has not been ridden for three days, and is already saddled. Hasten, dear! Remember, three knocks."

While she had been speaking Charles Murray's quick ear had heard unwonted sounds outside. He groped his way to the front doors, closed them, and threw the heavy bar across.

"Yes! Yes! Remember Washington must have the letters if I fail," whispered Henry, as he entered the space and closed the panel.

At that moment Annette's merry voice was heard at the outer door leading from the lawn. Margaret's face grew white with fear. Through a hazy mist she saw Captain Peyton enter while Annette stood behind him. Had he seen? Had he heard?

CHAPTER VI.

"These clashing discords, these injustices, this fighting of
brother against brother, are all of earth. They belong not to
Heaven, as love belongs there."

IT was no slight task to regain control. Peyton
could not fail to see her agitation. His face
flushed hotly. "Madam, your pardon. I startled you. There is no possible excuse for my intrusion."

"No! no!" answered Margaret, breathlessly.
"'Tis I who should have pardon. Methought I
heard. . . . But there is naught to fear."

"To fear? What is there to fear?" and he put
his hand on his sword.

His words, his unconscious manner, restored her
confidence. She even smiled.

"Methought I heard soldiers coming."

"No British soldier would dare molest you."

"Perchance some rebels might stray hither," ventured Mr. Murray; "though 'tis scarce possible in
open day. But come, sir, into the hall. Tell me,
are our servants attentive to your wish?"

"We thank you," answered Peyton, and he involuntarily held out a hand to render help to Mr. Murray's uncertain steps. "We need to trespass here
but a few moments longer."

57

He was interrupted by loud voices outside, the clashing of swords, the clink of spurs.

"My daughter was right," said Charles Murray. "There are soldiers in the garden."

Peyton gave Margaret a quick, reassuring glance. But a change had come over her. Here was a calm, controlled woman, full of dignity and resource, — the shrinking, anxious girl was gone.

"Mus' I open de doah, Massa Murray?" asked Chloe, as she bustled down the stairway.

"Wait," he answered; "wait a moment."

Oh! how he longed to be able to see his daughter's face!

The same moment a loud voice was heard outside: "Surround the house. Watch every door and window."

Then a sword hilt struck the door. "Open to the King's men! the King's men!" shouted the same voice.

Peyton's hand had been lightly resting on his sword, and he had drawn nearer to Margaret. Now he smiled.

"'Tis Musgrave, the colonel of the Fortieth," he said. "He will not harm you. 'Twas to see him that I rode this morning from the city. We miscalculated, and rode too far north. Then came the mischance to Brown Bess."

"Shall I open, massa?"

"Yes, Chloe."

She went and threw back the heavy bar. Colonel Musgrave and six troopers stood without.

"You are far too slow, wench," Musgrave grumbled, roughly.

"You knocked so berry loud, massa, I thot for shuh you be rebels," and Chloe smiled hospitably.

The Colonel looked in at Margaret.

"Madam, we seek a rebel whom we traced to the shrubbery yonder. We found his beast, but he has disappeared. He had a close thing of it. He must have come into this house."

Years afterwards, Margaret oft heard chanted the praises of this gallant soldier, who, at the battle of Germantown, made The Chew House into an impregnable fortress, and defied the American army. She herself joined in the praises of his bravery. But she could never forget the day when she first saw him. She could never forget the terror, the turmoil — yes — and the joy of that day. On that day she saw Colonel Musgrave's weakness rather than his strength; and on that day she first saw Arthur Peyton, and knew that he lived in the world!

Standing behind one of the pillars near the big staircase, Captain Peyton was hidden from Musgrave.

The Colonel's voice was harsh and his manner bold. "Damme! madam," he exclaimed, "the rebel must have come into this very room."

"'Tis impossible," she answered. "No American spy would dare venture into a house ere he knew if it belonged to Tory or to Whig. My father and I have heard naught but now and then a horseman riding past. Our quiet village, sir, has seen many more of such than usual, since my Lord Cornwallis entered Philadelphia. O, yes, one of your men has but just taken his horse to our stables."

Musgrave turned impatiently. "There are other doors than this. We will search the house, madam."

Margaret bowed with dignity. "Certainly, at your convenience. People loyal to the King are most happy to be of service to his cause."

She pointed up the stairway. "The house is at your service. Send your men up there, or to the stables across the lawn, — whither you choose. My servants will not molest you. Or you may go to cellar and attic by this way," and she threw open the door leading to the spiral staircase.

Musgrave looked at her undecidedly, then took a few steps down the hall. He started back in astonishment when he saw Peyton.

"Zounds, man! you here? Of a truth, I looked for you in camp yester-eve."

"I could not leave till daybreak. Where is your station, Musgrave?"

"Across the road, not far from here. I saw a man dashing helter skelter from the Market Square. There were shouts of 'Stop the rebel!' Six of my men sprang to their horses. I followed. Damme! Peyton, you saw him. Came not a rebel through yon doorway?"

"Methinks you saw Captain Peyton himself but a few minutes ago," said Charles Murray, hurriedly. "Of a surety, sir, your eyesight must be well-nigh as bad as mine when you mistook Captain Peyton for a rebel."

Peyton smiled. Musgrave looked vexed and puzzled, then forced a laugh.

"Ha! ha! Peyton would make a pretty rebel. Methinks he would be an easy target for our bullets. But tell me, Arthur, saw you not a man, without hat or coat, rush through yon doorway?"

It seemed to Margaret that she could hear the

throb of her heart, as she waited, breathlessly, for Peyton's answer.

The Captain smiled again. "I had been here but a moment when you came riding up so furiously. Wherefore all the trouble, Musgrave? I have seen no one but myself and Shipton."

"Whom my daughter-in-law called a right comely and pleasing youth," said Charles Murray.

Peyton glanced around for Annette, but she had disappeared.

There was a moment of silence, then Musgrave frowned. "Methinks you are all blind or nicely fooled. We saw a man clearly. No mistake, egad! No mistake. Atkins? Grove?" Two troopers saluted. "Go outside. Search the shrubbery well. Go to the stables. Go everywhere. Find the rebel."

The troopers went out the rear door. At the same moment were heard hurried footsteps on the gravelled road in front. Then the gleam of a scarlet coat in the doorway.

"Ah! Captain Baines!" shouted Musgrave. "'Tis late you come. The rebel is gone."

"'Tis not possible. I have his horse. He must have come into this very room." And the newcomer glanced around the spacious hall.

"We have given permission that the house be searched," said Charles Murray.

Captain Baines laughed harshly. "Permission! Permission, old man? I like that well!"

"And why not permission, sir?" asked Peyton, sternly. "'Tis a good word, well and aptly chosen."

With a smothered oath, the captain of the Fortieth put his hand on his sword.

"Tut, tut!" said the Colonel, sharply. "No time

for that now. Baines, be kind enough to take a trooper and search those outlying buildings at the back of the house."

Baines looked into the stern face of Peyton once more, then sullenly motioned to a trooper who followed him out. Musgrave turned to Charles Murray.

" My father, sir, can scarcely see you. He is nearly blind, due to valiant service fighting for the King."

The Colonel looked at Margaret sharply. Then, with bold admiration, " Where, fair lady? At New York?"

" No, with Wolfe before Quebec."

The Colonel gave a slight whistle, then resumed: " From my camp across the fields, I had heard that this lordly mansion belongs to Benjamin Chew, of legal renown in these parts. Have I the honour to speak with Madam Chew?"

" No; Madam Chew is at present in Philadelphia, entertaining, I doubt not, my Lord Cornwallis, with convenient dignity. Mr. Chew is away. He is spending his summer — " Margaret stopped. She would not make capital out of her friend's misfortunes. Not so her father.

" And Mr. Chew has paid well for his loyalty," Mr. Murray hastened to add. " The Congress has banished him to Virginia."

Under stress of excitement there was a rough eloquence about this gallant Musgrave, which inspired the soldiers under him to do great deeds. But in ordinary conditions he had few words at his command. His usual resource was " Ah!" He made use of that convenient word now, then turned to the three troopers remaining with him:

" We must be on our way in pursuit of the rebel."

" Some refreshment, and your men can easily follow him," said Margaret, hastily. " How far, think you, could he go without a horse?"

" True, Mistress — Mistress — "

" Murray, at your service." And Margaret swept him a curtsy.

" Mistress Murray. A prettier name than Chew, by my troth."

Margaret smiled at her father. " Yes, my father did well to choose his name."

" Be not obstinate, sir; you do no harm to tarry," said Mr. Murray, with quick intuition grasping Margaret's plan. " Have you any troopers without?"

" Templeton?" One of the men saluted. " Templeton, see if the men outside have discovered aught."

" Of a surety, sir, you will permit them also to come in and have refreshment."

" With pleasure, mistress, if it pleasures you."

The Colonel motioned to Templeton who went quickly out. His errand took him not long. The mention of refreshment had stirred his martial spirit. Perchance he consulted with the men outside. But in a moment he stood once more before Musgrave.

" The men have searched the trees and shrubs, the stables and the garden to the rear. There's naught been discovered. All is quiet. Naught is heard but the hum of bees."

Margaret assumed concern.

" Now, Colonel, if your troopers have disturbed my hives, I much fear me — "

" If they have, Mistress Murray, they will be the ones to suffer." Charles Murray smiled.

" Where is Captain Baines? " asked Musgrave, authoritatively.

" He is searching the servants' quarters."

" Look the servants as if they are harbouring a fugitive, or is there aught suspicious about them? "

" I know not, sir. There is the Captain. He will tell you." And the trooper discreetly withdrew behind a pillar near Chloe, who had been standing there absorbed and well-nigh panic-stricken with vague fears of she knew not what.

Musgrave looked at Baines searchingly. There was an ugly frown on the Captain's face.

Margaret motioned to Chloe.

" Chloe, a dozen bottles of your best wine, some mulled wine also. We entertain these guests."

" Yes, Missy Margaret." But she did not stir.

" Didst hear her, wench," whispered Templeton. " Mulled wine, wench, an' quarts of it. His Majesty's soldiers are thirsty."

" Have you thoughts to stay? " asked Baines, his brow clearing as if by magic. He, too, had a martial spirit, awake to the call of duty. He looked at Margaret with bold admiration, and came nearer to her. She drew herself up with dignity, and almost instinctively walked nearer to Peyton. Why was it that this man's presence gave her courage, strength, — courage to play her difficult part, strength to do all possible for the anxious, waiting fugitive, listening behind the secret panel.

A trooper appeared at the rear door of the hall. Templeton met him on the threshold.

" We are to have wine, Grove. Egad! an' yet that wench there has lost her hearing, an' goes not for it."

Despite the libel cast upon the acuteness of her senses, Chloe heard him.

" Wot you t'inkin' 'bout wine for, you ole red-face, when you's got to catch rebels for shuh? I 'clare to goodness some ob Massa Murray's ale de bes' for you."

Her indignation took away her vague forebodings. She bustled to the dining-room door. By that time the importance of her air and step was quite restored. With her accustomed sober dignity, she went to do her mistress's bidding.

For a moment Margaret stood motionless, looking on the floor, deep in thought. Then she became aware of Musgrave's eyes upon her searchingly. She roused herself.

" Pray, sir, send one of your troopers to our stables across the lawn," she said, smiling bravely up into his face. " One of your countrymen has but now gone thither to repair some damage to his captain's horse."

" Who was it, fair lady? "

" Methinks you know. 'Tis a gallant and right comely youth."

" He raved over the virtues of a certain captain, — one Peyton who fought at Brandywine," said Mr. Murray, with a smile towards where he supposed Peyton to be standing. Peyton smiled in return. Musgrave began to laugh boisterously.

" Ah, 'tis Shipton — Bob Shipton! By my faith, where Peyton is, there will Shipton surely be. Ha! ha! He follows him like a dog. Ha! ha! and many a wild ride doth his captain lead him. Ha! ha! I doubt not he be already out of breath, seeking to keep up with Brown Bess. Ah! mistress, there be no need to send a trooper for Bob Shipton. He will be here anon, for he is of a prying temper, and he will long to know what brings us hither. Ha! ha!"

" But you will send for him. It were a pity to leave him out of our humble entertainment." Margaret tried to keep an anxious tone out of her voice. Captain Baines had been gazing at her with yet bolder admiration. Now he came quite near to where she was standing, but, half startled, she moved away. Then bethinking herself, she tried to smile, as if to conciliate him. He paid no heed to Peyton's warning look, but came quite near to Margaret again and bowed low : " Mistress, your most humble servant, an' it please you."

But Musgrave saw the look on Peyton's face. He gave a loud laugh.

" By my troth, Arthur," he exclaimed, roughly, " you have made quick progress in gallantry. Our army has not been long in this region ! " He turned and went over to examine one of the portraits on the wall, and called Captain Baines beside him.

Margaret flushed hotly. Had she even glanced at Peyton she would have seen how the coarse jest pained him.

" Mistress, your pardon," he said, softly. He stood and entreated her with his eyes. Then almost against her will, she looked at him and smiled. He seemed content and went up to the big doorway in front. The smile in his eyes had been like the comfort of sunshine.

CHAPTER VII.

"Ah! Madam, these be troopers of our army. They are seeking a rebel spy — and they hope to find him lurking in the bottom of Mistress Murray's delicate goblets."

MARGARET had brief chance for a hurried word with her father.

"I must get that lieutenant away from the stables," she whispered under her breath. "And I must get them all within, and then close the shade of the dining-room window, so they may not see out towards the stables. 'Tis not likely they will stray into the office and look from the window there. They will have the wish to stay where the refreshment is. Could I make it natural to serve it in the parlour? No, that would not do. Go you and sit by the dining-room window, father. I must be there that I may give the signal."

As she moved away, he caught her hand and gave it a hasty kiss. Then, as he slowly found his way across the hall to the dining-room door, he called out to Peyton: "Those portraits which your friends are examining are well worth careful attention, but there are two in this room whose colouring is thought to be unmatched in this country. Will you come, gentlemen? The pictures will serve till we have our wine."

67

Peyton turned.   Then he and the others followed Mr. Murray.

Mr. Murray had some dim idea of Margaret's plan, for there was strong mental sympathy between father and daughter; but he puzzled himself in vain to guess how she would manage to give to her brother the expected signal that it was safe for him to steal down the hidden staircase to the cellar, then through the underground passage to the stables.

As we know, the kitchens and laundry-rooms were connected with the main portion of the house by a narrow corridor, with open pillars towards the side of the rear garden, but a solid wall of masonry on the side towards the stables.   The stables were some distance across the lawn, in a stone building almost as large as the main portion of the house itself.   The underground passage leading from the secret panel had no connection whatever with the corridor to the kitchens, or with the kitchens themselves.   Had there been an outlet there, Margaret would not have had so much to fear.   Her brother would have been entirely concealed from view by the thickly growing shrubs in the rear garden.   But the secret way ran underneath the lawn, and came to an end just this side the entrance to the stables. There, at its end, was a small opening in the lawn almost entirely concealed by a thick clump of bushes, to be sure, but they were not so high as a man; and were any one to be watching from the dining-room windows, a man could be distinctly seen as he emerged from the opening in the lawn, — seen before he could find refuge in the friendly shelter of the stables.   Thus it was not only essential that no enemy be in the stables at this critical time, but that no enemy be looking out the windows facing the lawn. When Henry Murray would hear Margaret's signal, and would hasten along the underground passage and come out from behind the bushes, he might be seen from these windows. Even if he escaped observation here, he might be seen as he rode Selim either to the garden at the rear of the servants' quarters, thence to the road in front; or more directly to the carriage drive which ran from the stables to the front portico, then through an avenue of stately trees, down to the front gate. There was naught but the lawn between the stables and this rear garden. It was, therefore, in full view of the dining-room. And there were no trees beside the driveway from the stables to the front portico: the avenue leading down to the front gate began just beyond the portico.

The front windows of the hall did not cause Margaret quite so much anxiety, for she felt sure her brother would choose the pathway to the front road through the rear garden. Nevertheless, she resolved to keep these unwelcome guests away from the front windows. The big front doors must of a truth be closed.

This brave girl of twenty-two had a hard task before her.

As Chloe and Jake opened the door leading from the corridor, the eager Templeton saw that they were bearing trays, on which were pitchers and glasses. A small youth, with a big head and queer-shaped feet, followed meekly with the wine-bottles. Was this the redoubtable Clem?

Templeton gave Grove an eager push with his elbow. It brought Grove nearer the dining-room door. Templeton thought it wise to follow. They paused on the threshold with eager glances at Jake and Chloe and the little Clem.

As Clem marched gravely to the big mahogany sideboard, he saw the brilliancy of these wonderful guests. He saw and marvelled. His wide-open eyes danced and shone as they caught the gleam of the gold lace, the flash of the red. Peyton's heart warmed towards the lad. With a furtive look to see that no one was near, he put out his hand. There was the glint of something in colour much like the gold lace on his coat. It was slipped into the lad's hand. Then came the gleam of something white — something far more precious than the gold. And Clem showed this precious ivory white generously, as if he scorned concealment.

The troopers who had been searching outside passed the front windows and came to the big doorway. Chloe bustled past Templeton and Grove, ignoring them completely. She walked gravely up the hall. " Gemmen," she said to the newcomers, as she pointed back towards the dining-room, " you's wastin' time. Dare's wine on de table dare. Bettah use your legs to some 'vantage 'stead o' scourin' roun' our garden an' tramplin' down de flowers."

They paused with eager glances at her smiling face; then hurried down the hall. They heard Margaret's clear voice addressing their colonel.

" I have here some most excellent mulled wine and some choice grape, pleasant on a chill October day. The grape wine is in the bottles."

The Colonel smiled. " We thank you, Mistress Murray. Baines, Peyton? "

Then he saw the eager faces of the troopers just

outside the room. He motioned consent. They came crowding in. Margaret looked up at Peyton.

"I pray you be seated. You are tired from your ride." She someway felt that she could not give this man the same invitation she gave the others.

"We have his beast, and even if he is hiding near, he cannot go far on foot," said Musgrave to Peyton. "We do no harm to tarry."

"As you please, Musgrave," Peyton answered, smiling. "What is one paltry rebel in comparison with the pleasure of his Majesty's colonel?"

"Ha! ha! Peyton. I thank you well for your consent."

And then, as if he could not resist, he went to the table. When Colonel Musgrave once began on work like this, he carried it through with a zeal befitting such a gallant soldier. And Captain Baines showed scarce less zest.

Peyton went out into the hall. As the troopers and their officers reached and poured the wine, Margaret kept glancing nervously out the open windows. Then she uttered a joyous exclamation, as she turned to Musgrave, "See, sir, your lieutenant has left the stables and comes hither."

"Yes, mistress."

Margaret went nearer her father.

"How careless of me to leave that window open upon you, father. This October air is chill, and the sun is not good for your eyes."

She shut the window, and drew down the shade.

"There! that is better." And she gave her father a tender smile. Then she went to the other window.

"Now, gentlemen," said Mr. Murray, "have no hesitation. 'Tis not every home in the neighbourhood of Germantown, or Philadelphia for that matter, can offer you such mulled wine as that!"

For emphatic answer, Musgrave took up a pitcher and poured a glass, holding it up to the light. Captain Baines did not stop to do that. He drank steadily from first to last.

And Peyton, Margaret saw, had wandered about the hall, till now he was standing in the open doorway, looking thoughtfully out into the front garden. How could she get him away? But Margaret felt a strange reluctance to invite him to join those eager men at the table. She *could* not do it. Her mind was in a whirl of indecision and anxiety. How was she to give the longed-for signal that her brother might escape?

CHAPTER VIII.

"It has been to my father and myself a most peculiar pleasure to entertain some of his Majesty's soldiers this morning."

THE door from the narrow passage opened softly. Annette had brought the Lieutenant back the same way she had conducted Peyton. He held the door open for her to enter the hall. She heard the voices in the dining-room, the clink of glass, and looked at Margaret in surprise. Margaret smiled bravely.

"His Majesty has sent us some of his soldiers for our guests this morning. We entertain them."

"Whom were those men seeking when they came out to the stables?" Annette asked again.

"Ah, madam," said Captain Peyton, smiling. "Ah, madam, these be troopers of our army. They are seeking a rebel spy, and they hope to find him lurking in the bottom of Mistress Murray's delicate goblets."

Musgrave came to the dining-room door. "Come, boy. 'Tis rare old wine."

Margaret saw that the Lieutenant shook his head. Baines looked up and gave a shout intended to be friendly.

"Come, Shipton! be not a fool. 'Tis a chance rare enough in this beastly country."

73

Peyton's lips tightened. Margaret saw the stern look coming again into his face.

"What is the mission on which you are bent?" asked Shipton of the trooper in the dining-room near the door.

"A damned rebel fox got possession of some letters from General Howe to his brother, the Admiral; naught else I know," the man answered. "We were in our tents when — "

"How did he get them?" interrupted Margaret.

"Stole them methinks."

"No, lady, the man who stole them was shot dead," said another trooper, who seemed more willing to explain. "We were in camp when a horseman, who had ridden quietly through Germantown, came out into the open country. We took no heed of him, till down at the Market Square we heard a big uproar. One of Howe's aids had dashed out from headquarters and hurled himself on a horse. Galloping madly up the street, he kept shouting: 'There's a damned rebel ahead. Stop him! Stop him!' Of a truth, we saw the horseman, but thought him not the rebel till, egad! he put spurs to his beast and was dashing past us, when another man shouted to us, 'After him, catch him, dead or alive!' Our colonel and captain, with six of us, rushed to our horses, and dashed helter skelter after the rebel; but by the time we got to the shrubbery yonder, he was gone, and naught but his beast was found."

"Yet we had seen him till he was hidden by the beautiful garden there," said another trooper, pointing to the rear.

"Where went the man who shouted to you to catch him?" asked Shipton.

" He vanished into the bushes near an old wall."

Margaret struggled to conceal her agitation, but her voice trembled as she spoke.

" Of a truth 'tis mysterious. . . . But you will find your spy. Where are the rebels encamped? "

" At Skippack Creek, unless the cowards have retreated," said Templeton, drawing near.

" No," said Captain Peyton, pausing on his way to the front doorway. " The enemy have not retreated. They have been drawing nearer. They are more than five miles nearer than when we came."

Peyton spoke quietly but with authority. Templeton saluted.

" Your pardon, sir, I knew naught but the gossip of the camp."

" You have intelligence, Peyton? " asked Musgrave, willing perhaps to stop one brief moment in his pleasant task.

" Yes," answered Shipton, with dignity. " My Lord Cornwallis has already written Sir William."

" Damme! those rebels got such a drubbing at the Brandywine," said Baines, loudly, " they will scarce venture to meet us so soon again. You will hear on the morrow that they are miles away."

" How far away are they now? " asked Margaret, quickly.

" From fifteen to eighteen miles methinks," answered Captain Peyton, with a smile.

" 'Tis a long way for that rebel to go without a horse," said Annette, as she flashed him a brilliant smile in reply.

" Damme! he will never go," said Baines, as he filled another glass. " We will catch him ere he goes a mile, and swing him to the first tree."

"Be not too sure of that," said Shipton under his breath. "Seen him have I not, but as he was heavy enough to lame his horse, methinks the first tree might, perchance, not hold him till —"

The Lieutenant was interrupted by Baines's loud laugh.

"A clever wit, by my troth," he exclaimed. "Come, Shipton, this wine will make it sharper."

"The shortest road towards the Skippack Road would be the one leading right over Chestnut Hill, would it not, Mistress Murray?" Musgrave seemed willing to stop another brief moment to ask this question. Margaret answered with decision.

"He would not likely take that road, thinking you would be sure to take it. But he would strike across the fields to the right. Strike the old Limekiln Road. Here, I will show you." She started to cross the room to the fireplace.

"But first permit me to offer you wine, Lieutenant."

She motioned Shipton to the table with grave courtesy. He smiled, looked irresolutely at the troopers, and made a step nearer, just as Peyton came to him and took his arm.

"Have you seen that portrait of Doctor Samuel Chew in the front hall? 'Tis a fine one methinks."

The boy's face flushed. Then he whispered back:

"Come, let us go, Arthur. 'Tis better that I shun the danger. All my nerves are on a tingle."

"Yes, we will go in a moment, Bob. Musgrave will be ready soon. But he must go first."

Peyton's lips tightened. None knew better than he the effect of good, generous wine on men like these troopers of Musgrave's. As for their captain — of a truth, 'twere better that the wine be not too generous.

Putting his arm within the Lieutenant's, he drew him nearer Mr. Murray.

"The walls of your house seem unusual strong, and the doors are thick as fort walls," he said.

"It is the strongest house on the country-side," answered Mr. Murray, pointing towards the richly wainscoted wall. "Note the thickness of those stone walls. A foot at least. Then there are windows up-stairs, from which a dozen men might hold a regiment at bay. These walls would stand even cannonading. I was through the French and Indian wars, and we made use of a house not so strong as this, and it withstood musket-balls and cannon. Even the efforts of the Indians to fire it were unavailing."

Peyton bowed, then looked towards one of the windows. "Those shutters might hold a thousand years, were they not opened from within," he said to Shipton. Musgrave heard him, and exclaimed in a loud tone:

"We'll remember this, boys, if we should have a battle here near Germantown."

A battle! Here, near Germantown! Margaret's heart's beating nearly stifled her. No, such a tragedy could not happen here! Here in her home. Her beloved Cliveden!

She felt relieved that the Captain had not returned to the front hall, but how best to keep him engaged with her father? Her thoughts were anxious and perplexed, as she went swiftly out into the hall to the front doors and closed them softly. But the watchful Colonel saw her as she turned back.

"Mistress Murray," he said, "what road would he be likely to take to reach the enemy's camp?"

"Who? O, I forgot — You mean — "

"Yes, that rebel fox we are after."

All at once an inspiration came to her. She might perchance give the expected signal without arousing suspicion. She went to the dining-room fireplace and took up the blackened poker.

"Let me give you a slight idea of the country. I know it well."

But though her voice was steady, her hand trembled.

"Now, gentlemen, here on the floor let me map out the roads for you."

"Nay, nay, sweet mistress, that will spoil your pretty floor," said Musgrave, hastening nearer to her.

Margaret smiled with effort, and glanced restlessly at Peyton and Shipton, as if in fear of their leaving the room.

"'Tis in a good cause. . . . There is too much soot on this." She gave two violent blows on the hearth with the heavy poker, and had raised it to strike a third blow when Musgrave stayed her hand.

"Nay, nay, Mistress Murray — your floor."

Margaret grew impatient. She glanced at Musgrave, who stood beside her, glass in hand. The troopers and Captain Baines were busied at the table. Peyton and Shipton drew nearer. She *must* give the signal now.

"Here, Peyton, drink. 'Tis rare old wine." And Musgrave held out his glass. "Where is Brown Bess? Hast broken Brown Bess's delicate ankles yet? Shipton, I needed not to send for you, you curious tempered youth. I told Mistress Murray so. . . . 'Tis well you are here to help us in our search of the rebel fox. But you were to show us the road, sweet lady." The gallant Colonel found it easy to talk now.

Margaret took another blackened poker, and this time succeeded in giving three violent blows on the hearth of the wide fireplace.

" There! that is better. Now, gentlemen, see, here is the Germantown Road — the villagers call it the Main Street — it runs past this house, as you know, straight up to Chestnut Hill."

She began to trace distinct lines on the floor, and her guests crowded around her. Even Captain Baines left the table.

" At Chestnut Hill a road starts, which runs in a straight line, due north. 'Tis a road leading to Bethlehem. Three or four miles north you come to the Skippack Road which crosses it, runs down in a southeasterly direction to the Limekiln Road, crosses that, on to the Old York Road, crosses that, and so on down. But that way it concerns us little. Methinks you know how the Limekiln and the Old York Roads run, both to the east of the Germantown Road. Here is the Limekiln Road, running parallel to it here, then branching off this way. See, away over there is the Old York Road, parallel, or nearly so, then branching, and it finally runs into our road away south of your general's headquarters at Stenton. . . . You have sure intelligence that Mr. Washington's camp is somewhere on the Skippack Road? Now, after going the three or four miles north from Chestnut Hill, and coming to the Skippack Road, you turn to the left, go some distance in a north-

westerly direction, and you are sure to come soon
near the rebel camp. Now, Colonel Musgrave, think
you that your rebel spy would choose that direct way
to Mr. Washington's camp?"

Margaret's eyes were very bright as she looked
up into the Colonel's face.

"Egad! why not, mistress?" Musgrave exclaimed. "He would have strong wish to reach the
rebel camp as fast as time would serve."

"Damme!" shouted Captain Baines. "Of course
the fool would go that way."

"Methinks he would not," Margaret said, de-
cidedly. "See you not what the man's thoughts
would be? Why turned he aside from the Main
Road? See you not that his plan was to avoid that
way, of a surety, thinking his pursuers would choose
the shortest way to Mr. Washington's camp?"

"Damme! the lady has the right of it," muttered
Templeton to Grove. Grove pushed his neighbour
aside that he might get a better view of Margaret.

The signal had been given! Before her mental
vision was a figure stealing down the steps behind
the secret panel, now along the underground passage
— out! out to the stables! Then she could see her
brother fling himself on Selim. Away, away along
the sheltered garden, out from behind the thick trees,
to the road in front. Up the road, lost behind the
knoll. Off again! A mere speck in the distance.

CHAPTER IX.

"Washington is not many miles away, and some of the British are encamped only across the fields to our left."

MARGARET for ever blessed her father that at this critical time he called Captain Peyton's attention to a fine miniature of young Benjamin Chew, who was absent in London, studying law in the Inner Temple. Captain Peyton left the group gathered around Margaret, and conversed apart with Mr. Murray.

"What road, think *you,* would the rebel take?" queried Musgrave.

Margaret drew again the dark, mysterious lines upon the floor.

"See, here is the Main Street, running from Chestnut Hill down through the village, on towards Philadelphia. At the Market Square, the centre of the village, there is a street running to the right, — that is nearly eastward. 'Tis called by some Luken's Mill Road, by others Church lane. At Luken's Mill it strikes the Limekiln Road. I know little of your camp, but my brother — " Margaret's voice trembled a little in spite of her mastery of herself — " my brother has of late ridden much around your camp, and he tells me that your guards and dragoons are stationed at the junction of Church Lane and the Limekiln Road. Further north on the road is the

First Battalion of Light Infantry. But your rebel could strike across from behind our orchards and farm-lands, and reach the Limekiln Road beyond the place where that battalion is stationed. Of a surety, there are no sentries beyond. Now, what think you? Could not your rebel, after eluding you among the shrubbery, as you say, have struck across our orchard and farm-lands to the woods north of your infantry, then taken the Limekiln Road up to the Skippack, thence to Mr. Washington's camp?"

"Egad!" exclaimed Shipton, excitedly, "Mistress Murray has a clever wit. She has the right of it, of a surety. Besides, he would not go by the Main Road, because he could not pass the sentries at Mount Airy. But over there he is free to strike across country."

"Yes, I see, I see," said Musgrave, eagerly. "We have time to catch him on the Limekiln Road."

Had Musgrave, the troopers, Margaret, been in the hall, they could not have failed to see a man passing the front windows. He tarried to look in, then stole off around the house. Had Margaret seen him, her heart would have almost stopped beating. The man was not her brother.

"Peyton, Peyton!" called the Lieutenant, "methinks we should be going."

"Time, time to catch him on the Limekiln Road," said Captain Baines, thickly, as he went back to the table.

Margaret's tone grew anxious.

"Will you not all drink to the health of the King?"

"A most loyal maiden, by my troth," said Templeton, under his breath.

" Yes, yes, a health to the King," shouted another trooper.

" And success to your ride of this morning."

" It will be their ride of this evening if they tarry here much longer, taking your excellent wine," said Shipton.

" Hard to find — find such wine. Ha! ha! By my faith, 'tis a merry jest," shouted the captain of the Fortieth.

A trooper, who had been serving himself with unblushing freedom, suddenly looked at Margaret. She was still near the fireplace, her glowing, excited eyes fixed on the group of busy soldiers. She had proposed the toast, hoping that even Peyton and Shipton would be diverted from their purpose of soon taking their departure. She paid no heed to this man who had left the table, and was on his way towards her. When she saw him, she could not suppress a breathless exclamation. Peyton turned quickly. The man put out his arm as if to throw it around her. She evaded him, but he repeated his venture. The next moment he was hurled to his knees, and Peyton stood over him with dark and stern face.

" Bethink yourself, or you will feel my sword."

The man picked himself up in shame. The troopers near him laughed. He went over to the table, and with savage eagerness broke one of the bottles on it. The wine flowed over the table. Grove and Templeton held their glasses underneath.

" By the King! the man shows excellent taste," said Baines, holding himself steady by the table, and looking over at Margaret. " Fine wine — hard to find finer. Ha! ha! Fill the glasses, and fill the

men. A clever wit, by my troth. Bright eyes of
our hostess, Mistress Margaret Murray, at your service. Ha! ha! 'tis a merry jest."

"No jest, sir, an it please you," exclaimed Peyton, a dark flush on his face, his hand raised, as if
he would strike the speaker on the cheek. But he
was stopped by Musgrave's loud, authoritative voice:

"Arthur! no offence is meant, of a surety. Have
patience. Egad, sir! we have scant time for quarrels."

"Scant time for quarrels," muttered Shipton,
"but sufficient time for insults."

"Be silent, boy! No insults, by the King! but
honest truths, ha! ha! Fill the glasses and fill the
men."

Peyton looked a moment irresolutely at the unsteady captain, then, with a smile half of pity, half
of contempt, went back to his talk with Mr. Murray.

Shipton again made as if to go to the door, but
Annette smiled and motioned to the table.

"You have not tasted the grape wine. Methinks
you must be tired from your ride. You do not the
justice to my sister's hospitality that do the others.
May I not offer you wine, Lieutenant?"

"Thank you, sweet lady — no. My friend and
myself drink little wine, and we throw the dice for
neither love nor money. I would these men were led
by my friend, rather than by Colonel Musgrave,
lady."

"And if they were?" asked Margaret, coming
near.

"And if they were, sweet lady, the rebel spy were
already in our hands, and the letters safely back with
General Howe, who writ them."

Peyton did not hear this enthusiastic speech from the youth who loved him. Mr. Murray kept him busied talking.

Meanwhile the troopers began to pledge each other.

" Here's to the success of his Majesty."

" Here's to the success of our hunt for the rebel."

" Here's to the brave lasses left behind in England," shouted a trooper, filling his glass to overflowing.

" Here's to the bright eyes of our hostess." It was Baines who gave this toast. The troopers raised a shout as they lifted their glasses. Baines looked around for Margaret, then moved unsteadily nearer her. Then came suddenly against Peyton. He frowned, then smiled guiltily.

" Zounds, man! I'll not touch her."

Peyton went back to Charles Murray.

Annette was puzzled at the eager hospitality evident in Mr. Murray's manner, and she wondered much at the lavish use of his precious wine. But she was too wise to show her wonder. She was annoyed, too, at the admiring glances she won from the bold eyes of these soldiers of King George. After a silent curtsy to Lieutenant Shipton, she hastened across the wide hall to the parlour opposite. The bolt was heard drawn after she had closed the door.

Shipton went across to Peyton and seized his arm: " Come! Of a truth, we have trespassed here far too long."

" Ay, we should be going." But the Captain looked longingly over at Margaret. He liked not the thought of leaving her.

"There is no need for haste, Lieutenant," said Charles Murray, coming slowly near the two friends. "Methinks there is little for his Majesty's soldiers to do but enjoy the fruits of their glorious conquest of Philadelphia and Germantown." Then he turned to the troopers: "Wipe off the cobwebs. You see, of a truth, 'tis old, rare wine."

"Fit for kings," answered Musgrave, with elation.

"And the loyal subjects of kings. You may have a long and weary ride before you. It may be nightfall ere you are back in camp."

"And you may be by nightfall in the hands of Light-Horse Harry or Captain McLane," said Shipton, smiling.

"Forbid such a misfortune," answered Margaret; and in her heart she meant it.

"Ay, ay, sweet mistress," said Templeton, "but we would not be captured without some of the damned rebels falling headlong from their saddles."

Margaret's hands clutched a chair nervously, as if the strain were getting beyond her. "Heaven forbid that also."

Peyton went to Musgrave and grasped his arm. "Come! Bethink yourself, man! You'll catch no rebel now."

"Here's to the success of what is righteous, and holy, and just," said Charles Murray, groping his way to the table, and seizing a glass. "Captain Peyton, Lieutenant, here, give us a toast ere you go. Drink success to your enterprise, to your brave troops, and to your fellow officers."

"Ay, ay! a toast, a toast!" shouted the troopers in unison.

Shipton glanced at Peyton. The latter shook his head gravely.

" We thank you, sir."

Charles Murray held out a glass to Shipton. He was about to take it from his hand when Margaret stepped forward for the glass. She smiled at Shipton. " Your pardon, Lieutenant. We honour you all the more." She tossed the glass under the table. It fell in fragments, and the wine sprinkled up over Musgrave's feet.

Margaret felt rather than saw that Peyton's glowing eyes were fixed upon her. But she gave her hand to Shipton with a smile that went straight to the boy's heart. He bent to kiss her hand, saying, softly :

" I thank you, I thank you. You know not what the wine does for me. It makes me — makes me — " He broke off suddenly, in confusion, then added, earnestly, " You are most kind, Mistress Murray. We shall not soon forget the hospitality at Benjamin Chew's beautiful home."

" Thank you, Lieutenant. It has been to my father and myself a most peculiar pleasure to entertain some of his Majesty's soldiers this morning. Tell me, was your Brown Bess, as you call her, carefully attended ? "

" Thank you, yes. Your servant, Jake — I think his name? Yes, Jake did marvels. Your permission Mistress Murray." Shipton bowed again over her hand. " Farewell."

Musgrave turned reluctantly from the table. " Fill the glasses and fill the men! Show us to our horses! Zounds, man! Show our horses to us."

He looked at the diagram on the floor ; the marks were almost gone.

" The road across the fields — fields — to the Limekiln — believe you said, Mistress Murray. We thank you."

Captain Baines bowed unsteadily over her hand. " Bright eyes, I said, bright eyes, egad! bright eyes."

He spoke as if in the effort to convince himself of some forgotten truth, then smiled into space. Peyton stood beside her, as if on guard. Musgrave laughed.

" Good boy, good boy! Put up your frowns, Arthur. He'll not touch her. Ride you with us, Peyton ? "

" No, my horse is not fit."

" And the curious-tempered youth? Shipton, Sir Robert Shipton at your service — stays he with you ? "

Shipton bowed.

" Ride to my camp across the Main Road. I will meet you on our return, and have our conference." Musgrave, the colonel, the gallant soldier, the man of dignity, of action, was evident now. " How long, Shipton, can you be spared from my Lord Cornwallis? "

" I am to be on the staff of Sir William Howe if I choose to take the commission."

" 'Tis well. I will be back before sundown, Arthur."

They all hastened out together. There was a clatter of swords and spurs, rough voices, Musgrave's loud laugh. Margaret seemed to hear nothing but Peyton's low-spoken farewell. It seemed as if she saw nothing but the tender look in his eyes. She softly closed the big doors, and then turned and threw herself, sobbing, into her father's arms.

CHAPTER X.

"An open foe is not to be dreaded; 'tis he who stabs in the dark."

AT last Margaret asked in a faint voice: "Think you he has gone far enough?"

"Yes, he must have reached the knoll. It will hide him from their view. Besides, if they remember your diagram, they will go in the other direction. Heaven be with him, be with him. He will soon be in the camp."

Her sobs grew fewer and quieter.

"Can we but keep from Annette his danger and our fears."

"We must, my brave girl, we must."

Margaret left her father, and began pacing up and down.

"She may come any moment and question us." she whispered, hurriedly. "I would I could go to the stables to see if he took Selim in safety. If I could but open the panel and go thither the way he went. Methinks 'twould help me to be assured of his safe flight."

"Go not, dear, 'twould give her all the more cause for question. He must have heard the signal, and all been well. 'Twas hard for you, dear, to keep them busied with the wine, and in the room that suited best your purpose. . . . My brave girl!"

"Please, father, say no more, or — or — " She broke off, suddenly; then after a moment of silence: "Of a truth, when I saw the temptation 'twas for that poor lieutenant, I felt degraded in my own eyes, that I — I would condescend to tempt a man — and those bold-eyed troopers. . . . Oh! I hope, I hope I shall not have to waste any more wine on any of the King's troops. I want to save it all for our army, our sick men. I hope I shall never, never in all my life see a British officer here again, father — " Then she faltered. It was well that Mr. Murray could not see the hot flush that swept over her face. Did she really in her heart wish never to see — at least one again?

"You will likely see many a British soldier here before this cruel war is over." Mr. Murray's tone was bitter.

"How fresh they are! how bright their red coats! how strong they look! It makes my heart ache, ache! for the poorly clad, the ragged, the hungry, the glorious men, who are fighting for liberty." Margaret's voice trembled with passionate feeling. "These British! They ought to stay at home, and let us be free, free!"

Mr. Murray sighed.

"Father, come, you are tired from the turmoil and the uproar and your fears for Harry. Come, sit by the fire, and I will stir it into a blaze."

Ah! there was that face again at the window, peering in, — curious, anxious, expectant. But Margaret did not see.

She led Mr. Murray to the fireplace in the little room at one end of the front hall. She threw on the almost dying fire one of the logs Chloe had let fall. Ah! so much had happened since! Then she turned to comfort her father, for by a quick thrill of sympathetic affection she knew his thoughts; knew that he was lamenting his helplessness — this passive endurance of events irritated and fretted him — he wanted to make events himself. He wanted to fight, to be active, to conquer. He wanted to help, rather than be helped. Margaret knew that in a time of stress and danger like the present the bitterness of his regret would be especially keen.

She had oft occasion to comfort her father by the tenderness of her sympathy; but he scarce knew the effort it cost to talk just now. She longed to be silent, to recover from the tension of nerve of the last half-hour. But she paid no heed to her own wish. Sitting on the arm of his chair, and giving her father loving, tender touches on the head and cheek, she tried to cheer him; and when Annette, in a few moments, appeared at the door, she turned to her a smiling face.

"Ah! at last they have gone. I liked them not, with their rough ways," exclaimed Annette. "Wherefore so much wine to the enemy, Margaret?"

"'Tis no new thing for The Chew House to be hospitable," said Mr. Murray, with well-assumed impatience. "They came because they fancied a rebel spy had taken refuge in our shrubbery. But you heard them, girl, 'tis no need to repeat. Methinks their eyes saw not well because of the wine drunk yester-eve by their camp-fire, and Margaret's entertainment would scarce work improvement in their eyesight."

"That lieutenant was comely and pleasing," continued Annette, thoughtfully. " Could you but have heard him tell me how his friend has saved him from ruin. ' I know not why I tell you all this,' quoth he, ' but I feel as if I wanted to.' And then to see you tempt him, Margaret."

One of those swift changes came to Margaret's face which made it have for many people so much charm. " Think you not, child, that I, too, was pleased with that gallant and comely youth? Of a truth, I hope that no harm may e'er befall him."

" Nor his friend," added Mr. Murray. " I had much profit in my talk with Captain Peyton."

Annette laughed merrily. " We are loyal rebels, in truth, chanting the praises of two soldiers of King George. . . . Come, come, Margaret, know you not how hungry I am? Dinah must have a finely broiled wing for each of us, and I have been wishing those redcoats would but hasten. Why let those soldiers have all the refreshment? I was up so early, at the time Henry rode away, that it seems as if the day were fairly spent, yet I know well the noon-hour has not yet come. Can you not call forth from your inner consciousness a zest for food, father? "

" No, child, but I will go back to the dining-room with you, an it please you. After giving satisfaction to that surprising appetite, Annette can betake herself to the summer-house for a quiet time of self-communion."

" Could you not come to the summer-house, too? We cannot have many more such perfect days."

" If happily Dinah, who is making candles, and Keziah, who has met with certain difficulties in her soap-making, can spare this model housekeeper of ours," said Mr. Murray. " Bethink yourselves," he continued, with an effort to be jovial, " bethink yourselves of Margaret, the toast of Charleston, New York, and the City of Penn, not to mention her conquests of the British while absent in London, — of Margaret, the ruler of a country-house, with farmers, gardeners, and dairymaids to keep from mischievous idleness."

Margaret swept her father a fine curtsy. Could he but have seen her! Then she gave him both her hands.

" Come, father, let us have a merry meal together, and *this time* let us drink to the health of *General,* not of *Mr.* Washington."

She led Mr. Murray gently across the hall, and, as Annette followed, she trilled a few bars of a merry song. The door through which they passed was shut. The merry song ceased. The big hall grew quiet. Then once more the man outside stole past the windows, and peered in cautiously. When he saw that the room was empty at last, he opened one of the front doors softly and came in. His slouch-hat was well down over his eyes, the collar of his short cloak drawn up. The disguise served him well. Even had he met Captain Peyton then, it is probable he would not have been recognised.

His manner showed he feared discovery; and yet this man was of a character so determined that he would scarce have retreated from his purpose even had Margaret appeared before him.

But the Fates were busy that October morning weaving a thick web of misfortune for poor Margaret. She did not appear at the door. She was safely in the dining-room; the walls were massive, the doors of the thickest oak. No sound could possibly penetrate thither. We build not such houses now.

Swiftly up and down the left wall went the intruder, feeling of the wainscoting, listening to it, with his ear close. Then swiftly to the right wall, bending, listening. Then into the schoolroom — but he spent little time there. The " office " at the opposite side of the hall — the side nearest the stables — detained him longer. He came from it, looking puzzled and thwarted.

" I've heard of secret panels in these fine old mansions," he said to himself. " But where? Is it in this room? Where is the wall hollow? Had that black rascal not been in his stables, I could have caught the rebel at the other end of what must be a passageway running underground from somewhere in this house. The cellar, perchance, but how to get there? When he stirred the bushes, ready to spring out, I could have made an end of it then and there, but I feared that black rascal of a servant, so I could only lie among the bushes till the troopers left — curse their tardy legs! Methinks the stone I put there will not be easily moved. That end's safe. Now for this."

He opened the door leading into the passageway. He glanced sharply up and down the spiral staircase, then went to the outer door and bolted it. He took care, however, to see that the door leading back to the hall had been left open. Then up and down, feeling of the wainscoting as before. He reached the region of the secret panel, and listened intently.

" Ah! this is it. The wall is thin. I hear him coming."

He drew himself up close to the wainscoting.

The panel slowly opened a few inches, and Henry Murray looked out. The light seemed to dazzle his eyes. But seeing, hearing nothing, he came out, sword in hand. With a bound the man was upon him. The sword fell from his hand, his arms were held down in a grip like iron.

"If you make one outcry, if you call for help, this knife will go through you," whispered a voice close behind his ear. Twisting his head around, to see, if possible, who the enemy was, Henry Murray beheld naught but a hat drawn down over a face; only two eyes were visible, two blazing eyes — eyes blazing with passion and a deadly purpose.

"Turn around. You have no time to look at me. Go out that door, cross the hall and out the front doorway. I will follow."

Henry Murray refused to stir.

"Go out that door!" The stern voice grew sterner. "Obey me, or my knife goes into your back."

The tone of the voice, even more than the words, made Henry Murray feel that it were well to obey.

"Step softly. Call for no one. Make no noise, or you will rue it. I stab you. You will rot, and I will escape. I can get out that doorway long before any one could come. Now go!"

And go he did. Once outside, and by thickly growing trees hidden from any chance observer from the house, the man spoke once more. And he loosened the iron grip of Henry Murray's hands.

"So you are caught at last. By my troth, you had to remain in your hole longer than I wot."

"Who are you? Push up your hat and let me see your face, you coward."

" Give me those letters ! "

" I have no letters."

" You lie! I saw you take them from Washington's messenger, who was shot from his horse."

" I have no letters."

" You lie! I heard that Quaker talking to you in the Green Tree Tavern. I was on the watch to save the letters. I shot the fool, only to have you thwart me by your wild dash up the street. Turn around. I want your back to me. There! Now, listen. I saw you enter that house. You did not leave it. I saw you try to get out from your hole. Give me those letters."

Henry Murray shook his head.

" On my faith, I shall have them, or you will speed to hell. Give me the letters, and your life is yours. Refuse them me, and it is mine! "

" I have no letters."

" Damnation! I lose patience. Give me those letters, you miserable, treacherous rebel! "

" Ah! 'tis a precious packet of letters, which Howe would be so loath that Washington see. Howe will give you solid gold for it, you spy."

Well was it for Henry Murray's wife and sister that they did not witness the desperate struggle which now took place. Had Murray's arms been free, he had been a match for this unknown assailant; but he did not succeed in freeing his arms. His enemy, too, was at a disadvantage, for he dared not loosen his hold in order to get at sword or pistol. And Murray was in desperate plight to elude the swift lunges of that terrible knife.

The two men fought and struggled together through the shrubbery, back and forth, on and on, till they reached the lane below the Cliveden groun's. Here Henry Murray showed failing strength. Seizing this advantage, the enemy succeeded in dealing him a heavy blow. He fell headlong. But it suited not his enemy's purpose that they should be seen by any chance wayfarer in the lane. Glancing furtively up and down, he saw no one, except a long way off on the highway. He dragged the prostrate man some distance to where the trees grew thicker by the wayside. Then he threw off his hat and cloak.

"At last! The rat had fire in him, but it was no use thinking he could escape me." The man's tone, even to himself, was fierce. "A pretty chase he led me, clear across country. Damn him! Who can he be? Some friend of that rebel Johnson; but he seemed a stranger in the village."

The man's thoughts were swift, and his fingers were still swifter. He began a skilful search of Henry Murray's pockets; muttered a curse, and turned the pockets inside out.

"Where are those letters?"

He glanced up continually and listened.

"Where in hell are those letters? Where has he hid them? In his boots perchance."

The man showed frantic haste, for up the lane he saw two horsemen. He found nothing in Henry Murray's boots.

"Redcoats, by Jove! Where are those letters? Ah! perchance, they are hidden in the saddle of the horse the troopers seized. If so, then they are not on the way to Washington. They are going back where they came from! No, he were not such a fool! If he gave the letters to any one else, they may be soon in Washington's hands. Howe were right angry with me for my failure."

He gave the prostrate form a savage kick, then began his search over again, turning up the sleeves, ripping part of the coat up with his sword. The hoofs were heard nearer.

"I must get away. Sold! sold! Naught for all my breakneck ride, and the killing of the rat!"

Another savage kick, then the man bounded towards a clump of trees, where he had concealed his horse. The creature gave him a warmer welcome than he deserved. It was impatient to be off.

CHAPTER XI.

"That Englishman seems a most kindly disposed and courteous gentleman."

"HEAH! dis litter mus' be got away befoh Missy Margaret come back. I'se been lookin' for you, Jake. Pity de little missus got so hungry couldn't gib us time to clear dese t'ings away. Now she's gwine to de summer-house, an' Missy Margaret an' her fadder come back soon," said Chloe, opening the door from the corridor. She found Jake already in the room.

"Dose flashy redcoats drink a pow'ful sight wine, an' dat cunnel! Augh! Wot you stain' dare, an' look so pale. Be it wid 'thusiasm 'bout somethin' or 'nother?"

Jake was evidently strongly moved by that form of pensive thought to which Chloe gave the name of enthusiasm. He stood with his fingers tightly interlocked, his eyes, with a far-away look in them, fixed upon the sunlit lawn to be seen through the windows, now wide open. Chloe passed her hand over his eyes, then stood back from him, patiently waiting. Then he rewarded her by saying, softly:

"If Missy Margaret could only have seen dat Brown Bess. Oh, she was a beauty! beat Selim or Tempest all hollow."

"No, no, you cawn't say dat!"

"I do say it. Her mane so soft an' glossy! Hebben send dis house such a hoss some day, honey."

Now Jake turned, and succeeded to some extent in casting off the reminiscent mood. He slowly took up a bottle from the floor, but he held it idly in his hand, and suffered his companion to work unaided. Then the mood overcame him once more, and he continued, in a soft, plaintive tone:

"An' her master! I 'clare to hebben dat he's a good man, dat he's too good for our sojers to kill. I feel sorry now, honey, dat men like dat cappin come ober de ocean dus to get killed by Gen'al Washington's sojers. It makes me feel bad, Chloe. My heart's all a-screwed up in my insides, so I can hardly breeve. But dare seems no help for it. Washington's sojers mighty brave an' pow'ful. Dey's irresist — irresistabul, Chloe. I t'ink I shed a tear now when Cappin Peyton an' dat Brown Bess fall on de bloody field."

Chloe nearly dropped a pitcher, her hand shook so.

"Wot bloody field you mean, Jake?"

"Dare'll only be one moah battle, Chloe. De angel ob de Lord will come down an' wipe out all dese British dat's come ober de ocean to beat Gen'al Washington's sojers."

Chloe stood in open-mouthed astonishment. In her excitement she put a glass down hastily, and was in no hurry to take up another.

"De 'Mericans will make an attack on dese British. Ebbery day I look ober de hill yonder, an' I spec' I see de banners flyin', an' de cannon roarin', an' de muskets flashin'. I feel sorry for dese British. Dey's got to perish."

" Ain't any ob dem gwine back to England? " asked Chloe, sadly.

" Not one," answered Jake, solemnly.

" Not dat Gen'ral Howe we seen passin'? "

" Nebber."

" Not dat Cornwallis dat's tuk Philadelphy wid all dose grenendeers? "

Jake shook his head.

" Nor dat lieutenant wid de pretty waves ob hair ober his ears? "

Jake was decided when he once made up his mind. Now he did not flinch.

" Not one, not eben my Cappin Peyton will ebber get back to ole England. Why, it's Providence, Chloe. It's wot de Lord wills. It ain't deir fault, poor t'ings. Dey's a-doin' de bess dey know how, an' dey fight well — no prevaricatin' dat. Dey's brave. Now it's prob'bul dat Cappin Peyton fights like de debbel. He looks though he could. He's got a flash in his eye, a spurrit 'bout him dat I 'lows warrior-like, an' brave an' c'rageous — but — he's British; he wears de debbel's own colour shuh. Dey will all leave deir bones heah, honey."

Chloe gasped. " Heah? Heah in Germantown? "

Jake nodded wisely. " Ay, ob a shuhty, deir bones will all lie heah."

" I lub dat little lieutenant," Chloe said, plaintively. " I tuk scarce notice ob de udder. But my! he tuk plenty notice ob Missy Margaret. I seen dat plain 'nuff."

" An' he tuk notice ob me," said Jake, drawing himself up proudly. " Look heah! "

Chloe bent over Jake's hand.

" He gib ye all dat? "

" All dat, an' he said he'd gib me moah when he come anudder time."

" Jake, dat Cappin's no fool. Ye make mistake 'bout his leabin' *his* bones 'roun' heah. He knows too much to do sech foolish t'ing as dat. Met'inks Massa Murray doan' want no British bones a-lyin' 'roun' loose heah."

Chloe stopped and glanced out-doors. " Dare's Missus Annette a-gwine long de garden paff to de summer-house. Spec' Missy Margaret be long heah soon. Heah, you, you make haste and pick up dose broken bottles, and quit your 'thusiasms. Dis disorder ain't proper. He, he! spec' dose British like de mulled wine too well to throw deir bones 'roun' promiscous. Bones ain't fit to drink sech wine, an' clank sech swords, an' make all dis fuss 'bout. Spec' — "

But Chloe's confidences were cut short by the entrance of Mr. Murray. He came across the hall slowly, then paused to wait for Margaret.

" Till now we have kept Annette from knowing," said Margaret, as she overtook him.

" Yes, dear child."

" Jake, when my brother came out from the secret way, and flung himself on Selim — "

Jake turned with a startled air.

" Your brudder, Missy Margaret? Wot you a-sayin'? Massa Henry been heah, missy? "

Margaret dropped Mr. Murray's arm.

" Jake! has Master Henry not been seen by you? "

" Whar, missy? Whar, missy? I hain't seen him since las' night."

" Entered he not the stables? Took he not Selim,

and rode fast across the rear garden to the road in front?"

"No, no, missy. Selim, he munchin' oats now dis berry minit in his stall."

"Jake!"

"Missy! Wot you look like dat for?"

"Father!"

"He must be still in the underground passage," said Mr. Murray, with trembling voice.

Margaret hastened to the door leading to the spiral staircase. To her consternation, the panel in the wainscot stood open, disclosing the darkness beyond.

Charles Murray followed her slowly, taking hold of the chairs for support.

"Chloe, a candle, quick!"

Chloe rushed back to the mantel, took one of the candles out, lit it by the fire, and rushed with it to Margaret.

"Stay there, Jake, beside Mr. Murray; I will go within."

Margaret seized the candle and entered the dark space. For a moment the candle-light flickered fitfully, then was lost. Margaret had gone down the steps. Charles Murray and Jake and Chloe stood without the open panel expectant.

CHAPTER XII.

"You are most kind, Mistress Murray. We shall not soon forget the hospitality of Benjamin Chew's beautiful home."

A LONG the dusty highway, Peyton and the Lieutenant had ridden slowly till they had come to the shade of some tall trees. They tied their horses and threw themselves upon the fragrant grass. For a time they were both silent; then Shipton spoke suddenly.

"There is no need to hasten to that noisy camp. Musgrave will not be back for hours yet. What boots a delay?"

"An you get not hungry, boy."

"Hungry! Who hath thoughts of eating? Let us eat air and feed on the winds of heaven. Is she not beautiful, Arthur?"

"Beautiful? Who?" But Peyton's heart gave a big thump.

"Why, that little lass who showed me where to take Brown Bess. She is the wife of Mr. Murray's son. Fortunate son of Mr. Murray! Happy son! Man to be envied, of a truth! 'Tis marvellous, Arthur, how she won me. I felt impelled to speak out my heart. I told her all that sad history."

"No, boy! no!"

"Yes; I told her of all you have saved me from, — ruin, disgrace."

" Of a truth, 'twas most unwise."

" Nay, Arthur. It did me good. It helped me. It helped me the way it helps me when I talk to you. Methinks when you go back to England next week, I shall sadly need all the help I can get. Had it not been for my coming, you might be in England now."

In England now! The Fates forbid! This Margaret Murray, who had so stirred the depths of his heart, was not in England.

" If 'twere wise to throw up my commission, I would I could return with you."

" Think not of that, Bob. There is a future before you in the army."

" Not here in this war, Arthur, not unless our leaders " — Shipton glanced around cautiously, then drew nearer to Peyton — " not unless our leaders work together and show more competence. Even I, young and ignorant as I am, can see the one supreme mistake."

Peyton raised himself on his elbow, and looked at his companion sharply. " Be careful, Bob; 'tis best to have strong opinions, but never best to express them freely."

" I will have care of my tongue, Arthur, but here, alone together, we may speak freely. Perchance it may be our last time alone together."

Peyton reached over and touched the boy's hand.

" You have the right of it, Bob," he said, gravely, " when you call it a supreme mistake. I see it well, and have not hesitated in telling Howe that the capture of Philadelphia is of slight moment compared with his junction with Burgoyne. And yet Howe's army has been travelling further and further from

Burgoyne, instead of moving up to help him. Disaster is sure to come."

" Methinks this Washington has had intention to keep the two armies apart."

" This Washington," answered Peyton, warmly, " is a genius in his strategy. He is not beaten yet."

" Was it from that spy of Howe's that intelligence came of Washington's movements on the Shippack Road ? "

" Yes; the man has exceptional advantage. He has access to both camps to serve the wounded. He was of great aid to Howe before the battle at the Brandywine, and at Paoli. He was the chief cause of Wayne's surprise. But, Shipton, I have slight liking for the man; yet, as fate has made me the confidant of Howe, I can but acquiesce in his making peculiar use of this Tory. I have the feeling, Bob, that were Howe's gold to fail, the man could be bought by him who would pay a higher price. This, to you alone, Bob. And remember, too, that no one, except you and me, and Howe himself, has knowledge that this man is aught but a common surgeon."

Shipton nodded gravely.

" I had not troubled you with certain of these matters, were it not that Howe has wish for a trusty youth at his hand when I am gone."

Shipton's eyes glowed.

" I thank you, Peyton; I thank you again."

A long silence fell between them. Peyton lay with his hands behind his head, his eyes fixed on the flying clouds, the brilliant sky. At last he spoke.

" Bob, I return to England with sorrow in my

heart. The trouble between the King and these colonists is not understood there as it ought to be."

"But your report, your study of the country,
your effort to get at the truth of things."

Peyton's face saddened.

"I have worked hard to get at the truth of things;
but I have slight hope that aught I can say will have
much influence with my cousin, Carlisle, or with
any other of the peace commissioners whom the King
intends to send out; though, indeed, Chatham
thought otherwise when he urged me so hard to
undertake this mission. Dear old man! How I
love him! 'Twas to please him that I came; and
now what I shall have to tell him will be that even
his plans for conciliation would not content these
colonists. Burke's opinions are nearer the truth. If
the King had but listened to these men! If he would
but listen now!"

"Then you think that Carlisle and these peace
commissions will do but little good?"

"But little, I fear me — unless they offer that
which is different from their intention now. But
yester-eve came to me a letter from my cousin, in
which he says that he may, perchance, sail soon after
my return, but that he and the other commissioners
will have no authority to offer to the Congress here
that which they insist upon, — an acknowledgment
of independence. But, methinks, Bob, we will talk
politics no longer. Let us enjoy this soft air. See
how it moves those tree-tops. And those clouds,
how fast they sail over the blue! 'Tis a beautiful
world, Bob. O, that we men would not spoil it
by our hates, our discords, our cruelty, our hard
selfishness."

There was another silence, then Peyton suddenly sat up, shading his eyes and looking intently on the road they had come.

"I have dropped my cloak. Can you see it on the roadway? Your eyesight is better than mine."

"No, 'tis not there. But we will walk our horses back."

They untied Brown Bess and the other horse that had been grazing beside her. Bridles in hand, they walked slowly back. Arrived at the lane below Cliveden, Shipton exclaimed:

"There's your cloak up there, beyond that clump of bushes. The breeze must have carried it off the highway. No, 'tis a man lying in a heap in the glaring sun. Ah! see! Some one is bending over him. Damme! he is kicking him."

"Your eyes are like telescopes, Bob," exclaimed Peyton. "I can see no man."

But they sprang on their horses. It took them not long to reach the prostrate form of Henry Murray. Peyton was the first to spring down beside him.

"Who has done this?" His voice was stern, his lips set.

"In truth, it could not be the man Musgrave seeks?" said Shipton.

Peyton looked again at Henry Murray, then up the road.

"No, this is no work of our men. An Englishman would scorn such work as this. Besides, they took the Limekiln Road."

"There! There! See the cowardly thief!" shouted Shipton. "'Tis he who has done this." He pointed down the lane. "There! See him be-

yond that rise in the ground. He's riding as if
the fiends were after him. I would like you to give
Brown Bess a chance to catch him, the cowardly
thief!"

Peyton stood for a moment, as if in doubt, his
hand on his sword. Then he looked sorrowfully
down at Henry Murray once more.

"Poor fellow! Of a truth, we cannot leave him
here. We shall have to let the man go. I wonder
who this is. He's not a soldier. He has no uniform. His sword has been torn away; also his
pistol from his belt."

"How fine that lace is around his wrists."

"He has been treated most shamefully, Shipton.
See the bruises! . . . 'Tis a mean, bad world. How
little love there seems to be. How little! And we
all need love. O God! we need it sore."

Peyton knelt down on the grass and touched Murray's hand.

"Shipton! Shipton! He's not yet dead!"

Peyton put his ear to his heart.

"He is yet living! His heart is beating, Shipton! We cannot leave him here; we must take him
somewhere."

"It will kill him to move him."

"We must take the risk, Shipton. 'Tis too far
to go to camp. We are very near Mr. Murray's.
There is love there; there are kind hearts there,
Shipton. They will take him in. They'll find his
mother for him. For he *must* have a mother somewhere! A mother or a sister!"

Here was this strong soldier, who had fought
so gallantly at the Brandywine that the story of
it was on the lips of every common trooper, bending

now tenderly over this stricken stranger, speaking of him with tears in his voice, caring not whether he was friend or foe.

To Shipton, who had seen this man with the wounded at the Brandywine, this occasioned no surprise. Shipton himself had felt this man's tenderness.

"Come, now! Let us lift him on Brown Bess. She will walk slowly if I tell her to. You lead her, and your horse will follow. And we'll find this boy's mother for him. No, we shall have to carry him. Never mind the horses. Tie them behind that clump of bushes. Methinks they will be well out of sight."

CHAPTER XIII.

"But love is a gift sent down from Heaven itself to bless this sad, distracted world."

THE candle-light was seen again, and Margaret came out from the dark passage. Her face was startled and white, her eyes excited.

"Father, he is not there, and at the other end there is something heavy, like a stone. I could not get out."

"I go see, missy." And Jake hurried away.

Chloe's quick ear had caught the sound of steps outside. She hurried across the hall to one of the windows.

"Missy, missy, dare be British redcoats walkin' up de paff."

"Those troopers back again. Curse them!" said Mr. Murray.

"No, massa, I see no hoss. Dey both carryin' some one. Dey got some one in deir arms."

Margaret stood pale and motionless.

Voices were heard without. Then the sound of a sword-hilt striking one of the doors.

"Chloe, open it!" said Mr. Murray, with an imperative gesture.

One of the big doors was opened softly. A great beam of sunlight entered and fell in glory across

the floor. In the sunlight stood the two Englishmen. In their arms was — could Chloe be sure? —
yes, 'twas Massa Harry — dead — and where was
the poor young wife?

"Your good services, girl. This is the only house
near," said Peyton, quickly. "We were on our
way to camp when, on the road there, we came upon
this poor fellow, lying in a heap. We could not
leave him. Pray crave admittance for us from your
mistress."

Back in the shadows, beside her father, stood Margaret. Chloe, with trembling hand, pointed to her.
Then Peyton saw her.

"Whether he be friend or foe, it matters not.
He must have help at once, or he will die."

Margaret simply bowed her head.

The two Englishmen brought Henry Murray in,
and laid him gently on the settee at the left. Then,
with a stifled cry, she flung herself down beside him.

Peyton turned anxiously to Charles Murray.

"You know him, then?"

"He is my son. Tell me! tell me!"

Peyton gently supported the trembling man, to
whom the sunlight was but a gray mist.

"It is not death. Take heart."

At that moment Jake entered, hurriedly.

"Missy, missy, dare's a big stone 'gainst de end
ob de passage." He stopped and looked wonder-
ingly at the group before him. Margaret rose.

"Heed it not now, Jake. But ride Selim in all
haste to the village, and summon a surgeon."

Jake made as if to go.

"Stay! If that young surgeon, Doctor Worthington, who has but recently arrived in the village

to care for the wounded, can be found, bring him also in haste. Much have I heard of his skill."

Jake made for the door. Margaret turned to her brother, then started suddenly. He had failed! What had he told her to do? She turned again and stopped Jake by an imperative gesture.

"Stay! I shall need you myself, for I ride forth in but a few moments. Send Sam and Tom on Tempest and Kit for the surgeon, and you bring Selim and Prince, well saddled, to the portico in all haste."

While she had been speaking, Charles Murray had knelt down beside Henry Murray, feeling his heart, stroking his hair, — all marks of trembling, pathetic tenderness. Margaret put out her hand unsteadily. Peyton started forward to help her, but by a supreme effort of will she controlled herself once more.

Shipton sprang to Henry Murray and supported his head.

"Egad! Peyton, something must be done at once to stop this blood."

Peyton touched Margaret's arm gently. "Of a truth, your brother needs help ere the surgeon arrives. Your pardon, but permit us to carry him up-stairs. I am very strong, and no stranger to illness."

Margaret looked at Henry Murray irresolutely.

"Consent, consent, sweet lady; Captain Peyton may save his life. Let him do all he wishes," said Shipton, eagerly. "He has saved many a life for your King."

Her King! Then they did not know. They did

not suspect. She felt Peyton's wistful, questioning eyes upon her.

"Chloe, the big bedroom over the parlour," she said, faintly.

Up the stairs, slowly, carefully, went the two Englishmen. How tender they were! how strong and helpful! Margaret followed them with her eyes. Mr. Murray came and grasped her arm.

"Daughter," he said, faintly, "what of the letters he gave you?"

"Father, I must go at once. 'Tis a long ride, you know. I cannot even wait to be of much help to them. And Annette! Poor girl! I will not be here to comfort her." Margaret's voice trembled.

"O daughter, if you would but send Jake."

"I dare not! I dare not! No one could suspect what I carry. Whereas Jake might not have wit even to be able to get through either the British or the American lines. O father! I must not stop to talk. You know I *must* go. There is no choice. I'm the only one."

"Jake must carry arms."

"Yes, and I have my pistol in my saddle. I shall be perfectly safe, dear father. Father, dear father, look not so troubled. Reck you of aught else that can be done? I *must* go. O father! I must not stop to talk. You *know* I must go. There is no choice. Come up-stairs now. Chloe will know what to do to help them after I go."

But Mr. Murray shook his head. "I would be but a hindrance, daughter. Stay with them as long as you possibly can."

When Margaret was in her own room, alone with her anxious thoughts, her courage almost failed her.

" It breaks my heart to go before he regains consciousness, but I must. The safety of our whole army may depend on those letters," she kept saying to herself, as with numb fingers she fastened the buttons of her riding-habit. Then she seemed to hear her brother's voice once more: " Quick, Margaret! Take these letters! Hide them in your gown. If aught happen to me, they *must* go to Washington. His camp is at Skippack Creek." " Quick, Margaret! Quick, Margaret!" kept repeating itself in her excited brain. " Yes! yes! Washington *must* have the letters if I fail."

CHAPTER XIV.

"She could never forget the terror, the turmoil, — yes, — and the joy of that day."

CHLOE stood a moment alone in the hall. She had been sent for bandages, and in her excited mind conjectures as to the best and quickest way to get them ran riot with thoughts of the two soldiers to whom this stricken household already owed such a heavy debt.

"Talk ob deir nebber gittin' back to ole England," she muttered to herself. "Dat cappin now; he's safe! *He* won't nebber be killed by Gen'al Washington's sojers. Ef he was wounded now, like Massa Harry, he'd cure hisself, an' eben ef he was killed, he'd manage to crawl out de bad fix. *He* won't nebber leab no bones in dis country."

"My! ain't he a pictur' now in his glitterin' red," she continued, as she came face to face with Peyton at the top of the stairs. "He *ain't* wearin' de debbel's own colour. He's an angel ob light, he is, an' he's pow'ful kind to Massa Harry, an' met'inks de Lord tuk notice how he comforted poor Missus Annette when she come in, white an' scared, t'inkin' Massa Harry dead. . . . An' he's mos' as tall as my Jake. Ay, I t'ink so."

"Yes, Massa Cappin, I'se got dem," she said aloud. "I'll gib dem to Missus Annette. . . . Massa

Murray pow'ful worried, an' wants you down dare one minnit."

Peyton leaned over the stairs. He could see Mr. Murray at the foot.

"Yes, Mr. Murray," he said, softly. "Take heart. There is much hope." Then he went back.

As Margaret hurried down the staircase, her heart gave a quick throb of pain as she saw the grief in her father's face.

"Father, be not troubled. It may be well into the night ere we return, but I shall be safe, father, dear father! I shall return as soon as — "

For a moment neither of them could speak. Then the father said, brokenly: "That Englishman seems a most kindly disposed and courteous gentleman; we owe him much."

"Yes, father, he has saved Harry's life perchance. And the Lieutenant, too. Of a truth, he is equally kind."

"Jake has not yet come with the horses. O Margaret! The mystery of all this trouble, the mystery!"

"And we dare not question these Englishmen. They might suspect."

"Hush! He is coming."

Mr. Murray raised a warning hand.

Captain Peyton showed a trace of surprise at seeing Margaret Murray in riding-hat and habit. His face was grave, and there was unmistakable anxiety in his eyes. She gave him one swift, imploring look. How she longed to explain, to set herself right as it were. She could have borne reproach in his manner more easily than this gentle, grave dignity.

"Mistress Murray, bethink yourself. Go not

away from your brother. I am at your service. Let me go for you."

Margaret's heart nearly stopped beating. " Oh! it must be done. I must go."

" Let me go for you."

" No! no!"

" I can find twenty surgeons within the hour."

" Oh! it is not that," answered Margaret under her breath.

Peyton smiled. " You can trust me."

" I know it. I know it. But you cannot go. No! No!"

Margaret's voice was almost inaudible. He looked at her with sympathy and deference. How she blessed him in her heart for this unquestioning courtesy.

" Then I will stay here," he said, softly. " I may be of service. I can help you. Let me stay."

" We already owe you much," said Mr. Murray.

" I have done naught, sir," Peyton answered, as he looked inquiringly, eagerly at Margaret. Her eyes were blinded by a sudden mist of tears.

" But we have no right to keep you," she said, brokenly.

" There is naught to take me back till nightfall, unless the trumpets blow for battle. And there is no sign of that. I am not in this country to fight. I have no command, though, in truth, when I am with my friends, and they have to fight, I help them."

He smiled, then there came a great longing into his voice. " Ah! dear lady, you love him; you love your brother. There is not too much love in this sad world. Love is beautiful. It is of heaven. Let me help you."

She gave him both her hands, with a quick, self-forgetful impulse. She found voice after a pause. " I thank you; I hope you will stay."

There was a look in his eyes which made her own droop. A soft flush came into her cheeks. " How dear, how sweet she is," he thought.

" Thank you, thank you for all your kindness," she said, faintly. Then she went towards the big doorway.

" There is Jake with the horses. Father, good-bye; I shall be back ere midnight, I hope."

" Mistress Murray! you ride not through the night? 'Tis dangerous. No! It cannot be." Captain Peyton looked quickly from father to daughter.

Something in their faces told him that this was no common errand which took her away thus. Something in their faces told him also that they would brook no intrusion upon their reserve.

" Mistress, your pardon."

She bowed in silence. Then Charles Murray took his way slowly up the staircase. " Good-bye," he said. Margaret's eyes lingered on him a moment, then came back to Peyton. He spoke eagerly.

" You will permit me to put you on your horse? Were it not for aiding your brother, I would I might have the honour of going for you, or at least guarding you on your journey."

Her face softened. " I fear me, sir, that were impossible."

" The roads are full of lawless troops. Go not into danger, Mistress Murray. Remember you are needed by — by your brother."

He was standing in the doorway. The light fell full on his face. His uniform sparkled. It seemed to Margaret that she had never looked on a goodlier face. Her whole heart went out to him there. Then she spoke, as if to herself and under her breath. "How hard to go! How hard it is!"

"Would it be more bearable for you were I to promise to remain till your return?"

She gave him a long, searching look. The look changed suddenly. An unlimited trust in him came into her heart.

"Thank you, no; it is too much. But stay till the surgeon comes, and comfort my father."

There was a pause.

"Yes, comfort him. He sorely needs it."

Peyton stood and entreated her with his eyes.

"I hope, — yes, — I hope you will stay — till I return, — stay with him."

She gave him her hand again, and, as he held it, she said, in a voice which he could scarcely hear: "Oh, sir! could you but know how we thank you. We thank you from our hearts."

The next moment she and Jake were dashing towards the gate. The thick trees soon hid them from his view, but just before they disappeared, she turned in her saddle and looked back. He waved his sword. Then, with set, stern face, he went back to Henry Murray, to wage a desperate fight with the Angel of Death.

CHAPTER XV.

"Yes, that is one of the bitternesses of this war. It is not between alien countries, but between men who are brothers."

IN the late afternoon of that same day, Washington sat in his tent. It had been a day of many perplexities and cares, and now he was trying to snatch a few moments' rest in order to write letters and to talk to young Alexander Hamilton, who sat on a rough stool before a board supported on two barrels, which served as a table. Papers, quills, and ink-wells were scattered over the table. Directly in front of the General was an empty glass and a bottle filled with water; further back on the table was another empty glass. Four unlit candles were beside it. As the two men wrote and talked, camp noises could be heard from without, — an occasional shout, the tread of the sentries, the neighing of steeds.

"I am not without hope," wrote the General, "that the acquisition of Philadelphia may, instead of his good fortune, prove General Howe's ruin. The loss of the city is an event which we had reason to wish had not happened, and which will be attended with certain ill consequences; but I hope it will not be so detrimental as many apprehend, and that a little time and perseverance will give us some favourable opportunity of recovering our loss, and of putting our affairs in a more flourishing condition."

He looked up and caught Hamilton's eye.

" The discouragements of the campaign are wearing upon the nerves of the army."

" True, and my own hope burns faintly at times," Hamilton answered, gravely.

" But if we can but all keep together. We should all — Congress and army — be considered as one people, acting on the same principle, and to the same end."

" Yes, yes," answered Hamilton, with a sad inflection to his rich voice, for his thoughts were busy with the men who were jealous of the great general, and doing much to weaken his influence with the Congress and with the people. He was thinking of Conway, of Gates, of Lee. He knew more of the evil they were doing than Washington himself. In truth, Hamilton's heart was sore to-day; but he kept his own counsel.

Then Washington spoke again.

" The cause for which we are struggling is just and right. We are fighting for our homes, our children, for our very existence as a nation — a nation in its infancy. Only one year old!" Washington's voice grew husky. He threw down his pen, and went to the side of the tent, seizing one of the ropes dangling down and replacing it in its position. He stood with his hand on the tent-pole and continued:

" But we are destined to become one of the greatest nations the world has ever seen. To that end let us be patient, and do what lies in our feebleness and weakness to hasten the great future; and, though we make mistakes, or have reverses, are misunderstood often, and harassed on every hand, let this be forgotten when we ourselves are dust. Let the bright deeds live in our history. And the suffering and the toil and the cruelty and the bloodshed be forgotten."

He began pacing up and down, his arms folded over his breast, his eyes bent in thought. Then he said, slowly: "Though the people and the Congress think we are defeated, we have yet cause for self-gratulation."

Hamilton's eyes glowed.

"You mean, sir, that we are keeping apart the two great armies of the enemy."

"Yes; I cannot yet fathom the cause of General Howe's not making effort to join General Burgoyne. He will gain little benefit from Philadelphia, except a comfortable housing for his troops. Without him, Burgoyne is lost. I wait the chance to strike him a blow that will be felt. The forts on the Delaware are still ours. Germantown has too strong a force for us to make an attack, but occasion may yet serve us."

Just then an orderly appeared at the entrance to the tent. Hamilton rose and took a paper from him.

"Light-Horse Harry desires to inform your Excellency that he has returned from a skirmishing expedition, and has brought in nineteen prisoners," he said, approaching Washington.

"Inform Captain Lee of my appreciation of the service, and order the disposal of the prisoners in the usual manner."

Hamilton had not been seated long ere another

orderly appeared. They spoke together, then Hamilton again addressed Washington.

"That physician who has been around the camp so much since the battle of Brandywine — "

"Ah! Worthington, you mean. He brings news from the Marquis?"

"I know not if he has the Marquis's wound in charge, but he is without, and earnestly wishes to speak with you."

"Admit him."

Hamilton ushered in a tall, distinguished-looking man, with piercing eyes, deferential, polished manner. He bowed to Washington gracefully and respectfully. The General returned the salute with grave courtesy.

"I come direct from Germantown, your Excellency. There are rumours which may be of some service to you. You know my profession gives me many opportunities. I am thought to be neutral. But as you well know, I have our great cause at heart." Worthington's voice was pleasant. It had a sincere tone in it.

Washington bowed.

"Be seated, sir," he said, as he himself sat down.

"I thank your Excellency. I have ridden hard."

"Now, sir, your news; time waits not."

"I well know that you watch but for a chance to attack the enemy when he is off guard. There are rumours current in the British camp that you purpose to attack soon. Intelligence has been brought to Howe of your moving five miles nearer him than you were at the time he took possession of the village."

Doctor Worthington did not add that 'twas he

himself who had brought this intelligence to Howe. He went on in an earnest tone: " Now, I have ridden hard hither to tell you that the British camp at Germantown has but to-day been strengthened. Troops are pouring in fast from Philadelphia. This is no time to strike."

Washington closely observed the speaker. But his face was impassive.

" This morning, early, I was at Howe's head-quarters at Stenton. There is a wounded officer of his staff who is under my care. Egad! sir, my chance was not to be lost! I heard the General have speech with Sir Henry Stachey as I passed through the big hall. They were of the opinion that, after the drubbing our army had at the Brandywine, you would scarce venture an attack; but, lest you had such intention, they would strengthen their force in Germantown, and take especial precaution. Now, I assure your Excellency that General Howe's forces are so strong, our army would be certain to suffer disaster were you to make the attack. Now, you will not do so, General?"

" I am not in the habit of communicating my plans, Mr. Worthington."

" Pardon me, sir."

" But I thank you; I shall bear your words in mind."

Hamilton gave Worthington a penetrating glance. Worthington met his eye unflinchingly, half haughtily. Then Hamilton turned and went out slowly, returning the next moment with a paper, which he laid before the General. Washington laid his hand on the paper, Worthington watching him furtively.

" Pardon me, your Excellency, one reason I spoke

of your perchance attacking Germantown was that, when I left the village, there were vague rumours that one of your men had seized letters from a private messenger of Mr. Howe's."

Washington glanced through the paper.

"I could gain no certain information; but, as I left the village, some troopers shot past me in pursuit of the man who had the letters. He was doubtless on his way to your Excellency. You have probably received them."

Washington glanced up with interest, but remained silent. Worthington was getting anxious.

"His face is a mask," he said to himself. "How am I to find out if he have heard aught of those letters?"

Then he added aloud, "Methought that if perchance you had received the letters, they might change your plans, sir."

"They probably will do so, Mr. Worthington."

"But I warn you, General, that I heard rumours at Stenton that those letters, written by General Howe to his brother, the Admiral, were a feint, designed to fall into your hands. The enemy would act directly contrary to their import."

"Ah! heard you that, Mr. Worthington?"

"Yes; the British being strengthened, and you decoyed to make the attack, 'tis easy to see the argument, your Excellency."

"I see it plainly, sir." Washington glanced again at the paper in his hand. "Mr. Hamilton," he said, "Captain Trumbull is in the adjoining tent. He has had another bleeding from his wound, and earnestly wishes to have speech with us ere he grows weaker. Your indulgence, Mr. Worthington. We will soon return."

Hamilton held the flap of the tent aside, that the General might pass out. Doctor Worthington was in the tent alone.

He listened to the receding footsteps, then glanced around cautiously. Drawing from his pocket a small packet, he held it in his hand a moment, and listened again. Nothing could be heard but the noises of the camp in the distance and the steady tread of the sentry near.

He went over to the rude table, and with skill and swiftness poured the contents of the packet into the empty glass on the side nearest him. He replaced the packet in his pocket, while glancing furtively towards the entrance of the tent. Then he walked with steady step and nonchalant air to the rear of the tent. He had not long to wait. And he turned an expectant, deferential face towards Hamilton, as he once more lifted the canvas flap for Washington to enter.

" What is your proof of these movements you describe? Have you naught in writing?" asked Washington, coming over to the table and seating himself.

" No, your Excellency. This morning I was in the British camp. This afternoon I am here. I kept my ears open for news. I saw the troops pouring into Germantown. I heard several officers in the Green Tree Tavern discussing their plans, of which I have already informed your Excellency." Worthington drew up a stool and also sat down.

" You brought information to me on the twenty-first that it was Mr. Howe's intention to turn the right of my army. I followed him, as you know, on the opposite side of the river. But you informed me not that, on the night of the twenty-second, he was to make that countermarch, by which he got to the ford below, and pushed on towards Philadelphia. If your means of information are what you claim them to be, I should have been notified of this."

"After I left Mr. Howe's camp, he must have changed his plans. Egad! your Excellency, a man cannot do more than possible. I desire to serve my country, and I risk death by hanging. Of a surety, what you pay me for my services is not much compensation for that risk."

"True, sir! Our country pays her servants very little in these unhappy times."

The General rose and began pacing up and down, his brow contracting in serious thought. He apparently had forgotten Worthington's presence. He sighed deeply, as if his heart were oppressed. Then he went to the rude table, and took up a quill. He held it idly in his hand and spoke again.

"Find you the country round about affected to the patriot cause?"

"There be many Quakers and neutrals, as you know." Worthington smiled blandly.

"And many Tories, too, methinks."

"Many men are loyalists because they are entrapped by the brilliancy, the dash, the fine array of these British."

"Think you not that many look with a rueful eye on patriotism in rags?"

"Ha! ha! Yes; very good, your Excellency, very good."

Washington did not smile. Worthington's face grew serious.

"Ah! you refer to the time when the patriot army marched through the city only a few weeks ago?"

Washington bowed.

"The men were in partial rags. Where there were uniforms, they were faded and dusty. They had sprigs of green in their hats to make an harmonious array."

"I was in the crowd of onlookers, your Excellency, and rejoiced at the enthusiasm of the Whigs."

Worthington smiled somewhat cynically. "But the women were the most taken by the British," he added.

Washington flung down his pen, impatiently. "You wrong them, sir."

Worthington's smile became indulgent. "Your pardon, your Excellency, but I wrong them not. Could you but see how the women in the city are welcoming these fops, these perfumed officers, these gold-laced, bepowdered men, with their sparkling red — these — "

"You wrong these women of our land," thundered the General. "Without them our hearts would indeed grow weary. Our patriotism would lose its fire. Our blows would lack power."

He turned to Alexander Hamilton, who stood beside him with a slip of paper. Hamilton's face was flushed. His eyes shone. His voice was not as steady as before.

"Your Excellency, a young girl was stopped at the outer posts. But she insisted that her news was of much moment, and demanded that she be allowed to come here under guard. They have placed her servant in custody. She is without, and desires that this be given you."

On the slip of paper he handed Washington were the words, " Margaret Murray, The Chew House, Germantown."

" Will you speak with her without? " he asked, with a significant glance in Worthington's direction. He could not conquer a vague distrust of the General's visitor.

" Yes, yes," answered Washington; and as he hastened out, he said to himself, " The daughter of my old friend, — one of the truest friends I have, — one of the few, the very few true friends. A sweet maiden, truly. I well remember her that night I tarried with them. How warm was her heart with love of liberty. 'Twas a memorable night when we sat by the big fire and talked. 'Twas a night to make us young again; to make us forget grief and pain and loss and disappointed hopes; to make our hearts glow with enthusiasm, with courage, with high and holy purposes. Will ever occasion serve that we have such a night again? "

CHAPTER XVI.

"And though we make mistakes or have reverses; are misunderstood often and harassed on every hand, let this be forgotten when we ourselves are dust. Let the bright deeds live in our history. And the suffering and the toil and the cruelty and the bloodshed be forgotten."

THE light was growing dim inside the tent. Hamilton went to the table and lit the candles upon it.

"Of a surety, Colonel, you like not darkness," quoth Worthington, laughing. "Methinks 'tis most time I rode back to the British camp. But 'twere best that I wait till the twilight fall. Though considered neutral, and my care for the wounded furnishing excuse for visiting both camps, I can serve our cause best by *to-night* going under cover of darkness."

Hamilton gave him a swift, penetrating glance. "Why to-night?"

Worthington lowered his voice. "There are Tories round about your camp, Colonel Hamilton. I can perchance learn if they seek to find out if his Excellency intend to move his army to attack Germantown. I can learn if they have discovered aught of his plans, and if they have, I can ride back and warn the General."

Hamilton bowed gravely. "Think you not that many of these Tories play a dangerous game?"

Worthington looked at Hamilton furtively. A gleam of anxiety came into his eyes. " I know not your meaning, sir."

" Captain Lee caged three of these spies outside the camp only two hours ago. No! News will not be carried to Germantown to-night of any move of our army."

Worthington smiled. " No, Colonel Hamilton, there will not. We will make that sure."

" His Excellency has had some experience of spies and traitors to our cause. He has also learned the value of true friends. Know you aught of his friend, Charles Murray, of Germantown?"

" Murray, Murray? I first fell in with these British at Wilmington whither the sick and wounded from the Brandywine had been conveyed. I know few of the people in Germantown village. Where lives this true friend of the General?"

Did Hamilton notice the slight tone of sarcasm in Worthington's voice?

" He lives in The Chew House. Cliveden, 'tis called. We slept there — the General and two of his staff — last month."

" Oh, yes! yes! That is a fine mansion, as rumour hath it, on the Main Road, about a mile from the village. I may have passed it oft, not knowing the owner. But Chew — Benjamin Chew believes in the redress of grievances, not in revolution. He has not been in favour with the Congress."

" Benjamin Chew and his old-time friend, Charles Murray, think not alike."

For once, Alexander Hamilton forgot to be reserved with this talkative physician. He added, with a warm glow in his rich, musical voice:

"He has a most beautiful daughter. She has been the toast of every patriot youth in city and village for many a day."

Worthington smiled. "And the British are in the village and have possession of the city. She will now be the toast of many a gay redcoat."

"God forbid!" exclaimed Hamilton, fervently. "Margaret Murray would scarce favour the enemies of her country. She has scant liking for sparkling red, methinks."

"These Chews are rich, as rumour hath it," continued Worthington, insinuatingly.

"Perchance! In truth, Mistress Murray has come into inheritance of a handsome property from her mother, and a large estate in Virginia belongs to her, also."

Worthington's eyes gleamed. Hamilton turned quickly. The General stood in the doorway of the tent. Beside him was a young girl whose riding-skirt was spotted with mud. There were signs of weariness in her face. She was breathing rapidly. Washington held up the flap for her to enter. The rays of the setting sun streamed through the open space behind her and touched with beauty her face and figure.

Worthington's eyes fixed themselves upon her with an intensity characteristic of the man. Hamilton hastened forward with a stool.

"Your business is done with me, is it not?" asked the General, turning to Worthington. "If in your care of the wounded, you can continue to bring me word of the strength of Cornwallis's forces in the city, and of Howe's movements in Germantown, I shall esteem it well."

He handed Hamilton a slip of paper. Hamilton went to the tent door, and these were the words he read: —

"Direct that this man be closely watched. Have him conducted immediately to the outer posts, and if he do not leave at once, I am to be immediately informed."

"Mr. Hamilton?" Hamilton crunched the paper in his hand and turned to the General. "Conduct Mr. Worthington."

Margaret had passed Doctor Worthington without looking up; but now at the General's mention of his name, she started, showed agitation. Then she exclaimed:

"Doctor Worthington! Oh!"

Worthington stepped forward. "Ah, mistress! Pardon me if my remembrance is at fault."

"No — you know me not. But many soldiers visiting my home have told me of your skill with the wounded. I had sent — "

She broke off suddenly, and turned away to hide her agitation.

"You had sent for *me?* Tell me — " He showed eagerness and much admiration for her; though his manner was deferential and courteous.

"It is a desperate case — at my own home — "

She put out her hand blindly to catch the table. Hamilton sprang to her help. The General hastily poured from the bottle of water into the glass on the table in which Worthington had put the poison. A horrified, startled look came into Worthington's face. Washington stepped forward, the glass out-

stretched towards Margaret. With a quick movement, Worthington hit the General's arm, as if
by accident. The glass fell to the ground, shattered at Washington's feet. Washington and Hamilton looked at Worthington in surprise. He bowed
low with a well-simulated air of chagrin and apol-
ogy.

"Your pardon, your Excellency, a thousand pardons. I knew not I was yet like an awkward
schoolboy. Zounds! what a misfortune." He
looked dubiously at the fragments of glass on the
ground.

"But 'tis not beyond repair." He seized the
glass at the other side of the table and poured
water into it, offering it to Margaret with deference. "An accident has befallen at your home, fair
lady? It pleasures me to go thither as soon as possible. Where is it?"

He looked at her eagerly, almost boldly. But
she paid no heed. She regained self-control with
difficulty.

"'Tis at Germantown," she said, faintly. "At
Benjamin Chew's summer home. I pray you, go
at once."

Worthington glanced at Hamilton and smiled.
"Colonel Hamilton was but speaking of you before you came in. May I not wait and escort
you home? My way lies with yours."

"'Tis better that you wait not for her. Her
horse is spent, and herself in no condition to ride
for a full half-hour." The General's tone, for all
its courtesy, had authority in it.

"I implore you to hasten," said Margaret, faintly.
"Captain Peyton is still there."

"Captain Peyton!" The surprise in Worthington's tone was unfeigned. But Margaret could say no more. The General gave Worthington an imperative gesture of dismissal. The latter started to go; then turned impetuously.

"Pray hasten, Mr. Worthington. You had intention to return to Germantown at once, I understand. Have the great kindness to hasten. Mistress Murray will follow you within the half-hour."

The General gave Hamilton a significant look.

Hamilton bowed Worthington out. Washington and Margaret stood a moment listening to the receding footsteps. Then he turned to her.

"My dear Mistress Murray, you have done a service for your country to-day. I thank you."

He gave her his hand.

"I trust occasion may serve for me to thank your brother. Now you must rest."

"I am not tired, sir. I must get back before daybreak. My father needs me, and my brother, — I know not even if he be living."

"Ah, Mistress Murray — women as well as men sacrifice themselves for their country."

She covered her face with one hand and turned away. Washington's voice grew very gentle and yet was firm. "Your horse must be bestowed and fed, and you yourself rest."

He took her hand and guided her trembling steps to a pile of cloaks and coats in one corner of the tent which served as a rough couch. One of his rare smiles lit up the General's face, and he won from her almost a smile in return.

"You have acted with judgment, Mistress Murray. I commend your discretion. But you must remain a few moments. You have had a long and perilous ride."

" I have been preserved from peril, Mr. Washington." But she felt she had no will to combat his. She sank on the rough seat and buried her face in her hands.

" Colonel Hamilton? " called Washington, sharply. He had heard a footstep outside the tent. " Colonel Hamilton? "

Hamilton appeared at the entrance to the tent.

" An orderly has been sent with Mr. Worthington to the outer posts? "

" Yes, your Excellency."

" He has intention to depart at once? "

" Yes, your Excellency."

" Is no one outside? "

Hamilton went to the entrance and looked out into the deepening twilight.

" No one is within hearing," he said as he turned again.

" Mr. Hamilton, letters are here of much moment. They are from General Howe to his brother, the Admiral. They intimate that the Britsh cannot feel secure in the city till they have driven us from our forts on the Delaware. A large force of the British troops at Germantown moves out tonight to form a junction with the Admiral's forces. Their object is to attack the redoubts at Billingsport, and thus march on Forts Mifflin and Mercer up the Delaware. Have the goodness, Mr. Hamilton, to take note that General Varnum be directed to be on hand with his brigade to render reinforcements at Forts Mercer and Mifflin, as occasion may require. Now is our time to strike the blow for which we have been waiting. The camp at Germantown is in a weakened state. Now is our time to strike the blow. Another letter reveals a plot of deadly import. But take the letters, Hamilton. They will tell you the mischief."

Hamilton took the packet Margaret had brought, and as he read, he frowned; then said, thoughtfully:

"Ah! Worthington spoke of these. Rumours that they are a feint, he said; act directly contrary to their import? No! It is well, well, indeed, that we have these letters. But — but — "

He stopped and looked at Washington, and then at Margaret. She raised her head from her hands.

"*You* brought them, Mistress Murray?"

"Yes, Hamilton, she brought them."

Hamilton's eyes glowed.

"My brother," she said, quietly, "has long been on the watch to be of some service to you. This morning he gained possession of these letters. How I have not yet had time to learn. Nor know I how he came to be suspected. He had started to ride to you, when he was suddenly pursued. He read the letters that he might happily tell them to you, but he hurried to me with them, that I might, if he failed, see them in your hands. He failed. . . . I am here with the letters, Mr. Hamilton." A faint smile crossed her face.

But before Hamilton could reply, the General said, quickly, "Mr. Hamilton, bring me that map of Germantown and the roads roundabout."

Hamilton went out hastily.

"Now rest, Margaret," the General said, imperatively. Then he turned to the table, and busied himself in gathering up the papers and articles upon it.

"My servant Jake?"

"Mr. Hamilton will see that he be sent for and will attend you in safety. Now, Margaret, you are not obeying me, and I expect obedience in all my soldiers. Your father is my friend. Rest, child, rest."

She went back to the pile of cloaks.

"I trust you as my own daughter, Margaret. You have heard these secret orders. When you arrive at home, 'tis possible you may find that surgeon there."

"That man is not for our cause?" said Margaret, hastily.

"Happily so — I have no cause to doubt it. But we are all on guard these perilous days. Mr. Worthington has seemed disposed to give us good service since we came into this region." Washington laid down a paper and examined another. "But we have known him so short a time, and have had no occasion to test his allegiance to our cause. Besides, the Tories are as thick here as the oak-trees on yon hill. I feel we can trust so few around us. But I can trust you as were you my own daughter."

Margaret caught the General's hand from among the papers and kissed it softly. Her eyes were full of tears.

"Here, Mr. Hamilton, lay the map on this side of the table."

Hamilton obeyed.

"Now, Mr. Hamilton, see, the village of Germantown, as you remember, consists chiefly of a single street about two miles long, with stone houses fronting the street, with gardens and orchards in the rear. The centre of the village is at the Market Square, an open space, you remember. Mount Airy is about two miles from the Market Square, Chestnut Hill another mile nearly north. At Chestnut Hill, the road branches, one branch going to Reading, the other to Bethlehem. The village can be approached not only by this Germantown Road from Chestnut Hill, but by the Manatawny Road or Ridge Road which runs down by the Schuylkill bank, crosses the School House Lane, and on towards Philadelphia. The Limekiln Road, coming from the northeast, becomes at Luken's Mill continuous with Church Lane. The Old York Road, still further eastward, joins the Germantown Road about two miles below the Market Square at the Rising Sun Tavern. Now the good patriot who drew this map for me tells me how strongly and to much advantage Howe has entrenched his army. Our only hope is to attack him on all sides, and simultaneously. The right wing under Grant, stationed on Church Lane, with advance-posts on the Limekiln, must be attacked by a portion of our army which will advance along the Limekiln Road. Other of our brigades must go by the Old York Road, so as to get in the rear of this right wing and cut it off. Agnew and Grey, with the Hessians under Knyphausen are in School Lane, extending to the Manatawny with extreme pickets on the Wissahickon. They must be attacked by our men who will march down the Manatawny Road. The main portion of our forces will march on the village by Chestnut Hill, and drive the enemy down on the main encampment at the Market Square."

"And below at Stenton, where Howe has his headquarters," said Hamilton, looking up from the map.

"Yes — and in some manner we must send advance forces to cut off Howe's headquarters from possible communication with Cornwallis in the city. Now, Mr. Hamilton, send an order at once with a request to Captain Allen McLane to attend me in my tent immediately, and, Mr. Hamilton, do me the favour to send messengers at once to Generals Sullivan, Greene, Wayne, Armstrong, and Maxwell. Our army will make preparations to march to attack Germantown. Hasten, Mr. Hamilton, to send the messengers."

With a farewell glance at Margaret, Hamilton hastened away.

"Oh! General, General Washington," she cried, breathlessly, and she laid a shaking hand on the map lying on the table. "Our home is but a mile from the Market Square, on the way to Mount Airy. The Fortieth Regiment is near us. Oh! there will be a battle! It will be near our home!"

"Yes, unless the enemy will move within the next two days. And I have information that they seem to be well satisfied in Germantown. They will be off guard. If we can but force in the pickets at Mount Airy, surprise the Light Infantry there and the Fortieth Regiment stationed below, and force them to retreat to the city, they will flee past your house. The beautiful garden will be destroyed, but happily your house may not be touched. 'Twill be the houses in the village that will suffer most. Could you but hasten to a place of safety. There may yet be time."

" Oh! we could not, we could not!" Margaret's voice was husky and strained. " My brother could not be moved."

There was a pause, then Washington said, gravely:

" Oh, Mistress Margaret, this is a cruel, cruel war!"

He took up a letter and glanced at it. Then tore it to small bits. He dashed his hand across his eyes.

" O that there might be a way for peace!"

And Margaret hid her face in the pile of coats in the corner. She was trembling with weariness and passionate emotion. Washington looked at her with concern a moment, then he spoke, and his tone was one of sternness and indignation.

" Peace has been offered to us many times, but on what terms! Terms which are but insults. We shall have war, not peace, unless the peace come with freedom and liberty. Not until the King of England acknowledges that we are free, that these States are independent, separate from his crown, will we lay down the sword."

Washington dropped his papers. His eyes flashed. He drew himself up. His voice became stronger, more vehement.

" The very last drop of our blood will flow for liberty, for our country, our land. We shall fight until there is no more fight in us. We shall fight, barefoot, our feet weary and blood-stained. We shall fight, — ragged, hungry, cold, without pay, without uniforms — many times without bullets or bayonets; — even if I am misunderstood, slandered, persecuted. We shall fight against overwhelming, bitter, cruel odds. We shall fight, and we shall win!"

CHAPTER XVII.

"There is not too much love in this sad world. Love is beautiful. It is of Heaven."

THE journey homeward had few terrors for Margaret. She bore with courage the spectral shadows of the trees by the roadside and the dim outlines of the hills; the dark streams they had to ford; the deepening glooms of a forest, with the strange calls of the night birds when they were aroused from slumber by the sounds of the horses' hoofs.

It was only as she passed through Beggarstown, and was near the garden gate of Cliveden, that dread and terror began to torment her heart. What was she to find at home?

Grief and desolation and loss?

Before her horse had fairly stopped, one of the big front doors opened, and the gleam of candle-light streamed out across the steps of the portico.

"Father! Father!" she called, tremulously.

But it was not her father who came out.

As the Lieutenant helped her from her horse, he said, softly: "I have comfort for you, Mistress Murray. Captain Peyton bids me tell you that your brother will do well if he can be kept in absolute quietude through the night. His wife is beside him,

brave, sweet woman that she is. Captain Peyton
begs your indulgence. He will remain there also."

"Came the surgeon in time to be of help to you?"
Margaret asked, as they entered the wide, shadowy
hall.

"Your servants could get no one in the village.
They are all engaged with the wounded."

"Of a surety, my father sent again?"

"I rode thither myself, Mistress Murray, but to
no avail. There had been sharp skirmishing beyond
the Schuylkill. Allen McLane, with a troop of
horse, attacked one of our foraging parties, and
many wounded were brought into camp at sundown."

"And came not Doctor Worthington?"

Shipton looked at her in surprise. "Doctor
Worthington? No!"

"I saw him about sundown, and methought he
would remember his word, and be here when I
came."

"His services were of a surety engaged the moment he entered camp."

Margaret stopped. Her face was soft with tremu-
lous tenderness. "O sir, how much you and your
friend have been to us in our great trouble." She
laid her hand caressingly on the youth's arm.

His face flushed hotly. "Say nothing, dear lady,
I implore you. 'Tis our happiness to serve you."

"I shall never even hope to repay you," she said,
brokenly.

Then she turned to meet her father on the stairs.

It was not till two hours had passed that she saw
Captain Peyton. After persuading her father to try
to get some rest, she had come out into the garden.

The hushed and breathless autumn night was there, the calm stars, the trees, seen but dimly, but whose presence was companionship. She drew her cloak tight around her, for the night chill made her shiver, and walked on slowly, glad of the stillness and the peace; yet with that misery, that dread feeling of coming disaster, deep in her heart. What was soon to happen? This hushed and comforting gloom would be filled with the flash of muskets, the roar of cannon, the screams of wounded horses, the groans of dying men.

If she could but get away! If they all, — her father, Annette, Henry, these helpful strangers, the trusting servants, — if they all could but flee, away, away to a sheltered refuge, where the sound of battle could not come, — away from the hatred, the blood-shed, and the tears.

She looked in the direction of the sleeping village: those little children; those farmers and stocking-weavers; those millers and tanners; those thrifty Germans; those Quakers; all the quaint folk, with their quaint ways and odd beliefs. If she could but spare them that which was to overwhelm them! If they could but be warned! But she must give no warning. Even the man, for whose step on the portico she was waiting, must not be warned. She could not tell him of this new trouble, and get the comfort for which her soul was starving.

Margaret was standing under a big oak, which was at the head of the avenue of trees leading down to the front gate. The light from the open doorway fell across the portico in a broad band. Beyond that, between the steps and her, there was complete darkness. Nothing could be heard but the soft rustle of the night breeze that moved the dried leaves underneath her feet. Suddenly, in the midst of her absorption in her unquiet thoughts, she became conscious that there was a movement other than the soft rustling of the leaves. What sounded before like shadowy footfalls now resolved itself into the measured though stealthy step of something that was the substance, not the shadow. Startled and surprised, Margaret's first impulse was to dart across the gravelled driveway in front of the steps and enter the open doorway. Her second impulse was to draw back further into the shade of the oak. Up the avenue the stealthy footsteps came. Then across the band of light falling from the doorway she saw the figure of a man sharply defined. He went swiftly across, then was lost in the gloom beyond. She had scarce time to wonder what the intruder sought, when down the avenue she heard other stealthy footsteps — then whispering voices. The footsteps and the voices drew nearer. Then two men halted near her hiding-place.

"Where went the spy?" whispered one voice.

"Around that building, methinks," she heard the other voice make reply.

"Damme! he has been in hiding here all day. How is it that we missed him this morning when we searched?"

Then the truth came to Margaret. The man who had gone towards the stables was but a common thief; but these troopers of the Fortieth had seen him skulking around the grounds and had drawn their inference.

"We will get him now of a surety," whispered Grove. "Templeton says that General Howe has offered a big reward for the safety of those stolen letters."

The voices and the footsteps passed on, and Margaret was under her tree alone.

The next moment she saw a tall shadow strike across the band of light from the doorway. She walked swiftly across the drive, and met Peyton on the steps.

"Captain Peyton," she cried, breathlessly. "Two of your soldiers have gone along towards our stables. They are following a thief or a spy. They evidently think 'tis that spy of whom they were in search this morning. I beg of you that you permit no firing of pistol or musket. You have said we must have perfect quiet through the night."

But she spoke too late. A shot rang out in the solitary night. Then a man ran past them, and sprang into the gloom of the shrubbery.

Margaret's heart gave a leap of thanksgiving at the man's escape, stranger and outcast as she supposed him to be; but her relief was short-lived, for the soldiers came in a mad rush down the drive and into the thicket. Before Peyton could reach them, they had caught the fugitive, and were roughly dragging him out.

"Who are you?" asked the Captain, sternly. "What are you doing in private grounds at this unseemly hour?"

One of the men was about to make a rude reply, but the other, who had caught sight of Peyton's tall figure in the light from the doorway recognised him. He saluted awkwardly. "Colonel Musgrave was unsuccessful, sir, in his search on the Limekiln. We returned to camp at sundown; but we felt sure the man might be hidden about these grounds, else he was the devil to get away from us all so sudden. We were detailed to watch. Damme! sir, the rebel has been sly, but we have bagged the game this time."

And Grove gave the prisoner a rough shake.

" You must fire no more shots," said the Captain, gravely. " Take the man off quietly, and report at once to Colonel Musgrave."

Then the prisoner spoke breathlessly: " I protest, sir, against this arrest. I am no spy. I am not even a rebel. I came into these grounds because of an agreement with Mr. Henry Murray, who lives here. He promised to leave a horse tied outside the stables. Go and fetch him. He will vouch for me."

" You are a clever rogue," Captain Peyton said, sternly.

Grove laughed brutally. " A pretty story. Why not come in open daylight for your horse? "

" Go and tell Mr. Murray," the prisoner repeated, earnestly. " Tell him that the man who lives in the Wissahickon Cave, who calls himself the hermit, whom he befriended, and to whom he promised a horse, is outside. He will protect me. Go and fetch him."

" The hermit, the hermit! " laughed Grove. " Look at his odd clothes, the dog of a spy! "

" You mean Mr. Murray, — the old man, the blind man? " asked Captain Peyton, not unkindly.

" No, the son, Henry Murray."

" He is up-stairs. An accident befell him. He is in great danger unless, happily, we can turn aside the danger. He is unconscious. He would not know you."

Bingham started back in horror. This, then, was the meaning of Henry Murray's failure to keep his promised word. He could scarce speak, because of his passionate feeling of surprise and grief. And he himself was lost. These men would not believe him now.

Grove laughed again. "You see, Mr. Rebel, you must come with us. And unless you produce those letters you stole from Howe's messenger, you will swing for it, of a surety."

"I have no letters, and I know naught of any letters. If you persist in this delusion, you will have the blood of an innocent man on your hearts — an ye have any hearts. If Mr. Murray could speak, he would confirm my word. Oh, sir! you are an honest man! Help me!"

There was something about Peyton that won Bingham's confidence; and something in Bingham's tone appealed to Peyton.

"Would Mr. Charles Murray know you?" he asked, kindly. "He is blind, but would he not know you by your voice or your name?"

His name! Here was a dilemma. It was absolutely essential for the success of his service to Washington that he should not be known as Rodney Bingham, whom all his friends supposed to be at Lancaster with other dangerously well-known patriots. Mr. Murray and Margaret had no suspicion of the part he was playing, unless Henry Murray had told them, and that was scarce possible. This terrible accident must have befallen soon after the secret meeting on the Wissahickon. Bingham thought quickly, and decided quickly. No! neither Mr. Murray nor his daughter would be likely to

know him, he said.   Mr. Henry Murray had been
kind enough to interest himself in his misfortunes.
He had given him money, and had promised him a
horse.   It had been merely his whim to come for
it at night.   He feared that the British might see
the animal, and it be pressed into service for the
army.

The prisoner's story seemed absurd enough, and
Peyton feared he could do nothing more.   But, as
they talked, they had been getting nearer the house,
and now in the doorway appeared Margaret, holding in her hand a candelabra with many branches,
every candle blazing.   The light fell full on the
prisoner's face.   His hat, which had formed his
principal disguise, had been lost in the struggle
with the soldiers.   Rodney Bingham's face was not
one easily to be forgotten.

Margaret gave a perceptible start of recognition,
but stopped when she saw the look in Bingham's
eyes.

" What are you doing to that man? " she asked,
abruptly.

" 'Tis the spy we were looking for this morning,
lady," answered Grove.   " He is telling a cock-and-
bull story about your brother helping him.   But he
will swing all the same."

" That man is no spy," said Margaret, hurriedly.
" My brother knows him well.   He received from
him a letter yester-eve."

" Will you tell me his name, Mistress Murray? "
asked Captain Peyton.

" Are you not — Rodney — "

" Yes, yes, Rodney Kelper, a villager of Germantown, who has a whim to be called a hermit.   He

wanders around the rocks of the Wissahickon, mistress, you know — "

" Yes, and your letter asked my brother to meet you."

" Ay, and he came, Mistress Murray. 'Tis glad I am that he told you of it. When this gentleman asked me if you would know me, I feared me that, perchance, you would not, and that your brother had not told you. 'Tis glad I am he did. He gave me aid, Mistress Murray, and he promised me a horse. I was to find it tied outside the stables. I was delayed in coming."

" Come with me, and I will get your horse for you," said Margaret, making as if to go down the steps.

But Grove held Bingham fast.

" These unmannerly soldiers, who caught me, seem not disposed to let me go, Mistress Murray."

" They have been doing but their duty, Mistress Murray."

Grove's sullen face brightened at Captain Peyton's hearty praise.

" You will let me go now? " asked Bingham, appealing to the other trooper.

The man looked at Peyton irresolutely.

" Damme! " Grove exclaimed. " We must report to Colonel Musgrave, and take the man with us."

" For what profit? " said Peyton, in his quick, authoritative way. " The man is clearly not the spy you seek. Release him. I will add my testimony in your report. The Colonel is my friend. He will understand."

" I thank you very much, sir," said Bingham, earnestly. " I know not who you are, but I shall not forget your face. Perchance it may be my good fortune to serve you."

Peyton smiled. "You have Mistress Murray to thank, not me. Had she not known you, I would have been powerless to help you."

"Nevertheless, I shall hope to serve you some day."

"'Tis not likely, sir, that we shall meet again. I sail for England within the week. But I thank you."

His words, "sail for England within the week," fell like lead on Margaret's heart.

"'Tis likely I can find the horse my brother had intention to give you, Mr. Kelper. My servant, Jake, sleeps on the second floor of the stables. He must have been roused by that pistol-shot. We will make short despatch of the matter if Captain Peyton will grant indulgence."

Margaret made her speech as formal as possible, but try as hard as she might, she could not make her voice steady.

"Wait, Mr. Kelper, I pray you, and I will get the key to the stable door. No — meet me at the stables. I will be there in but a moment."

Peyton slipped into the troopers' not unwilling hands gold pieces, which were of vast comfort to them, and were ample compensation for disappointment. He bade them betake themselves to camp, and tumble into their huts, to get the sleep of which they must stand sore in need, such faithful soldiers of the King as they both were.

The Captain's kindness cheered them, and they vowed to him eternal fidelity in their honest hearts.

And after they were well on their way down the avenue, the Captain seated himself on the steps, to wait for Margaret's return.

" Rodney! "
" Margaret! "
" Rodney, are you in truth a spy? Wherefore this concealment, this disguise? "
" I call myself by no such name, Margaret. But I am doing Washington a service which could not be done if I were known. There seems to be no one else in Germantown to do it for him. And I must keep my own identity hidden. Were it known, I would not only be hampered and thwarted at every turn, but, perchance, arrested. The Binghams are radical Whigs, as you well know. We have gone far. But let us not talk of me, but of Henry. How happened it, Margaret? It grieves me to the heart."
" Rodney, I know not myself how it happened. He was brought in from the highway by that Englishman and a young friend, a lieutenant on Cornwallis's staff. He has nursed my brother, for we could get no surgeon. He has saved his life."

Margaret would keep her own counsel. She said naught of the hurried arrival of her brother, a fugitive with those fatal letters. She would not even take this old friend into her confidence, and tell him of her perilous ride to Washington's camp. But she could speak freely of this Englishman's help and kindness; and her voice was warm with feeling as she spoke of him.

When she returned to the house, she found the Captain waiting.

"Your father sent the young German girl to say that he is in the big parlour, and a good fire is burning, and we must come, as the morning chill is in the air, and there is some marvellous coffee to be brewed; and methinks, Mistress Murray, we had better go."

His voice was so full of cheer that her sore heart must needs feel the comfort of it. And as they went down the hall together, she thought how strong he was, how tall. Those firm, straight shoulders, that well-poised head, that glow of health in his face, gave her comfort, too. She felt a pride in it all, as if, in some mysterious fashion, he belonged to her.

"And my brother?" she asked.

"He is resting quietly. His wife is beside him."

"And the Lieutenant?"

"He will come, too, I hope."

Would this hour just before the dawn ever be forgotten?

On the settee before the fire, Margaret sat with her father. On the rug at her feet lay the Lieutenant. In the armchair in the chimney-corner sat Peyton. These strangers seemed like long-tried friends. There was such homeness about this quiet hour with each other. Captain Peyton felt the full influence of it; and even Margaret, with all the secret burden on her heart, felt some of its rest and peace. When the young girl, whom she had saved from the perils of her homelessness, came in with the steaming, fragrant coffee, there was given additional cheer.

Sometimes they talked, more often were silent. Once, Margaret, leaning against her father's arm, lost herself in sleep.

They talked of England, of the war, of the obstinacy of the King, of the greatness of Lord Chatham, whom the King neglected, but whom all England loved. Peyton said he learned much from talks like this with men and women of judgment and intellect in the Colonies, who had so much better knowledge of the difficulties and the problems than the theorists at home.

"My cousin, Lord Carlisle, is to come out here ere long, as one of the commissioners of peace. It was the wish of my father's dearest friend, Lord Chatham, though we like best to call him William Pitt, that I come out first, and try to study the country, and be informed in such a way that I might perchance help Carlisle in his work. But I fear me that he and the other commissioners will be hampered by the King's narrow policy. I have much hope that Chatham may be enabled to submit certain propositions; because anything from him is sure of respect from the Americans. I find they think most highly of Chatham. But whether the King will listen to him remains yet to be seen. His state of health, moreover, gives me profound anxiety. I sometimes fear that he will pass into the immortal life beyond this, ere I have opportunity to reach England."

There was another pause. Captain Peyton walked softly up and down the room. The Lieutenant dozed a little. Then Charles Murray spoke.

"If this has been your work in this country, how comes it, then, that you fought at the Brandywine — had active service, as I am told?"

"Lord Percy fell, Mr. Murray. I took his command at once."

" And saved the day," said the Lieutenant, rousing from his slumber.

" You are dreaming, boy. Go to sleep again, and meddle not with affairs of such moment," said Peyton, pleasantly.

" In truth, you will return to Philadelphia to-day," said Margaret, with a tremble in her voice. " You will not need to remain here if you sail so soon for England."

" I know not. I have many things to arrange with General Howe; and then, as Colonel Musgrave is our neighbour in England, he has the wish that I consult with him on some questions demanding attention. It is possible that I may be obliged to stay in this region for two or three days."

" I beg and implore you to depart to-day," said Margaret, almost wildly.

He looked at her in pained surprise. Why did she wish him to go?

Had he but known that when he had said that he was soon to sail for England his words had fallen like lead on her heart, he might have understood. But he did not know.

" I beg you to hasten. Go to-day, to-day, and the Lieutenant, too."

" That were impossible," replied Peyton, and in his tone there was a trace of hauteur. " He has of late been transferred to the staff of Sir William Howe, and his duties commence to-day. He will have to remain here."

Margaret noted the swift change in the Captain's face. She started up hurriedly.

" O sir! " she said, tremulously, " there are many dangers here. I beg you to go."

" There are dangers everywhere in these uncertain times," said Charles Murray.

" But there may be another battle. You all — Colonel Musgrave, Captain Baines — you all spoke of it here this morning. I beg you to hasten."

" If that rebel, Washington, attack us, he will rue it," said the Lieutenant, as he gave the fire a friendly poke. " We are strongly entrenched. But if there is to be a battle, we will have to be in it once more together, eh, Arthur ? "

But the Captain paid no heed to the youth. His eyes were fixed on Margaret's face. Something in the expression of her eyes told him that 'twas for him — for him she feared. His safety was dear to her. The message of her eyes took away the pain of her words.

" See, the day is breaking," said the Lieutenant, going over to the window. " We must be off, Arthur."

" Yes, yes."

Mr. Murray started up. " My friends," he said, brokenly, " I shall hope to see you again during the day."

" We thank you," replied Peyton. " If not to-day, then of a surety to-morrow."

To-morrow !

Margaret could scarce breathe.

" We shall want to learn the condition of our patient," said the Lieutenant, smiling.

" I will send a surgeon, if there is one to be found. I shall see Doctor Worthington at Stenton, as he has several patients there. He will of a truth desire to come if possible. He must come. But I beg you,

Mr. Murray," added the Captain, " I beg you to take comfort. Your son will do well methinks. . . .May I come to-morrow? " he asked, as he held Margaret's hand a moment. " I have your permission? "

But Margaret could not speak.

CHAPTER XVIII.

"Let Mad Anthony Wayne taste the salt and pepper of your muskets. Sprinkle hell-fire in your pans. Strike now a blow that will go down into history."

IN the darkness, over rough roads, amid choking dust and the chill air of a foggy October morning, the army of Washington approached the unsuspecting village. Down the Limekiln Road came General Greene, with Stephens's, Muhlenburg's, and McDougal's divisions. They were ordered to attack soon after daybreak the enemy stationed just beyond the woods.

Down the Manatawny came General Armstrong at the head of the Pennsylvania militia, with orders to attack the enemy encamped at the junction of that road with School House Lane; a portion of the militia being sent forward, happily to prevent the arrival of reinforcements from the city. But Cornwallis was to come by another road, and thus this plan miscarried. The militia of Maryland and Jersey under Forman and Smallwood were marching down the Old York Road, with intention to come upon the enemy's rear and cut it off from communication with the city.

Over the brow of Chestnut Hill came Conway and Sullivan and Wayne, with Maxwell's and Stirling's and Nash's troops in reserve.

Allen McLane, sent forward by Sullivan to attack the pickets at Mount Airy, got there just as the sun broke forth for one blessed moment; but almost immediately the black clouds spread once more over the whole sky, — the fog and the darkness settled down like a pall, — dense, confusing, impenetrable.

The pickets at Mount Airy were killed; the outpost driven in; but the Second Battalion of Light Infantry, though surprised, soon formed in line, and to its help came rushing up the brave soldiers of the Fortieth Regiment. But naught could check the furious onslaught of Sullivan's and Wayne's men, who held in vivid remembrance the horrors of the twentieth of September.

" Have at the bloodhounds! " came in loud cries amid the smoke and the fog. " Revenge! Revenge! for the Paoli massacre! "

The Light Infantry gave way, and the soldiers of the Fortieth, for all their heroic effort, were forced to fall back upon their camp. The road was soon filled with a confused mass of struggling men and horses, with cannon and baggage. And in a few moments the infantry, in a mad effort to escape the deadly fire coming upon them swiftly through the fog, broke through the gardens east of the road and swept onward like a flood.

The firing at Mount Airy and the shots heard to the right from the Limekiln Road, came almost simultaneously. General Howe rushed from his comfortable quarters at Stenton, and, with his staff close at his heels, galloped up to the Market Square.

" We are surrounded on all sides. We are lost,"

was his first thought; but he sent rapid messages to Knyphausen on the west, to Grant on the east; and Lieutenant Shipton he sent flying up the road with a peremptory order to Colonel Musgrave that the retreat must be stopped at once. But Colonel Musgrave had been swept on at the head of his troops. Near the camp Shipton could see in the dim light a tall figure on horseback. He was waving his sword and rallying the panic-stricken troops; and in response to his compelling, authoritative voice many halted behind fences and walls and sent back into the ranks of the pursuers shot after shot that told with deadly effect. A moment more, when Shipton looked, the horse and its rider both were gone.

The big front doors of The Chew House stood open. The windows also were open; but the fog made it so dark outside that naught could be distinguished but the flashes of muskets. In the distance was the rumbling cannonading, — the terrible, ominous sound of battle. In the house were sounds of hurrying feet, cries and moans. Fugitives kept coming in on all sides, many of them wounded sore; all smoke-begrimed or black with powder.

From the time when the first shots of the sentries at Mount Airy had been heard, Margaret had been in a fever of excitement. She had been everywhere, giving courage to the terrified servants — directing, helping, — yes, — and suffering more than she could ever have imagined herself capable of suffering. Now she had come into the big hall in an anxious search for her father, and had found

him wandering up and down restlessly. At sight
of him, her fortitude at last gave way. She clung
to him for a moment in silence; then she said,
faintly:

"Sometimes I have been about to order the doors
and windows all shut and barred, but my heart
has failed me. Some poor wretch may hasten in
for shelter. But I feel as if I could scarcely bear
it longer."

"Courage, dear, courage. It will soon be over."

"The kitchens are already full of wounded men.
We have tried to do for them. One poor fellow
died as we were giving him some brandy. I had
to leave him and come to you one moment. Father!
I shall never forget, never forget."

There was another burst of noise and uproar.
Margaret started back nervously. She was worn
out with the conflict of many passionate emotions.

"O father! that terrible noise! Think, every
cannon-ball tears some of those men to pieces. O
father! I feel as if I could bear no more."

She hid her face again on his shoulder.

"Courage, my brave, brave girl." And Mr. Murray held her tight.

"That first shot! How it went through my
heart! I will hear it always. It will haunt my
dreams. And it was I that carried those letters
and started this horror."

"I would give much, much, could I but know
how our army is faring. If the attack was made
as the General planned. But I fear me, I fear me.
This fog of which they all speak, 'tis bad, 'tis
bad. I fear me the troops may make mistakes,
may fire upon each other, or fail to strike at the

centre, at the proper time. 'Twas superbly planned, but this fog and confusing darkness of a surety will bring disaster."

"It is, in truth, so dark. The fog and the mist so thick I can scarce distinguish uniforms. But it looks as if it were the British who are fleeing through the garden. They must be retreating."

"If the British are retreating, then it is our army that is victorious. This may mean much to our cause. It may help us win back the city." Mr. Murray's voice had the ring of a general who leads a charge.

Then he bethought himself of more personal cares.

"The servants have caused you trouble, dear?"

"All but Jake, brave, staunch soul that he is. The others are hiding in the cellar. And my dear little German girl insists on guarding the door of Henry's room. Should any soldiers flee up-stairs, she says they must not, shall not enter that room. She will stay there, and no one shall pass except over her. And, father, she holds the violin in her hand." It was with a sob that Margaret spoke.

Suddenly above the uproar outside there was heard an authoritative voice, shouting:

"Stop! Brave men of the Fortieth! Rally! Follow me! I am Colonel Musgrave!"

Mr. Murray pushed Margaret gently from him. "Hasten, dear. Bid Jake shut the doors and windows. Methinks we have afforded enough shelter to these fugitives. Hasten, love! Bid him do this service as quickly as occasion serves."

Margaret fled through the dining-room to the corridor beyond.

Into the big hall came the gallant Colonel of the Fortieth. A dozen of his soldiers followed him; but dozens more were borne onward by the mad crowd outside that rushed on into the gloom. Musgrave turned to Baines, who was behind him.

"Egad! 'Tis the strong, thick-walled house we were in before. It must be either our grave or our fortress."

He rushed down the hall to the rear door and flung it wider open. There was darkness and fog everywhere, and the flashes of the muskets were like big fireflies dancing here and there among the trees.

"Stop, men!" the Colonel shouted. "I command ye to stop! I am Musgrave, Colonel Musgrave."

A few of the redcoats obeyed. They crowded through the door.

Back to the front doorway the Colonel rushed. "Come in, brave men of the Fortieth!"

"Come in! Come in!" shouted Baines from one of the windows. "'Tis your only safety."

The uproar increased and drew nearer. Then all at once was heard a voice in that wild, dismayed, surging mass of men.

"Make way, there! damn you! make way!"

The crowd in the doorway was thrust aside, and there entered two men covered with dust, their faces black with smoke. In their arms they were bearing some one of a truth in most desperate plight. Baines and Musgrave and the crowd of soldiers fell back; one soldier who moved aside but slowly received a savage thrust from his Colonel.

"Egad! 'Tis Peyton," whispered Musgrave,

hoarsely, and he went to render help. Peyton was laid carefully down on the floor near the parlour door.

"Damme! who are you?" and the Colonel peered into the face of the taller of the men who had been carrying his friend.

"'Tis a stranger who helped me save him. Of a truth we were neither of us here had it not been for him," answered the smoke-begrimed Lieutenant. The stranger rushed to the table. Shipton looked sorrowfully at his friend.

"There, that will be better, Peyton, than lying out on that devilish road underneath the horses and the trampling feet."

"Bob! Dear Bob! I cannot understand how you ever reached me."

"I cut and slashed and got to you just as a beggarly rebel was about running you through. His soul has since flown up higher, — and on wings, too."

"They forgot not the way Grey's men used the bayonet," said Baines, with an oath.

"Then came this stranger to my help;" and Shipton put out his hand to Rodney Bingham.

Peyton moved his head feebly in an effort to look the stranger in the face. Then he saw Charles Murray, and exclaimed, quickly:

"Bob! Bob!"

"Yes, 'tis Mr. Murray's home, Arthur, where we were before."

"Musgrave, we have lost the day, after all."

The Colonel stopped on his way to the front doors.

"Yes, damn it all! Unless we can make a brave

stand. That devil of a Wayne! What fury was in his bayonets. ' Remember the twentieth of September! Revenge! Revenge! After the bloodhounds!' the men shouted. God! How they cut and slashed. . . . Feel you any better, Peyton?"

But the stranger who had been searching on the table saw what neither Musgrave nor Shipton saw.

"Here, can't we get some grog? Here, grog! some one! grog! Go for grog, he is growing faint."

Charles Murray called, sharply, " Margaret! Margaret!"

Margaret was not far away. She was seen at the far end of the dining-room. Shipton waved his hand to her. Then she came quickly out into the hall, bearing a bottle and a glass. Shipton rushed to her.

"Ah, Mistress Murray, we meet again. One of the bravest of our army lies dying there. Care for him, if you can."

A sob came into the boy's throat. He turned away quickly.

Margaret's heart gave a great bound as she recognised the figure huddled on the floor. Was it he? Yes! She handed the brandy to the Lieutenant, then with a stifled cry she flung herself down beside the man whom now she knew she loved.

" You see I am back again, all there is left of me," said Peyton, feebly, but with great joy. " I could not stay away, could I?"

The radiance of his smile was pain to poor Shipton. He poured hastily from bottle to glass, then thrust the glass into Bingham's hands. His own were trembling. " Egad!" he said, fiercely. " I am of little use."

Musgrave uttered an angry oath as he looked towards the open doorway and saw the men still rushing past into the darkness.

Margaret seized Shipton's cloak which he had thrown across a chair.

"Let me put this under your head. There! let me lift you. Try to drink this," and she motioned to Rodney for the brandy.

"It has helped many to-day."

"You are an angel of tenderness, Mistress Murray," said Shipton, as he turned away.

"Father! Father!" Margaret's voice broke.

"Yes, dear, I know."

"Oh! what can I do? Tell me, tell me what to do. He is suffering. Father! he will die. Tell me what to do."

Musgrave rushed from window to window, then glanced up the spacious staircase.

"Egad! unless we beware, we are all caged in ten minutes. The rebels are pressing us hard. They are close behind us."

The soldiers were crowding in the doorway in the wildest confusion. Troops were hurrying by outside. Shouts and groans could be heard; the flash of muskets seen outside. With a wild cry Musgrave rushed past the men already in the room and shouted to the men hurrying past the door.

"Stop, brave men of the Fortieth! Rally! I am Colonel Musgrave. Halt! I command you to stop. Will ye give up the day like cowards? Remember Trenton and Princeton! Strike a blow now that will go down into history. Stop! halt! Come in, brave men of the Fortieth!"

Soldier after soldier came rushing in. Musgrave lifted his arms authoritatively.

"Barricade the doors! To the windows — close and barricade them. Up the stairs. Up! Up! Fire from the upper windows! Fire on Wayne! Fire on the rebels! Let Mad Anthony taste the salt and pepper of your muskets! Could he but taste the sharpness of your steel! In his heart! In his heart! Strike, now, a blow for the King!"

CHAPTER XIX.

"Oh! how my heart aches with this love for him!"

WHILE Musgrave had been shouting the words that put fire and fury into every soldier's heart, Captain Baines had dashed to the front doors and slammed them shut. A sergeant threw the heavy bar across. Other men rushed to the windows, and swung to the heavy shutters.

Into the big dining-room, the " schoolroom " and " office; " into the passageway, the soldiers hurled themselves. Up and down the spiral staircase they rushed.

Ere the rear door of the hall could be closed and barred, Rodney Bingham dashed out from the group around Peyton, and flung himself out into the darkness.

Baines, at the head of a squad of men, hurled himself into the big ballroom, or " parlour," slammed the shutters tight and threw across the heavy bars. Six hundred men in the big house — six hundred desperate, vindictive men.

Then up the stairs went the soldiers in a mad plunge, Musgrave carried along with them. Even Shipton could not withstand that impetuous rush.

Sounds of sharp volleys were heard from a window above. Then the soldiers rushed from window to window, door to door, in different parts of the big house, slamming, barring, shouting, firing. Baines posted men at every window and door below.

"Bayonet any one who seeks to enter," he shouted, hoarsely, and a fierce and ugly oath soiled his lips. "Let the rebels feel the sharpness of your steel in their hearts! In their hearts!"

Peyton had been lying there, his eyes resting on Margaret, who had been trying to make his position easier. Her mind seemed closed to any thought of her own danger. Her whole thought was of him.

"Could I but spare you these terrible scenes," he said, feebly. "'Tis no place for you. Is there no more sheltered room? Go! I implore you."

"Hush! talk no more. If I but knew what to do for you. Could I but relieve you. . . . Drink more of this."

Peyton half raised himself up. Then, with a groan, he sank back. His hand went to his side.

He began to speak. She leaned down to hear.

"Should I die — "

He had to stop to catch his breath. She put her hand tenderly on his forehead.

"Yes?" Her voice was very low, but its tone seemed to give him strength.

"Should I die, could you write my father, Lord Castlereagh, Kent? Tell him I died in comfort, not out on the road under the horses; but in great and exceeding comfort?"

"Yes, yes. I will tell him you died bravely fighting for your King — "

"And thinking of dear old England."

"Yes. Be comforted. I will remember."

"Tell me. Should I not die — No! no! I must not — I must not — "

Peyton spoke in snatches, and as he spoke, the volleys of musketry, the sickening uproar, made his voice almost inaudible.

" In my cloak, you will find — a letter I have writ to Lord Chatham. I pray you — despatch it to him, and send a brief word with it — Tell him — how I love him — the dear old man. Pray Heaven he might have his way with the King. . . . My thoughts — "

A wild feeling of protest, of grief surged over Margaret, — protest against her own uselessness, protest against the cruelty of fate. She went over to her father. There was the tone of impatience in her voice.

" Oh, how helpless we are! Speak, tell me what to do! "

Charles Murray groped his way nearer Peyton.

" Ah, Captain Peyton, I am sorry. 'Tis often the best and the bravest whom we lose."

But this patient acceptance of grief did not satisfy Margaret.

" Father! Think, though you cannot see. Think! Tell me what to do."

Then she bent over Peyton. There were tears in her eyes — and in her heart.

" You knew what to do for my brother," she said, brokenly. " You helped him. Tell me. I beg, I implore you to tell me. I will do anything — anything — only live! Tell me, tell me! I will do it. I can bear it. I can bear anything. Only live! "

Shipton's clear voice was heard above all the uproar. He was shouting down the stairs.

" The enemy surrounds the house, Peyton. They

may send a flag for us to surrender. But the Fortieth never surrenders, Peyton."

"No, never — " Peyton whispered, then he looked
at Margaret sadly. "He cannot hear me."

"Peyton, Peyton, are you there? Peyton, Arthur, are you there?" shouted Shipton again.

"Tell him I am not gone yet."

The next moment, Margaret was at the foot of
the staircase. The Lieutenant had disappeared, but
she could see the Colonel standing above, waving
his arms aloft; she could hear him shout hoarsely:

"Fire, boys! another volley! Give the rebels a
hot taste of hell-fire! There! to that window!
See! see! Another volley, boys."

"Colonel Musgrave! Colonel Musgrave! can
you hear? Captain Peyton wishes me to tell
you — " but Margaret's voice was lost in the uproar.
Musgrave disappeared in the smoke. Margaret
started up the stairs, but had not gone further than
the landing when Shipton, running through the hall
above, saw her and stopped. His face grew white.

"Mistress! Tell me!"

"Take heart," she said; "he is living still, but
will you not do something for him? Leave those
men up there to do their fighting, and come down.
Come! I can do nothing. He needs help. He needs
you."

"Perchance we can take him out of the hall.
'Tis too dangerous a place for you, mistress. A
cannon-ball may strike through the hall at any moment. You must seek shelter in the big room."
And Shipton started down the stairs.

Meanwhile, Charles Murray had been walking
up and down — indecision, annoyance, horror, and

chagrin alternately depicted in his face. Now he halted opposite Peyton, saying, vehemently:

"It should not have been done, sir, — my house closed against my countrymen. I left it open to succour you all, to be a hospital for your wounded, not to be a barricaded fort against Washington's army. I command you to — "

Peyton roused himself, and looked at the speaker in amazement. Then a great light of comprehension dawned in his face.

"O sir! Pardon the hot impulses of war. We thought you were for the King."

CHAPTER XX.

"'Tis a mean, bad world. How little love there is, how little! And we need love. O God! we need it sore."

UP-STAIRS, in a sheltered inner room, whose heavy walls muffled many of the unwonted noises, Henry Murray lay. But every volley of musketry made him turn uneasily. In his delirium he was on a vast and lonely mountain, with a steep precipice at one side, the wild screech of the eagles the only sound that broke the stillness of the early morning. The eagles swooped down — down!

The door was locked and barred, and the young girl stood on guard outside. As the soldiers flew back and forth, one or two stopped to stare at her rudely, others with scrutiny or curious question. She looked at them with eyes that seemed not to see or be conscious of them. Once, when an attempt was made to open the door, she straightened up and said, firmly: " Es ist nicht erlaubt hinein zu gehen." When Musgrave himself, all unknowing, made attempt to thrust her peremptorily aside, she said: " Nein, nein, Mein Herr. Es ist nicht erlaubt. Sie können das Fräulein fragen. Ihr Herr Bruder ist da, krank, tod-krank. Gewiss Sie wollen nicht hinein. Gewiss nicht!"

And the Englishmen treated her with respect, though few understood her speech.

176

The volleys of musketry and the hoarse words of command were hideously frequent now. For a brief moment the wounded soldier lost himself in the faintness against which he had been struggling. When he awoke to consciousness, he saw Shipton bending over him.

" Courage, Arthur! Come back to us," the boy said with a sob. " If Worthington were but here, the rascally surgeon that he is. If he were but here! "

" But think you not of some relief? " asked Margaret. " My servants are of but scant service. They are hiding in the cellars, but methinks I could find Jake. Tell me quickly what can be done — "

She had to stop. Peyton stretched out his hand. She laid hers in it, and with an effort he raised it to his lips.

" You will be well in a few months," said the Lieutenant, forcing a smile. " By that time all this will have been forgot."

" A few months! "

" Yes, that wound is deep. I knew it when I stuck my handkerchief in. If Worthington were but here! "

" Think not of the future, sir. My father and I will take care of you."

And once more the wounded soldier raised her hand to his lips. But she spoke to the Lieutenant with a trace of passionate impatience.

" Why keep wishing for a man who is not here? What avail are wishes? I pray you bethink yourself of what your friend did for my brother. Would I had been here! Would I had seen, and known! "

She turned at a sudden, sharp voice shouting near

her. Musgrave had rushed down the stairs, and as he came he called back:

"Fire, brave men of the Fortieth! Keep up a hot fire."

At that moment a vigorous onslaught was made on the front of the house by the besieging Americans. The walls creaked and trembled. Then a cannonade began with fury. Musgrave dashed to the front doors, then to each window. His grim face lit up with a smile of triumph.

"They hold! They hold! Now let Mad Anthony rage."

More deafening volleys of musketry from the windows above.

"It is useless," shouted Shipton. "They cannot break through these walls."

"What fools these rebels are," cried Musgrave, with an ugly oath. "But they are getting a taste of British hell-fire, which makes them smart, I trow."

Peyton put out a hand, as if to stop him. He glanced at Margaret anxiously. Her eyes were fixed on the speaker, as if in horror. It had overwhelmed her at last, — the meaning of this attack upon her home. Her home was barred to her friends, her countrymen; Washington, Maxwell, Knox, Wayne were shut out.

"Look! look, Colonel! There! there! The front doors!" exclaimed Shipton.

A big splinter flew out from the middle of one of the massive doors.

"The miscreants are using a ram. Baines! Baines!"

Baines came tumbling down the stairs.

"More men there! Look! the splintered door.

Bayonet any one who tries to climb through. Damme! but here is special need."

"Up, boys!" shouted Captain Baines. "This table, that chair! There now! That settee! Pile them against the hole in the door. Higher, boys, higher. There! 'tis well. Guard the barricade. Let no one enter. Speed his soul to hell!"

"Here! here!" yelled the Colonel. And he threw open the door to the passageway leading past the spiral staircase. "There is a door there in the outer wall. It must open on the grounds outside. It may be forced! Egad! I hear voices." And Musgrave put his ear against the door.

"Fifty men here to guard the place. Bayonet any one who tries to enter."

"Look! look! to the window there," shouted a soldier, pointing into the "office," the little room at the right of the big hall. A tiny line of flame was seen creeping around the barred shutters of the window.

"Zounds! the miscreants have made damned headway!" shouted Baines. "Up, Shipton! Order a squad of men out on the roof of the third story, and fire upon them from above. The rebels will not stand our salt and pepper long. 'Twill make them smart and howl."

The Lieutenant dashed into the passageway and up the spiral stairway. A few moments more and a rattle of musketry was heard directly above. Then a soldier, black and grimed, came running down the big stairway.

"Colonel Musgrave! we can see them from above. They are forcing that window; they have piled straw and hay against it."

"I know it, you fool —" and the Colonel gave him an imperative gesture to go back.

Margaret had retreated near one of the pillars at the foot of the staircase. Her father was standing by the fireplace in the dining-room. A heavy frown disfigured his face. His lips were set and stern.

A second soldier came tumbling down the stairs. He hastily saluted Musgrave.

"Lieutenant Shipton bids me tell you he can see a flag coming towards us from the enemy."

"We never surrender. Shout it from the windows, and then pepper them with hell-dust."

The soldier dashed back.

Despite the hot shower of bullets falling from above, the Americans had succeeded in carrying enough straw and wood beneath the northwest window of the office, to cause a stealthy, creeping flame to ascend. They soon made a breach in the window, and two brave men forced their way through the flames, and reaching through the breach, managed to unfasten the shutters. The next instant, Captain Baines and a dozen men met them face to face. They were too close for bayonets to serve. A voice was heard shouting outside:

"Prime your flints well! Sprinkle hell-dust in your pans! Sprinkle it in the faces of the bloodhounds!"

Then came another voice: "The bloodhounds will soon taste the feel of our bayonets! At last! At last!"

"Surrender! Surrender!" cried John Laurens, of South Carolina, as he was about to leap in. Behind him was the brave Frenchman, the Chevalier Duplessis, and climbing up behind him, through the smoke and flame, came Rodney Bingham. The three brave heroes thought that their comrades on the lawn were following them; but just as Bingham thrust aside a bayonet pointed at his breast, he turned and saw that he and Laurens and Duplessis were alone. Baines seized a musket and fired, but the ball went wide. The three patriots were forced to fall back. They dropped to the ground. Musgrave's men slammed to the shutters, and through small rifts in the wall they could point their muskets. The next moment, volleys from below mingled with the discordant volleys from above.

A soldier appeared at the head of the stairs, and shouted: " Another flag, Colonel Musgrave! Colonel Musgrave, another flag! "

Musgrave dashed to the stairs. His voice was hoarse with passion.

" We never surrender. Shout it from the windows, and then spare neither grit in your pans, nor hell-fire in your hearts."

The soldier saluted, and was lost again in the darkness and smoke.

A few moments of dreadful uproar, which seemed like hours. Then another soldier came tumbling down the stairs.

" Another flag, Colonel Musgrave! Colonel Musgrave, another flag! "

Then again was heard that passionate, dominating voice: " The Fortieth will never surrender. Never! Though hell-fire burns. Shout it into the throats of the rebels, and then fire! fire! "

By a supreme effort, Peyton roused himself from the dreams that were overwhelming him.

" Musgrave, you are mad. Restrain your men! "

Margaret went near Musgrave and looked beseechingly into his grim, set face.

"Your men would not fire on a flag of truce? O Colonel! that is dishonourable."

The dreams and the visions hovered perilously near. The voices, the swiftly moving redcoats, the clang of the heavy muskets, seemed for a moment far off in the distance. Then Peyton's will triumphed.

"Musgrave, restrain your men!"

"O Colonel! you *would* not have your men fire on a flag of truce!" Margaret's voice rose in entreaty. Peyton's grew imperative.

"Musgrave! Recall that order!"

"Damn it all, Peyton, we have told these rebels we will not surrender. They send that second flag to gain time. We will not surrender, and those dogs may as well know it first as last."

Margaret drew herself up haughtily. Her eyes flashed. She went over nearer to her father.

"Musgrave, you are mad. Restrain your men," repeated Peyton.

Musgrave strode angrily to him.

"Damn you!"

Then Charles Murray spoke with grave and stern authority: "Colonel Musgrave, this is my house, and I rejoice to be of service to the suffering of both armies. But I protest against any outrage against the laws of honour. Your men must be ordered to fire no volleys on a flag of truce."

Musgrave seemed beside himself with rage.

"You miserable rebel, you! If you say another word, I will run you through."

"Musgrave, Musgrave, think! Stop a moment! Recall that order! Hasten! Hasten!"

Then Charles Murray spoke again: "If you restrain not your men before they fire on that flag, I will order my servants to throw open the doors."

Musgrave drew his sword, and rushed towards Charles Murray. But Margaret threw herself before her father. Peyton called sharply:

"Musgrave, Musgrave, beware! Mr. Murray is blind. You are forgetting. Restrain your men before it is too late."

"Damn it all, Peyton, I shall let my men pepper those rebels till they learn we do not mean to surrender."

And then there came the sharp rattle of musketry above.

Margaret learned afterwards that the young Virginian, Lieutenant Smith, who had been the bearer of the flag of truce, received a mortal wound. She had known him well. That his death should be due to treachery, to a shot fired from her own home!

She was standing in front of her father, one hand out as if to shield him. She drew herself up haughtily. Her eyes flashed. She pointed outside.

"Think you it gives us pleasure that our house be thus barred against our friends? It is our friends who are out there, our countrymen. Know you not that our hearts, our prayers are with them? Washington is out there, our Washington! Wayne, Sullivan, Greene, Maxwell, are out there. Fire no more volleys, Colonel Musgrave, or I myself will unbar those doors, and let our friends come in."

Musgrave stopped before her in astonishment,

then exclaimed, angrily, " Damn you, mistress, were you not a woman — "

He was interrupted by Peyton. Peyton's eyes, too, flashed. He rose feebly on his elbow and drew his sword.

" Musgrave, order those men not to fire! "

Peyton's voice thrilled Charles Murray's heart. It had the authority, the solemn dignity of a battle-charge. It was the voice of a supreme soul that for the moment had conquered weakness and suffering, and bidden even Death defiance.

Musgrave turned from Margaret, and strode across to Peyton. Peyton lifted his sword in his left hand. His skill at sword-play with his left hand was well known, but, ah! had that sword ever seemed before so heavy?

" Musgrave," he said, solemnly, " our men must respect the rights of that flag. We are Englishmen, men of honour. Order them not to fire."

" I shall do nothing of the kind. I am commander here, and you may go to hell."

" By the King! I will stand no more."

He rose to his feet, standing unsteadily at first, but strength came most marvellously.

Again and again that brave left arm struck out; and Musgrave, excited, passionate, distraught, fought with his friend as he would not have fought had he been himself. For a few moments it seemed as if Peyton would be victor. Once Musgrave was forced against the wall, and the Captain's sword flashed like a beam of light across his breast. The soldiers round about gathered in a circle, amazement making them all silent.

Margaret watched the fight with strained, hot eyes. She felt as if the blows were aimed at her own heart.

Then the circle of silent soldiers parted. Baines rushed through and impatiently struck up Peyton's sword. It flew from his hand, and hit the wall with a sharp clang.

Margaret sprang forward, her hands outstretched; but Musgrave threw away his own sword, and received Peyton in his arms as he fell.

CHAPTER XXI.

"Full of doubt and turmoil
And a wild unrest."

THE tide of battle had surged and tossed past The Chew House, down the Main Road, and through the village.

When Margaret Murray, in her passionate appeal to Musgrave, had said that Sullivan and Wayne and Greene were outside, she little knew that Sullivan was fighting his way down the road nearly to School House Lane; and that Wayne had got as far as the Green Tree Tavern. But, as her father had feared, the simultaneous blow at the centre had not been struck. Greene had advanced along the Limekiln Road, had withstood with desperate courage the resistance of the First Battalion of Light Infantry. Some of his men had, indeed, broken across the fields and farmlands, and arrived at Cliveden in time to join in the attack; but the main force had kept its original course to Church Lane. Handicapped, however, by the roughness of the road, by the thickets, the stones, the fences, and stoutly opposed by General Grant and his formidable battalions, they made but slow progress, and when the foremost of them reached the Market Square, they came too late. The British had rallied from the turmoil, the disorder, and despair of their first retreat, and naught could resist the excellent discipline they maintained. Many of the Americans fell; many were made prisoners. And, alas! their powder and bullets were running low.

Armstrong had failed to come to time. He had, indeed, engaged the Hessians and Yagers on the bluffs of the Wissahickon; but the fog and the mist hampered him as they had the others; and the confusion and lack of order brought disaster.

Sullivan and Wayne passed slowly down the Main Road, through the fertile gardens and orchards, over walls and fences and fallen trees, — firing, fighting, clubbing, bayoneting, — all confusion, horror, smoke from musketry and burning stubble fields, — mist and fog that made it hard to see who was friend and who was foe.

The doors of Cliveden had been shut and barred; volleys had been poured upon Sullivan's troops as they passed, and Wayne's, too, had had full benefit of the stinging bullets sent in such rapid showers from those upper windows. If the Americans had not lost time by halting to return that deadly fire! Every attempt to capture the house had proved in vain.

Well was it that the commander-in-chief came not within range of that fatal fire!

Out from the woods, over the brow of Chestnut Hill, the "reserve" advanced with steady, firm columns, under command of Nash and Maxwell and Stirling. Washington was with them.

Near the house above Cliveden a halt was made, and the officers called hastily together. Would they summon all their forces, leave this troublesome house to itself, and press on towards the Market

Square to the help of Sullivan and Wayne, and of those brave Virginians under Colonel Matthew of Greene's division, who had already reached the square, and were fighting against such odds?

While these officers were talking, a man, all smoke and dust and dirt, made his way to Alexander Hamilton, and thrust a paper into his hand. Hamilton could scarce make out the script, — words roughly scratched by the sharpened end of a burnt fagot : —

" DEAR HAMILTON : — Methinks the General may have doubts about the strength of the defence of the house. I was within the hall just before the doors were barred. I escaped with a grazed shin. There are five or six hundred men inside, under command of Musgrave and Baines. They are all well equipped with abundance of ammunition, and the walls are well-nigh impregnable. Our men have been storming them in vain. 'Tis a useless venture to besiege the house. Infantry, artillery will be of no avail. They are desperately in earnest. You will lose time if you stop to parley."

The letter was simply signed " R. B." But Hamilton knew well the writer.

If Bingham's advice had but been heeded! All the officers but one were in favour of pushing on to the help of Sullivan and Wayne. The opposing one, — that obstinate though well-intentioned Knox, with his excellent theories, but his lack of that flexibility of mind which makes a man accessible to new ideas, — Knox prevailed.

" 'Tis against all military rule," he said, " to

leave a garrisoned castle in the rear. We are told
that the attacks of infantry and artillery have both
failed. 'Tis no proof that Maxwell and his men will
not prevail."

And, therefore, Maxwell was ordered to remain
behind to besiege the house, while Nash and Stirling
pressed on to the village. Maxwell's men did good,
brave work. The assault was close. Forty-six
officers fell; the lawn was strewn with the wounded
and the dead; but, as Bingham had predicted, no
effort availed; not even when the detachment from
Greene's forces arrived and began a vigorous cannonading on the side of the house. Worst of all,
this sharp firing and cannonading in the rear of
Wayne and Sullivan were not understood by their
men; they thought the British surrounded them on
all sides; and when others of Greene's forces came
plump upon Wayne's men, each division thought
the other to be the enemy. Friends got entangled
with friends, and fired upon each other, and the
darkness of the fog made the confusion well-nigh
hopeless. A disorderly retreat commenced, and the
officers in command were powerless to check it.
'Twas a grievous and a lamentable error, for at
one time it had been feared by General Howe that
his army had suffered total rout.

" In good truth," exclaimed Mad Anthony, " we
were in possession of the whole encampment of the
enemy when this disaster came. Fortune smiled on
us for full three hours; the enemy were broke, dis-
persed, and flying in all quarters. A windmill
attack was made upon a house, into which six
light companies had thrown themselves to avoid
our bayonets. Our troops were deceived by this

attack, thinking it something formidable, and we ran away from the arms of Victory, open to receive us."

And as the retreat of the Americans became general, — the commander-in-chief, deeming it wise to withdraw all the troops in as compact an order as was possible, — General Grey, with his steady, firm columns, marched up the village street in close pursuit. Behind him came the gallant Agnew, who, alas! fell mortally wounded near the old Mennonite burying-ground. Close behind came Lord Cornwallis, who at first sound of noise of battle had rushed from Philadelphia with his grenadiers.

For a time, Musgrave knew naught of what was happening outside. He knew not that Cornwallis had come from the city. Nor did he know that with him was his friend André, a young man, then a captain, who afterwards — but at that time no one dreamed of the fate that was to be his.

Finally, Sir Charles Grey came to relieve Musgrave, and the doors of The Chew House were thrown open.

When Captain Peyton fell, Margaret Murray felt that she had reached the very limit of her strength. Dazed and bewildered, she watched the swiftly moving redcoats as they passed from window to window, or rushed up and down the stairway. Musgrave had little chance for aught but the furious onslaught on the enemy outside. Peyton lay there apparently forgotten, — it seemed hours to Margaret, but in truth it was but minutes. She saw a soldier hit by a ball that smashed through one of the front windows. He fell forward on his face, and there were red splotches of blood on the floor. But they seemed to make little impression on her benumbed senses. Once, when a cannon-ball came flying through the rift in the door, and whizzed over her head, and hurled itself out through the rear wall of the hall, she did rouse herself, and besought a soldier that he would hasten to find Lieutenant Shipton, and bring him speedily. But strange thoughts came to her while she was waiting. It did not seem much to matter after all whether he came or not. What was the meaning of these strange, terrible noises? Yes, there was a battle, — a battle. But where was it? Oh, yes! 'twas in her home, and her friends were being fired upon; and there was some one very dear lying there dying, and there was no one to help, or no one to be sorry.

She felt her father's trembling hands groping for her, and when he touched her face, she almost screamed. Was it her own voice that assured him that she was perfectly safe, perfectly well? Even in her dreams, her thought was unselfishly of him.

Through a dim mist she saw the Lieutenant coming. By one more supreme effort of will she shook off the darkness that was slowly but steadily creeping over her eyes. She caught hold of a chair to keep herself from falling. . . . Shipton gave her a swift look of comprehension and sympathy, then stretched out his hand. She caught it eagerly. Then she stood firmly. He said nothing to comfort her. Indeed, he himself was in sore need of comfort. The youth's heart was like lead in his breast.

" There is a little room yonder, beyond the dining-room. Perchance he could be carried thither."

" The cannonading is fiercest on that side."

" Then let us take him into a corner of the big room there. Of a truth, he must not be left here in this terrible hall."

The Lieutenant nodded; then stooped and lifted the unconscious man's head.

CHAPTER XXII.

"He has but been snatched from death."

HOW she lived through the next two days, Margaret Murray never knew. They seemed one mad, hideous dream. The screams of the wounded; the red blood everywhere; the confusion; the uproar; the hoarse oaths; the terrible work of the surgeons, — would she ever be able to forget?

When the doors were opened to Grey's men, and the gallant soldiers of the Fortieth rushed down the stairway and out into the air, what a sight met the eye! The lawn strewed with the bodies of the dead Americans, the wounded, and the dying. Broken muskets; torn helmets; splintered branches of trees; uprooted shrubs; the big log that had been used as a ram lying across the steps of the portico; the stone lions on the steps toppled over; great pieces of the house torn off; ornaments on the roof broken, urns smashed. Oh! 'twas a sorry sight. But it had been a gallant siege and a brave defence.

But this destruction, this suffering at Cliveden was nothing to that in the village. Especially at the Market Square were the misery and the desolation most apparent; though the whole village was a hospital, and there was scarce a garden for miles

around that had not in it a dead or dying soldier.

Margaret thought the villagers had enough to
bear without their being subjected to the visits of
streams of people who came out from the city, some
moved by pity, others by curiosity. But among
the former was the great Doctor Shippen, and Margaret had much comfort in his skill and kindliness.
This was the man who, when congratulated on
the number of cures he affected, and the few patients
he lost, replied, with a whimsical smile:

"My friend, Nature does a great deal, and the
grave covers up our mistakes."

He it was who now gave poor, distracted Annette the hope that Henry Murray would recover
health and reason. He it was, too, who gave Jake
some simple directions which helped him to serve
Captain Peyton with judgment and good effect.
Poor Jake's heart felt heavy enough at the fever
and delirium which had come to his beloved " Cappin," and were to last so many long weeks. But
Margaret knew not what she would have done without the help of Jake's honest strength and unselfish
devotion.

She would gladly have shut herself away from
all the heartrending scenes of those terrible two
days. But fate seemed to have its iron grip upon
her. She was needed. Her father needed her;
the servants were helpless without her; these suffering soldiers needed her; even the surgeons came
to her for aid.

In all the big house there was no place of retreat
for her. It taxed every effort to keep even her
brother's room free from the worst of the turmoil.

The peace and quietude of her beloved haunt in the woods at the other side of the lake could not be enjoyed now. She had no time, even had she had the wish, to go thither.

One moment she did snatch, that she might visit the stables to see what had befallen the horses locked in there. To her unspeakable relief she found them safe. Terrified as they had been by the uproar and the tumult outside, they had now settled down to a degree of comfort. It went to Margaret's heart to see Selim's unmistakable joy at sight of her. But she could not tarry with him. As she was about to lock the big door of the stable, she saw her whip lying on the floor. Mechanically she stooped and picked it up, and it happened to be in her hand as she was hurrying across the lawn to the house. She had nearly reached the kitchens when she heard a stifled scream. Then, Dorothea, her Deutsches Mädchen, rushed from behind the shrubbery, closely pursued by a rough grenadier. He reached her side just as Margaret came up. Margaret brought her whip in a stinging blow across his face. It came with such force that a band of red quickly showed itself. The man uttered an angry growl; but evidently feared to vent his anger on the haughty, indignant maiden with the flashing eyes and imperious air who had so unexpectedly become the champion of her whom he had thought to be his sure prey. He slunk away behind the shrubbery; and Margaret led the sobbing, trembling girl into the house.

The next moment, Margaret was holding the hand of a dying soldier, her face full of pity and tenderness, as she whispered to him a word of hope and of courage to speed his soul on its journey through darkness into the infinite light.

On the morning after the battle, she was watching beside her brother, that Annette might happily snatch a moment's rest, when a light step was heard in the room, and looking up she saw Doctor Worthington. Behind him was the Lieutenant.

"At last we have found our recreant surgeon," the Lieutenant whispered. "I captured him as he was sawing off a man's leg at Widow Deshler's up the road."

There was a dark flush on Doctor Worthington's face. His brilliant eyes looked troubled. Even this placid materialist seemed subdued by the solemn scenes around them on all sides.

"I have to crave a thousand pardons for my delay," he said, softly. "Of a truth, Mistress Murray, I forgot not the promise I gave you, nor my pleasure when I gave it; but I have had no moment that would serve me."

Margaret simply bowed.

Doctor Worthington looked at Henry Murray long and earnestly, then he turned to the Lieutenant.

"Tell me," he said, "the circumstances of the accident."

And Shipton told him.

"Is it known what caused it?"

"No."

"Bethink yourself well. Omit nothing."

"I have told you," said the Lieutenant, stiffly.

"Seems it not to you as if he had been attacked from behind? See! 'tis the back of his head that has been the most injured."

"I know not. Methinks it had occurred to us that he might have been struck from behind."

" 'Tis not necessary that you whisper. The man would not hear you if you blew a bugle in his room. Had Peyton no theory?"

"Methinks not. I heard him express no theory, only horror of the man who was coward enough to strike the blow."

The flush deepened on Worthington's face.

"We saw the poor fellow in sad plight. We could not leave him. We brought him to the nearest house. 'Twas surprise enough, in faith, to find 'twas his own home."

"Was no one seen by you?"

"No one. Yes, now I bethink me. We saw a man fleeing as though the fiends were after him."

"Who was the man?"

"How know I? We were too far away to see."

"Was he British or Continental?"

Shipton showed impatience. "What matters it, Worthington? The matter is to cure Mistress Murray's brother. The facts of his injury are a profound mystery."

"Then Peyton knew not the man who did it?"

"No. 'Twas of a surety a common thief, a rascally highwayman. And yet — and yet — "

"And yet?"

"Why, when we were dressing Mr. Murray's wounds we found that his money-belt, even his watch, had been undisturbed."

"How account you for that?"

"Methinks the thief saw us coming ere he had completed his purpose."

Worthington's face cleared.

"Well, well, it behooves us now to cure him and to leave conjectures alone. I must congratulate the man who put on these bandages. He ought to have been born a surgeon."

During the next ten minutes Margaret wished several times that this brilliant surgeon would talk less; but when she noted how skilfully he rearranged the bandages and placed her brother in a position that seemed to afford much relief, she decided that there were some men who had the power to talk and act at the same time.

While Doctor Worthington was thus busied, Margaret felt a light touch on her arm. It was Chloe. "Massa Kelper outside in de garden, missy. Go out de back door, he says."

It took Margaret but two minutes to reach the spot under a tree where Rodney awaited her. The smoke and powder-stains had been washed from his face. He had on his big hat, and he held a spade in his hand. His face was white and stern.

Margaret would scarce have recognised him for the man who had carried Peyton in but yesterday. Yesterday? Why, it seemed years ago.

"O Rodney, Rodney! 'tis not safe!" she whispered, breathlessly, as she looked apprehensively around.

"Yes, Margaret, it is. Have no fear; — only should any of those officers talking over there walk this way and come within earshot, remember I am Kelper and a partial stranger."

"Yes, yes."

"O Margaret! How is Henry?"

And she told him.

"Oh! I have been in a fever of unrest to know

if you are all safe. But I could not come before.
It has been awful here; but 'tis hell everywhere.
I was hurrying hither, when as I passed Reuben
Haines's I found that the whole house and grounds
are used as a hospital. Then at the taverns they
are taking down the doors and laying them across
chairs to serve as tables for the wounded. They
asked me to help them cut off legs and arms. I
could not. . . . I had to refuse. . . . 'Tis easy for
us to chatter about patriotism; to be enthusiastic
about our cause; to draw maps; study entrenchments; do all we can to bring on an action, but
God! after a battle! 'Tis enough to make one sick
of war. O Margaret! that men who say they love
our Father and believe in the gospel of love can
do such things! I tell you, Margaret, I will be a
Quaker in deed and belief, a hermit as I pretend to
be. I will retire from the world." And the patriot
made attempt to smile; then strong man as he was,
he burst into tears.

But Margaret had reached that point where she
had no more tears.

" I was in the thick of the fight; helped to kill men
right and left; clubbing, bayoneting. The darkness
was horrible, lit up only by the red flashes of muskets. But, Margaret, 'tis afterwards that the horror
comes. To see those terrified women crawling out
of the cellars where they had been hidden. I saw
some children running to shelter; and a cannon-ball
whizzed past them down the lane." . . .

Then he told her brokenly of General Nash, the
brave patriot from North Carolina, who, even when
mortally wounded, had led his troops on towards the
square. Then he spoke of Irvine and Turner, of

stout-hearted Lieutenant Smith and the dauntless Colonel Matthew, who was a prisoner. Then he told her of General Agnew, the noble Briton, who lay dying at Mr. Wister's, his blood staining the polished floor. There had been many heavy losses on both sides, and Margaret's sore heart was in sorrow for both.

Then they spoke of the retreat. " 'Twas managed with great ability, Margaret, after the first confusion and disorder were controlled. All at once the noise of battle hushed itself. It grew strangely quiet. Methinks the General's leadership was evident in the way the troops were drawn off, fully as much as in the planning of the attack."

" Father has been tormenting himself with wondering how the General feels at the failure of his plan."

" Ah! 'twas a magnificent plan, audacious, worthy of a great genius! "

Bingham's dark eyes glowed. " It has not been total failure, Margaret. We have taught the British many things. We can make the attack as well as defend ourselves when attacked. We can strike, boldly, aggressively, as well as use strategy. . . . Margaret, it will be the opinion of students of history who will write of this day, and of the patriots whose hearts will thrill at the remembrance of it, that not since Lexington has there been so important and significant an action as this same battle of Germantown, through whose horrors we are passing now."

At that moment, the Lieutenant appeared at the rear door of the house, and with him were Doctor Worthington and Captain André.

She motioned to Lieutenant Shipton, and he came at once towards her.

"This gentleman," she said, "is the stranger who helped you with your friend. 'Tis Mr. Kelper, of Germantown."

Shipton's sad face brightened. He offered his hand. "'Tis glad I am to see you again, sir. I owe you much."

"Will your friend get well?" asked Bingham.

"Doctor Worthington and Doctor Shippen both give some encouragement."

"Egad! Bob," said André, coming up. "If Arthur gets through this, 'twill be because of his clean living and strong health these years."

And then he turned to look at Margaret as she disappeared through the door. Doctor Worthington was following her.

"She's as brave as she is beautiful," John André said, and one of his most winning smiles came into his face.

"Ay, she is," answered the Lieutenant, fervently. "In faith, 'twere not possible to tell all she has done."

"I saw a poor wretch bless her as he stiffened his legs this morning."

"Many blessed her yesterday."

"Egad! Bob, methinks we should withdraw from this house as soon as the dead are buried."

And John André took off his hat reverently.

"We are to bury the dead here in the rear garden, and very soon, I am told."

The Lieutenant's tone was reverent and quiet.

"The men of the village have been busy at this work all the morning," said Bingham, as he leaned on his spade. " Your officers have been asking us to help. I have seen even the boys in the village working hard. Over there in that field across the road, seventeen Hessians were put in one grave."

" Poor souls, poor souls," said Shipton.

" There are many, many of my countrymen here," said Bingham, sadly.

" Yes, Mr. Kelper. There are many."

" I am here to help. I came for that purpose."

" 'Tis well," said André, " but remember that these poor fellows we are to bury in the garden here must not be put in with their faces up. Throw not dirt in their faces, for they also are mothers' sons."

" God bless you!" murmured Bingham, under his breath. And long afterwards he remembered those words of the genial, warm-hearted Englishman. And remembering them, he thought gently of John André's faults, and felt most sorry for his fate.

" Yes, Bob. We must withdraw as soon as Cornwallis can arrange it. God knows these people must be glad to be quit of us."

" Will your friend be able to go?" Bingham asked the Lieutenant.

But André answered for him.

" Egad, sir! He cannot be taken with us. He will have to be left to the care of these strangers, an they are willing."

" Doctor Shippen is of the opinion," said the Lieutenant, " that it may be months ere Arthur is fit to go."

The youth's voice trembled. André knew well

of the love he bore Arthur Peyton, but he knew not of the full strength of the bond.

He laid his hand tenderly on the Lieutenant's shoulder. "While we stay in the city we will ride out oft to inquire for him — and perchance, lad, the time may come when he will know us and be glad that we have come."

CHAPTER XXIII.

"There seems to be no choice in this matter."

THAT afternoon, Sir William Howe and Lord Cornwallis, with their respective staffs, visited the house that had been so gallantly besieged and so bravely defended.

"Of a truth 'twould be a grievous blow to many in England should Captain Peyton not recover," Sir William said to the Lieutenant as they stood together a moment. "It pains me much to see him in this state." And the kind-hearted General looked very grave. Then he moved near Charles Murray.

"If there is aught, sir, that can be done which would be of any service to you in this inconvenience of having our friend quartered upon you, I pray you, sir, command me. Sir Robert Shipton has told me of your exceeding kindness."

And Charles Murray in his stateliest manner made reply that, as 'twould be most dangerous to move the wounded captain, it was their pleasure to be able to tender to him the sincerest hospitality.

"I fear me that Sir Robert Shipton has not told you of his own and of Captain Peyton's kindness to me," he added. "So you see, your Excellency, that if a pleasant debt can be paid it ought to pleasure us much and make us grateful."

" But methinks you had slight intention to remain here throughout the winter. I am told that all these country-houses roundabout, Mount Pleasant, Bush Hill, Fairhill, Stenton, are deserted during the winter. What was your intention, Mr. Murray?"

" I know not, your Excellency. We are in the hands of God."

Sir William Howe lifted his hat.

" If you stay the winter here, 'tis possible you may be much inconvenienced. After I withdraw my troops to the city, the rebels will forage the whole country. I hope you may not be molested. 'Twill be my concern to protect any country people coming into the city on market days, that they may supply my camp without harass. I shall see that troops are so disposed that the rebels may not divert that which of right belongs to us. But I fear me that my protection cannot extend so far as Germantown. But I will send you a script that will pass you wherever our outposts are stationed."

Sir William Howe was ever generous in words, and he had most excellent intentions. Charles Murray felt the charm of the man, and realised why he was so popular among his officers and soldiers.

" I thank you, sir," answered Mr. Murray. " But as you perceive, I am severely handicapped by my misfortune. But if you will make out the script for my daughter and her grooms, we shall be glad of it."

" Their names?" asked the General.

" Jake, Sam, Tom."

" Sir Robert, have the kindness to take note that Stachey attend to this matter."

"Yes, your Excellency. Your pardon, sir, shall he not add an order that no horses on this place be pressed for the use of the troops? We are pressing all the horses in Germantown and roundabout. We might not be here to avert mischief."

"'Tis well you spoke of the matter. Have Stachey attend to it at once."

"Yes, your Excellency."

The next day an orderly rode out to Cliveden and left in Margaret's hands the document that was to prove so useful during the long weary months that were before her : —

"Mistress Margaret Murray, of The Chew House, Germantown, is to be permitted to pass and to repass the lines at Philadelphia at any time, accompanied by one or two of her three servants — Jake, Sam, or Tom. (She is under oath.)

"By order,
"Howe,
"*Commander-in-Chief.*"

CHAPTER XXIV.

"Perchance, lad, the time may come when he will know us and be glad that we have come."

THE days dragged on. Musgrave and his men had gone back to their huts and tents. Cornwallis had departed with his grenadiers. The British camp was as it had been before, except for the desolation roundabout, and the absence of those forever gone. The people of the village seemed too paralysed to set about the repairs of their ruined homes. The mills in the country roundabout were not running, — weavers, millers, tanners were idle. A spirit of torpor and of despair seemed to have been created by the war. Only the keepers of the taverns seemed to thrive.

One day the whole camp was in a state of peculiar excitement. There had been rumours that Washington, who was now at White Marsh, only a few miles distant, had intention to surprise the village as he had on that fatal morning of October the fourth. But evening fell, and the rebels had not appeared. Two days after that, a large detachment of Howe's forces marched up beyond Chestnut Hill to lure if possible that wily fox, the American general, from his lair. But he was safely entrenched, and would not come out to offer battle. But there was sharp skirmishing among the troops;

and that night many wounded were brought back
to the village.   Then there were dangerous expeditions across country after forage and horses.
Allen McLane and Light-Horse Harry Lee sorely
harassed these foraging parties; and many provisions were lost which were much needed in the
British camp.   The wounded soldiers, alas! showed
the fatal effect often of this dangerous sport.   These
skirmishes kept the village in a state of terror; and
every musket-shot heard at Cliveden was thought
by Chloe and Dinah to be the prophecy of another
judgment of the Lord.

On the eighteenth of October the British broke
camp and took up their march to the city.   They
had not been gone an hour before the Germantown
Street was filled with the Continental troops of
Light-Horse that harassed the rear of the enemy.

And this was the beginning of that constant action and reaction which throughout the winter were
to give Germantown little rest from alternate visita-
tions of British and Continental soldiers.

The country roundabout Philadelphia on both
sides of the Schuylkill might be considered neutral
ground.   He was master who had the larger force
or was the more adroit.   One day men from the
American army would meet in the taverns or visit
friends in the village.   The next day companies
of the British, or, perchance, small parties, would
sally forth from the city to forage or to skirmish.
Passing through Germantown, they, too, would
make use of the convenient taverns, sometimes of
the homes of the people.   As Charles Murray had
said, it was indeed a perilous time.

The day the British left, Doctor Worthington

had been busied with attendance upon certain soldiers whose wounds might make the journey most
distressing.   Finally word was brought him from
the Green Tree Tavern that two officers would
need attention ere they were fit to be put in the
carts which were to take the wounded prisoners to
the city.   He hastened to do this work; but ere
it was completed the last of the army had descended
the hill and were rapidly disappearing in the shadows
of the woods.   With an oath, he sprang down the
stairs to find that he and his charges had alike been
forgotten.   The cart with the prisoners had gone.
Hearing the clatter of hoofs in the street, he looked
up, and to his surprise he saw the American Horse
in full gallop.   A few minutes after, a trooper
sprang from his beast and levelling a pistol at the
doctor, shouted:

" You are my prisoner."

" Ho, ho, my good man, methinks not."

" Surrender, or I fire."

Worthington saw the man was in earnest.   " I
am but a surgeon," he protested.

" It matters not.   You are my prisoner."

A crowd collected — most of the men unsympa-
thetic, all curious.   No protests of the astonished
physician availed.   He was being carried off with
scant ceremony, when the crowd parted and a stranger stepped forth.

" Hold, man! " he said, pleasantly.   " Methinks
you are scarce aware that the two men in that inn
whom this surgeon has been nursing are of your
army.   Go up-stairs and see if you will not find
Captain Chester and Lieutenant Sprague.   A good
release for them, my boy.   Instead of going to the

city in a rough cart, they can go with you to White Marsh."

The trooper paused. Then with hand still grasping Worthington, and with pistol cocked, he dragged the impatient Doctor into the inn. He soon found that the stranger had the right of it. Worthington was let go, and the patriot army regained two of its bravest officers.

" Egad, sir, I thank you for helping me out of this scrape," said Worthington, as he and the stranger went down the steps. " I would have been soon released ; but the delay would have been most inconvenient for some of my patients. I ride to the city as soon as I have visited Cliveden. Were it not for the necessity of haste, I should insist that you have a bowl of punch with me and a quiet pipe."

" How fare your patients at Cliveden ? "

" Ah, know you them ? "

" But slightly. Mr. Murray was kind to me once in an extremity. Is he doing well ? "

" Marvellously well. He will soon be over his trouble."

" And the Englishman ? "

" He is yet in much danger. The issue cannot yet be foreseen."

The two men parted with the promise given that they should meet each other the following night, the place of meeting to be the King of Prussia Inn.

And it so happened that neither Doctor Worthington nor Rodney Bingham kept the appointment.

Now that the British were gone, there seemed to be slight hindrance in the way of the gratification

of Rodney Bingham's wish to visit his friends at
Cliveden; but he feared the presence of spies in the
village; and just now 'twas most important that
an enterprise in which he was engaged should suffer no defeat. This enterprise was concerned with
the fate of the forts on the Delaware. That it
failed was only due to the overwhelming odds
against which the Americans were struggling. On
the tenth of November the bombardment of the
forts began. The dull booming of the guns was
heard day by day at Cliveden; and for a whole
month the hearts of the patriots in city and village
were heavy with apprehension. When those guns
were silenced they sorrowed for the fate of the
brave men who had been forced to yield.

Margaret heard nothing of Rodney for many
anxious weeks. At this stagnant period in the
progress of the war there seemed little need for
secret service; and so he withdrew to Lancaster,
where in his true character he worked for the cause
of his beloved Washington. He was in direct communication with the members of the Congress and
also with the army.

Finally the winter set in, — the winter of the
suffering at Valley Forge, and of the contrasts in
Philadelphia. Patriotism in Rags in the one place;
gold lace, sparkling red, rioting and feasting in
the other.

A winter at Cliveden, when Stenton, the Wister
House, Doctor Shippen's home, and many other
summer homes were closed, would have been mo-
notonous at best; but in ordinary times the city
could with slight difficulty be reached. This winter,

however, was no ordinary time. A foreign army was in the city, — redoubts and fortifications stretched from the Delaware to the Schuylkill; few of the country people were allowed to pass the lines, and if allowed to pass 'twas difficult to get permission to return. Then the desolating hand of war had been laid most heavily upon the whole region stretching from the city to the village. The suffering of the people, the scarcity of supplies with which to relieve the suffering, and the daily pressure of many anxious cares, made this winter one never to be forgotten.

Cliveden was quiet, sometimes lonely. When her husband was past danger and began to recover rapidly, Annette felt some of the old craving for gay companionship.

"If Peg or Sophia could but come," she would often sigh, "or dear Dolly Stark. Methinks I should embrace even Susan Penter whose shoulder-blades stick out so much, and whose tongue is so sharp." Annette felt even a longing for a sight of the stiff old Quakers and their dames who had once caused mirth and merry chaff among the "younger set" in the placid, learned, somewhat humdrum though always self-satisfied city of Penn.

"Listen to this, Margaret," she said one day, after Margaret had returned home with letters. "Listen to this. 'Tis from Rebecca Franks,"[1] and Annette read in her clear, sweet voice:

"Oh, how I wish your husband would let you come in for a week or two. I know you are as

---

[1] This letter was written by Rebecca Franks and sent to a friend called Mrs. Paca. Miss Franks married Colonel Johnson of the British army and went to live in England.

fond of a gay life as myself. You'd have an opportunity of raking as much as you choose, either
at plays, balls, concerts, or assemblies. I have been
but three evenings alone since we moved to town.
I begin now to be almost tired. You have not
the slightest idea of the life of continued amusement I live in. I can scarce have a moment to
myself. I have stole this while everybody is retired to dress for dinner. I am but just come
from under J. Black's hands, and most elegantly
am I dressed for a ball this evening at Smith's,
the 'City Tavern,' you remember, where we have
one every Thursday. You would not know the
room, 'tis so much improved. I wish to Heaven
you were going with us this evening to judge for
yourself."

Annette sighed and picked up another letter from
her friend and kinswoman, Eleanor Trent.

"'Twould rejoice you, dear, to see how the old
theatre is transformed. No more stupid protests
from the Quakers will avail. We are amusing ourselves right well. Could you but see how well
Captain André acts. He is an artist, also, and has
intention to paint a drop-curtain which he will leave
to us even after the army moves. Yester-eve we
saw 'The Constant Couple,' a right amusing com-
edy, though less spicy than 'The Deuce Is in Him.'
Come when Henry has totally recovered. We miss
you more and more. Oh! Captain André and his
friend De Lancey have moved from Doctor Frank-
lin's house off High Street, and for a time are
quartered on the Bingham house, and they tell me
they are most comfortable there. The elegance of
the furniture, the convenience of the arrangements

appeal to these fastidious Englishmen. Mr. André has taken the south parlour as a painting-room. Methinks I can see Mother Bingham's horror were she to know. But the Binghams are safe at Lancaster, and well out of all these dissipations. Methinks such rabid Whigs would have scant comfort had they remained."

And at this point in the letter, Annette looked up and smiled at Margaret.

Margaret, daring, skilful horsewoman as she was, recked not of the miles between Cliveden and the city. The necessities of her household were many, and she went oft back and forth under the escort of her trusty Sam and Jake. When Sam could not be spared, she and Jake essayed the miles alone. Without him she never felt content to go.

That they passed unharmed through the many dangers of the roads was a marvel to Charles Murray. He had scant peace of mind while Margaret was absent; and when the hoofs of the horses were heard coming up the garden road he breathed a prayer of silent gratitude.

"Of a verity, 'twould be a happiness could Sophie or Peg come back with you," said Annette, one bright, clear day in December as Margaret was ready to depart. "Bring them back with you, I pray you, with some of the officers as escort. Of a truth, Lieutenant Shipton would seize the opportunity to come. 'Tis quite safe. There have been no Continental soldiers in the village for several days. Mrs. Chew has a big sleigh. 'Twould be a pleasure to see them. Be urgent with them, I implore you."

" Think you Henry would welcome these friends of Peggy's ? "

Annette smiled. " Why not? Henry is a strong patriot, but he has some vestiges of common sense remaining. It would pleasure him much to hear the sound of merry laughter and gay talk. . . . Methinks, too, Captain Peyton, though still in his own apartments, were not loath to see Captain André or the Lieutenant once more. Ah! he must be weary for the lad. . . . Jake informs me that the Captain has tried hard to write a letter to the Lieutenant for you to take to the city. Ah! There 'tis in your girdle. Let me see it, I pray you."

Margaret slowly drew it forth. " He made awkward work of the direction, methinks."

" Not so bad," and Annette scrutinised it curiously. " 'Tis marvellously well done for a man lying on his back both day and night."

Sophia and Margaret Chew came not that day; but a week later there jingled through the Germantown street a big sleigh, inside of which were three merry-faced maidens, — Mistress Chew, her sister, and a beloved friend. In one corner sat their mother, muffled in furs. Beside the sleigh rode a number of officers in full uniform. Behind were a dozen stout troopers as escort.

That day the old house became gay with laughter and merry voices. The big logs were piled high in the fireplaces — the flames leaped and shone.

Even Henry Murray gave André and Shipton cordial greeting. And Peyton, for one brief hour, was allowed to gaze into their friendly, sincere eyes and listen to their talk.

CHAPTER XXV.

"It haunts me so. It is as if I were in the land of dreams, — trying to clutch, clutch something which is for ever fading away into shadows. But it sometimes seems as if my imagination could piece out the whole picture and make it perfect."

THERE was another besides Margaret who recked not of distance or of cold. Scarce a day passed that Doctor Worthington was not in the saddle. Doctor Shippen oft commended the young man's energy as well as skill; and many a weary sufferer in city and village, many a wounded soldier at Valley Forge and at Philadelphia and in the country roundabout had cause to bless the skill that healed, the prompt decision and the courage that saved life.

And yet the man's success in his profession was not wholly due to his devotion to it, to his natural aptitude for the practical application of scientific knowledge. The emergencies of the sickroom and the hospital appealed to him, not because of sympathy, but because of pride. Ambition was the ruling motive of his life. He was seeking to make his work as a surgeon minister to his ambition. It had its obvious and its most useful purpose; but it would also serve as a stepping-stone to that which would bring in larger rewards, and richer.

From the day that he had taken charge of her husband, a warm feeling of friendship for him

216

had sprung up in Annette's heart; and as her husband gained strength under his watchful care, the feeling grew. How many weary hours the Doctor's frequent visits brightened, no one but Henry Murray and Annette knew. He brought with him the atmosphere of the gay world, of the world in which lived their friends — the world of warmth and plenty, of joy and of colour. And gradually Henry and Annette became convinced that here was a true patriot, of value to the new nation, animated by lofty ideals, ready to make sacrifices.

They were both clever and of quick wit, had acute perceptions and insight into character; and yet they were both deceived; and in that misfortune they were sharers with many others. But when distrust once began to blight the fair blossom of Henry Murray's faith in Doctor Worthington, it grew rapidly. Much mischief, however, had been brought about, ere the blight came.

For whatever he had done or planned to do, Doctor Worthington could give to himself abundant reasons that it was done in accordance with a strict sense of duty — but 'twas duty to himself, devotion to his own interests. He acknowledged no higher law, no more sacred duty, than to minister to his own welfare. 'Twas clearly to his own interest that he should serve the King. There was no harm in saying that the high principle animating him was patriotism. But 'twas no " Patriotism in Rags " he favoured; that which was adorned with lavish gold lace, sparkling red, was the patriotism that appealed to him.

He had been dazzled by the brilliancy of this

British army — the luxury, the wealth of its officers, their dashing manners, their air of owning all the earth and the kingdoms thereof. With these men of title he seemed to have kinship. His natural tastes were like theirs; given the same opportunity, he himself could be as irresistible as they.

Till they came, his life had been restricted and narrow; but that life in a small colonial town had never satisfied him. He had always felt 'twas foolish to stay in a pond when the full, rich, wide expanse of the lake might be his. He would cast off the old life, the old associations, even the old friends, and would steer out into the broad waters of the lake. If his boat struck the rocks or foundered, even then the venture would pay. But he would not strike the rocks. He would steer too carefully for that.

Months before, a great opportunity had been given him to serve the King — the way he served was, to be sure, somewhat perilous; but peril gave it zest, and it was fraught with more important consequence than he himself expected. His profession had given him entrance both to the camp of Washington and to that of Howe. In the former camp he heard much that was not intended to be heard. A duller man, with less sensitive perceptions, might have passed by these things and thought them of no consequence. Not so Doctor Worthington. The reception Howe accorded the news he brought taught him the value of his own perceptions. He gained confidence, and began to devise great schemes.

He intended to play for high stakes, and he risked much. But perhaps there was no man in city or village who enjoyed life and its excitements and uncertainties more than he. Should his schemes turn out well, his fortune was made. Thus he looked forward to a brilliant future, full of rich rewards to repay him for present sacrifice. In his plans he gave little hospitality to the thought of failure.

On one thing, however, he had not counted. He had won many friends and made few enemies. The belles and beauties of the city learned to watch for his coming; and his handsome face and figure, his assured manner, and his self-poise made him rival of many a gay blade; but he had had no thought of wasting time on love or love-making except as they might advance him in the success of his schemes. But now he was in truth wasting time; and sometimes he fretted against the passion that might possibly prove stronger than his ambition.

His fancy had been caught and held in thrall by a girl who was wholly unconscious of her influence over him. And yet his love for Margaret Murray was so blended with his ambition that it would have been safe to say that, had she been an obscure or lowly-born maiden, his fancy would have played truant at once. Her popularity, her assured position, the rumour of her large Virginia estate, increased his ardour. Worthington had the wisdom of the world. He was alive to its pleasures and its profits. He knew well the value of the material. He could never be the fanatic who would lay down his life for a conviction or the reformer who would suffer persecution for an ideal. Ideals had little place in his scheme of life. Money, power, social position were with him the important factors of happiness.

To such a man as he success was happiness, and they were the factors of success. He was not the man to march with enthusiasms, convictions, or ideals that would handicap him in his course. If he made any experiments with ideals it must be after he had got to the point that he could afford the luxury of them. " 'Tis easy," he said, " for a rich man like Captain Peyton, for instance, with an assured position, to indulge in the luxury of religious sentiment, or poetic delight in nature, or even, on fit occasion, to indulge in the delicate and alluring sentiment of tender melancholy; but the worker, the striver, — he must shut his eyes to sentiment. His whole task is to win. He has no time to think of the Infinite or the Eternal. He must be for the present. The fleeting hour with all its opportunities and its possibilities is the only tangible reality."

This materialism of Doctor Worthington, though never expressed to Margaret Murray, was vaguely felt by her. Had he but known it, that on which he secretly prided himself the most was that for which she had the least patience. She was grateful to him. She admired his skill, — his manner, his *savoir faire,* his brilliancy of mind made a certain appeal of their own. She was not blind to the charm of these qualities which made Doctor Worthington attractive to her brother. But Margaret Murray's mind dwelt in a large world. In truth she found little in Doctor Worthington's companionship to satisfy her. She was conscious of his narrowness of soul. And she spent little energy in thinking about him. When he was absent she usually forgot all

about him, unless in connection with matters relating
to the care of the invalids of her household.

'Twas well for Doctor Worthington's peace of
mind that he knew naught of the large world in
which Margaret's mind habitually dwelt, and in
which there was no room for him.

And 'twas well that Margaret was unconscious
of how desperate this man would be made by failure. With his iron determination and strength
of will he was capable of destroying anything that
stood in his way or threatened to thwart his plans.

This destructive tendency which, in less spacious
times with less gracious manners, would have made
him a desperate pirate or a successful highwayman, was in this year of grace 1778, and in the
placid city of Penn, modified and controlled by
caution and by worldly prudence, by a sensitive and
self-conscious regard for appearances, and an almost
morbid desire for approval.

There was to come a time when Doctor Worthington was to find that he could not always thus
control fancy and keep passion in check; but just
now his passion was so modified and controlled by
caution that he did not stretch out his hand rashly,
impetuously, as most fervent lovers would, to
take the prize he craved.

He waited and watched, he brooded and schemed,
— and the days slipped away.

CHAPTER XXVI.

"The whole land seems so full of treachery these days, we know not half the time who our foes are."

IT was the third of January, 1778. Big fires were burning in the generous chimney-places at Cliveden. The sunlight was streaming in the windows; but snow covered the lawns and garden paths; ice hung from the shrubbery and trees, and threw back the sun's rays in a thousand sparkles of beauty and colour.

In the big hall were Jake and Chloe. She was shivering, as if she could not forget the cold, and he had been piling the wood in great heaps before the fireplace in dining-room, parlour, and school-room. The door of the office at the other side of the hall was closed.

Chloe wore a bright-hued sack over a still brighter gown, and Jake was looking at her with evident admiration. Then he laughed softly, and held out his hand. She peered into it, and chuckled.

"Wot you want me to do?"

"You see dat? Dat's all youse."

"Wot fool-talk you sayin' now?"

"I ain't sayin' no fool-talk, honey. Dat's all youse, ef you get ebberybody out dat schoolroom dare, an' get Missy Margaret in."

"Wot you mean?"

"Nobody but Massa Peyton 'lowed to come. He hab Missy Margaret all to hisself till you cawn't help people a-comin', an' den only ober your dead body."

"My dead body? Massa Murray doan' want no darky's bones hangin' 'roun' loose heah."

Jake had a capacious pocket, and in it was some money, which he jingled most invitingly. Was it British gold? Precious, scarce British gold? Chloe's bright eyes shone gloriously.

"Keep um all out," continued Jake, solemnly, "an' let Massa Peyton hab his say wid de missy. He's been sick long time, an' he's gettin' most beside hisself wid de feelin' dat he's got to see de missy. Now, look heah!"

Jake took a little bag from his pocket, and put the shining pieces of gold in it. He held it up before Chloe's excited eyes. She tried to reach it. Did not succeed. Then she laughed.

"Now turn 'roun'," Jake ordered.

She began to turn around and around with bewildering swiftness.

"Turn 'roun' your back, I mean, chile."

She stopped with her back to Jake. He deftly pinned the bag of money to the sack.

"Now, Chloe, you cawn't hab dat till you's gwine an' done wot my dear Cappin wants."

Chloe kept twisting and turning, in vain attempts to reach the bag. The money jingled. Jake chuckled.

"Ef you doan' do it, chile, de money won't nebber be youse. I'll gib it back to my Cappin."

Chloe saw numerous difficulties in the way of her success. Her face clouded over.

" S'pose missy done gone to de city markets,"
she said, dejectedly.

Jake drew himself up proudly.

" Couldn't go widout me."

" Dat's shuh! " answered Chloe, meditatively.
" Now I bet'ink myself, Jake, de missy looked pow'-
ful pale dis mawnin'. S'pose she's sick. Couldn't
nebber manage it in dat case, Jake."

Jake looked disgusted. " She ain't sick, cos she
was jes' out in de stables lookin' at Tempest an'
Selim."

Chloe shuddered. " In all dis cole wedder. I
bet'ink myself dose hosses git 'long pow'ful well
wid you, Jake, an' you not trubble de poor missy
wid your work."

" I 'clare to hebben, Chloe, dat you try my patience pow'ful bad."

" Well, well, honey; be quiet now. S'pose Missy
Margaret's readin' dat ole Shakespeare to her
fadder."

" She ain't, cos Massa Murray's in his room all
by hisself alone."

Chloe began again to try and reach the alluring
prize pinned to her back, and, as she turned and
twisted, she talked on.

" I'se 'fraid dat Doctor Worthington frusterates,
fustates, fusterbates all my plan. He's mos' crazy
ober de missy, too. I 'clare to goodness, 'tis a pity
she doan' stay in de city moah, whar de Chews stay.
She'd make de hearts ob de redcoats go beatin',
beatin'. An' de balls dare. Wouldn't my missy
shine 'mong dem all! It makes my heart ache to
t'ink ob dem all."

With suppressed laughter, she stopped and looked at Jake invitingly. He laughed.

"You's cole, child. Le's hab a ball ob our own."

In the midst of their dance, Chloe stopped suddenly. A look of horror came into her face. Then she gave a low scream, and grasped Jake's arm convulsively. "Dare, look dare!"

On the floor of the big hall, on the white pillars, the walls, she fancied she saw the scenes that had made Cliveden, last October, a place of desolation and horror. Once more the soldiers were rushing up the stairway. There were blood upon their faces, powder stains and smoke. Blood from the dead and dying Americans, brought in after the doors were opened, lay in pools on the floor.

For one brief moment, Jake showed agitation, and the two cowered and shivered together, then he drew himself up proudly.

"Doan' feah, honey, doan' you feah no moah. I'se heah to take care ob you."

But Chloe felt that even this brave Jake, who feared no British or Continental marauder on the highway, was powerless to shield her from these ghostly visitants. Her terror made her voluble.

"Dare's dose big blood stains comin' out again. I washed dem all away only las' week. Dey's pow'ful deep in de wood. An' dare up de stairway. See! see! dose bloody han's a-stretchin' out. Dat's whar dat poah trooper, Grove, fell on de stairs. An' dare! See dose white faces a-peerin' 'roun' de pillars. Dey's all dressed in red, de debbel's colour, shuh. See! dare's dat bloody han' again. Dare's whar Massa Peyton fell like dead. See! see!"

But relief to her overwrought emotions came in

the shape of Captain Peyton himself, who opened
the door of the " office " and came out. He walked
across the hall very slowly. His right arm was in
a sling. He looked thin and pale. Close behind
him came Doctor Worthington. The physician
looked very debonair, dressed in the height of the
fashion, strong in health, confident in self, at peace
with all the world.

" I was in the city yester-morn," he was saying,
in his soft, insinuating voice. " I saw your friend,
Shipton, on Walnut Street. Musgrave and André
were with him."

Peyton reached the fire in the schoolroom, and
sank in Mr. Murray's armchair, as if glad to rest.

" My friend was well? . . . I would I had seen
him." And into the Captain's heart there came a
great longing for the lad.

Worthington gave Peyton a furtive look.

" Naught prevents your joining your friends, now
that the Americans have withdrawn to Valley Forge.
'Twere easy to avoid the skirmishing and foraging
parties that infest the roads."

" Methinks I can get to the city soon," Peyton
said, quietly. " But this first hour outside of my
own apartments gives me slight encouragement."

He laughed.

" I had need of Jake's strong arm to get down
yon stairway." And then he gave Jake a bright
smile, as he came to throw a big stick on the fire.

Jake followed Chloe down the hall.

Worthington began pacing up and down.

" Mr. Murray would lend you his calash, and I
could go with you, or Howe would send an escort."

" Thanks, sir."

Something in his tone made Worthington stop and look askance at Peyton, then he forced a laugh.

" Ah, Captain, you mistake me. 'Tis only I wish to serve Howe's friends."

" Yes, yes, I understand you fully, Worthington."

Peyton's tone was somewhat impatient. Worthington glanced around furtively. But no one could have overheard.

" Hist! I serve Howe best by working in secret. Only you and Shipton know that I am aught but neutral. Even Musgrave is not in Howe's confidence."

" You need fear naught. Our honour as British soldiers would not permit our betraying you."

" Affairs of much moment might depend on your prudence. These Murrays must not know."

Peyton shrugged his shoulders.

" Trust us. I have said enough."

Worthington came nearer.

" And if the need arise, you would lend me your aid ? "

Peyton looked at him in astonishment.

" Aid? What mean you? "

Worthington came still nearer.

" There is much chance for secret work, here, in this house."

Peyton started from his chair, exclaiming, vehemently, " I am a soldier — "

Worthington frowned.

" An Englishman — "

Doctor Worthington knew well that it was not to his interest to quarrel with this Englishman, whose influence in the British army seemed far beyond what his position as a mere captain could

possibly give. He did not understand all the ins
and outs of the matter, but he knew well that Sir
William Howe not only deferred to this captain's
judgment, and trusted him with important secrets,
but had been not seldom restrained from license
and error because of the Captain's delicate sense of
honour. Of a truth, here was a man of rank and
wealth, a man of authority, whose favour he must
keep. Worthington valued rank and wealth fully
as much as they deserved. In his heart, he had
scant patience with this man who bore his honours
so modestly, and he was determined that he should
stay in this hospitable house no longer than absolutely necessary. But trust him, he did. Doctor
Worthington's tone became once more bland and
soft.

"Of course, of course, my dear Captain," he said,
smiling. "But you serve England well by lending
me aid in my enterprise."

But Peyton did not smile in return.

"Howe were right angry were he to know you
were to extort aught from me."

"Sir! That is not the word."

"It is the word I use!"

Worthington showed difficulty in suppressing his
anger. He tried to smile once more.

"I have a scheme which will do much for your
cause."

"Keep your schemes to yourself, sir. I have not
asked for your confidence."

"Patience, patience, my dear Captain. My
schemes are not to be despised. By my troth, had
some of them not done well, your army were not
now in the city. Zounds! sir! 'Twas I guided

General Grey up the Swedes Ford Road, when he massed his troops near Wayne's camp."

"Yes. The Paoli massacre!"

"Massacre? Nay! The victory, the silent victory of the bayonet."

A great horror of the war and its hideous victories, and more hideous defeats, swept over Peyton. He grew impatient with this smiling, scheming time-server. Despite the importance of the work he was doing for Howe, he distrusted this Tory. He could not conquer the feeling that he might betray even Howe.

"I am a soldier — not a spy. Be silent, Worthington."

Worthington's face darkened. His fingers twitched. Then he muttered a curse under his breath. But he made once more a violent effort to control himself.

"Speak to me no more on this subject," said Peyton, vehemently.

"Be it so."

"I am a man of honour."

"And that is saying that I am not?"

"'Tis saying what you please to call it."

"Damnation! You will rue this."

Peyton shrugged his shoulders in disdain.

A welcome interruption came with Chloe. She bustled out from the dining-room, and closed the door behind her. As she arrived at the schoolroom door, both Peyton and Worthington turned to her expectantly. She smiled.

"Massa Peyton and Massa Doctah bettah rest in room whar you come from. De wind's dis side ob de hall. Pow'ful cole, met'inks. Bigger fire in dare. Missy Margaret serve coffee in dare ef you wish it dare."

Neither of the expectant men would give the other the satisfaction of asking why Missy Margaret did not come, but they were both impatient. Chloe looked plaintively at Worthington.

" Mus' take pow'ful care ob you' patient, Massa Doctah. Bettah go in udder room."

Then Chloe skilfully got behind Worthington's back, and sent a series of significant gestures to Peyton. He smiled and nodded, then rose slowly. Worthington watched him till he had reached the door leading to the " nex' room." Then he turned to Chloe and said, softly: " Of a surety, I must see Mistress Margaret soon. It is time she came."

Chloe turned him an inscrutable face. " Missy Margaret, you want to see her?"

" In faith, I told you so when you let me in."

" Shuh 'nuff, shuh 'nuff. Spec' Missy Margaret be at liberty soon. You go dare in nex' room."

" Zounds! He is going thither?"

" He? De Cappin? He ain't no harm. O yes; hab de honour to go den in de big parlour, an' I sen' her dare."

Chloe chuckled, as Worthington hastened out.

" Pretty cole in dat big room. Dat spruce doctah git tired waitin', I spec'. I 'clare to goodness, wish Jake now had some dat Cappin's boldness. Jake so bashful, he nebber know what to say. Jess wish Missy Margaret would help him out some, same way I'se a-helpin' de Cappin. A pow'ful good she'd do him if she'd only would take him in han' now. I cawn't bring him to terms. He jess be so bashful, he doan' seem to know whar to go an' wot to say.

But he lubs me. Dat's shuh. He looks at me so
lubly like, an' he comes an' leans near me when I
a-workin', an' when he goes to de city wid Missy
Margaret, he allays brings me suffin' choice. An'
he's pow'ful good to gib me dis chance wid all dis
money. Met'inks I'se gwine to hab hard time gettin'
dem two togedder. Dat spruce doctah allays in de
way. Bes' plan to get him outen way in big parlour,
an' sen' Massa Murray to keep him busy. Trubble
is, dis ole house so cole, only got two, t'ree rooms
safe for de dear Cappin. Oh, dis awfu' winter!
Dis ole house so cole, so cole, my berry bones froze.
Missy Margaret allays says, 'member de poor soljers
in camp. Trust her for lettin' us forget 'em! Wish
de cole would stop for once. Den perhaps we could
t'ink ob dose poor soljers in der rags an' sufferin',
wid some degree ob comfort."

And thus the thoughts chased each other through
her excited brain. Meanwhile, she must discover
the amount of the magical gold, which was still
pinned to her back. She trusted to the kind Fates
to bring her mistress soon. If they refused their
aid, she would go and seek her. But if she persisted
in defying ease and warmth and comfort, and tarried in those chill stables, Chloe felt perfectly justified in allowing some scope to the Fates.

With a cautious glance around the room, and
sundry shivers born of the cold and of the fear of
ghostly visitants, Chloe went down on her knees
before the fire. The sack was soon off, the little
bag on the floor.

"Three guineas! British gold!"

With a sigh of supreme satisfaction, the bag was
slipped into the capacious pocket of her bright-hued

petticoat; the sack was once more in its place, and Chloe went back to the dining-room.

She had not long to wait for her mistress. She came through the corridor leading from the kitchens. A breath of cold air entered with her.

"Dare she is now! — de honey — lookin' as bright an' fresh as de mornin'," Chloe said to herself as Margaret threw off her heavy hood and cloak, stamped the snow from her feet, and came to the fire. She gave Chloe a radiant smile as she held up her chilled fingers to the blaze.

"You's done gone to see 'bout dat sick hoss, missy?"

"He is doing well, Chloe. In faith I am much encouraged. I can ride him on the morrow methinks."

Chloe's eyes shone.

"De Cappin will be pow'ful glad to see you, missy."

Something in Chloe's tone made Margaret look at her in astonishment.

"What mean you?"

Chloe laughed softly.

"I mean, missy, dat Cappin Peyton feels pow'ful 'fraid you ride to de city, or go somewheres 'fore he hab de chance to come."

"Chloe! He has come down-stairs? At last? At last?"

"Yes, missy. Dey wanted to s'prise you, an' Jake watched till you's done gone out. Den Jake helped de Cappin."

From the heights of her superior knowledge, Chloe gazed ·compassionately down at her mistress. Then she added, vehemently: "Time he did come down-stairs. Oughten come befoh. Dat spruce doctah pow'ful 'fraid to trus' him by hisself alone."

"Doctor Worthington has been most prudent, Chloe, wise and kind," said Margaret, quietly.

"Oh, yes; de Doctah wise 'nuff, no prevaricatin' dat. He too wise to want de Cappin wanderin' 'roun' too soon, an' gettin' into mischief. Manage de Cappin bes' when he in de one room. Hard to catch a rabbit dat runs 'roun'. Put him in a cage, an' can feed him spry an' easy. Let him nibble all he likes. But de rabbit likes liberty pow'ful bad."

Perchance there might be hidden meaning in Chloe's words; but Margaret would not question her. Chloe knew that well, though her happiness would have been perfect had Margaret been willing to question her. Chloe loved to answer questions.

"Chloe, I ride to the city soon. Bid Dinah tell — "

"Oh, missy, you cawn't go now. De Cappin wants to see you. He hain't seen you by you'self alone all dis long, long time. An' he's been sick so long, an' been waitin' an' waitin' till he could come to you, an' — an' — He'll hab his happy chance, if my plan doan' git fusterated."

A hot flush spread over Margaret's face. She turned away, and reached for her cloak and hood. Then the virtuous Chloe thought she might make the Fates auspicious for herself, and she continued, in a plaintive tone: "Cawn't you do summit to change t'ings a bit wid me, missy?"

Margaret looked at her with a puzzled face, then threw down the cloak, and came back to the fire.

"Ah, Chloe, you mean Jake?"

" Yes, I lub him, an' I know he lubs me, but —
but — "

" But what, Chloe? "

" But he done gone an' not said nuffin' yet. When
his heart jes' a-achin', too, I know. Now, a word,
jes' a word from you."

If Margaret felt like smiling, she checked the
impulse. The pathos of it all appealed to her quick
sympathy.

" I understand, Chloe," she said, gently. " I shall
bespeak my sister to give Jake some good advice.
She will know better than I, forsooth, what to do."

" Oh, t'ank you, missy; oh, t'ank you. But you
know 'nuff you'self 'bout de feelin'. I spec' you do
well 'nuff you'self."

The flush on Margaret's face deepened. Chloe
started guiltily.

" I 'clare to goodness, I'se wastin' all my dear
Cappin's patience. Shuh you stay heah, missy. I
go tell him you heah by you'self alone. Warmer
heah den in dat windy schoolroom. Jake not
know de truff 'bout dat room."

But the Fates were averse to Chloe's innocent
scheme. She had just reached the door when there
was a fumbling outside. She opened it, and Charles
Murray appeared.

Margaret went to him, and led him towards the
fire.

" Good-morning, father. Another bright, clear
day. The roads will be well frozen. Methinks I
can go into Philadelphia soon. Dinah was but yes-
ter-night much concerned about the poor condition
of our larder."

" O that we might send something to Valley

Forge! Every mouthful I take seems to choke me, when I think of all the suffering there."

Mr. Murray paused by the fire.

"I saw several foraging parties pass down the road not long ago," said Margaret.

"Neighbour Wingfield lost his cow but yester-eve, Jake informs me."

Margaret laughed.

"And Chloe says that Mr. Johnson's pigs are getting beautifully fewer every few days."

Mr. Murray sighed. Margaret drew the arm-chair nearer the fire, and put her father in it gently.

"The last day I went to market, I met such a quaint little Quaker, who was driving his last cow into the city," she said. "He evidently liked British gold better than American paper. He tramped along quite happily, when a foraging party from Valley Forge dashed into sight. Jake and I pulled up, and were hidden by some trees. The sight we beheld was both amusing and sad. The troopers seized the cow, and answered the poor Quaker's protests with language more highly spiced than elegant. Much sorrow felt I for his distress, and yet I liked to think that the British were not to have that fine cow."

Mr. Murray smiled, then asked, "Heard you aught of Harry this morning, daughter?"

"Annette says he hopes to come down and drink coffee with you."

"Ah! That is good news. The world is bright and beautiful this morning, daughter."

"Yes, dear."

"And the Captain, I fear me, is not yet strong enough to come down."

"Father!" she said, tremulously, "Chloe tells me he is already down-stairs."

"Is it possible? Hast seen him, daughter?"

"No."

"Of a surety, Doctor Worthington was with him."

There was no answer from Margaret, then Mr. Murray continued, thoughtfully: "Ah! he has had so desperate an illness. We should feel sobered, thankful over his recovery. . . . Margaret, methought at one time we would have to lay him beside those heroes who are so quiet, so peaceful, there in the garden."

Chloe had intention to go and see how fared the rival suitors for her mistress's companionship; but Mr. Murray's words changed her intention. Out in the hall were those phantoms, peering at her from behind the pillars. She would not go thither just now. She would wait and give some opportunity to the Fates to work for her. She softly stole out into the corridor, and betook herself to the kitchens.

Mr. Murray's mood was not only reminiscent and grateful; but he had evidently some burden on his mind.

"Margaret! Daughter! I understand not why Henry feels that the Captain — that he — Margaret, we had lost him had he not — We owe Harry's life to him. He not only brought him in, but — "

Mr. Murray's confused words were cut short by Henry Murray himself.

"I have been looking for you, father," he said, as he came hurriedly to the fire, and threw a stick on somewhat impatiently. "Father! Captain Peyton is out of his rooms at last. Thank God! he is fast recovering. . . . I should like it not, father, were we to harbour in our house such an enemy longer than needful."

Margaret started. The flush on her cheeks deepened.

" He has but started on the road to recovery, my son; this is but his first day outside of his own apartments. It would be death for him to go yet. Believe me, he has a proper and courteous sense of his position here." Mr. Murray's voice shook.

There was a look of surprise as well as pain in Margaret's soft, true eyes. Mr. Murray spoke again.

" What has happened, Harry, that you withhold from him your confidence?"

" Post-horses bring him oft letters from the city. A letter which came within the hour bore the seal of Sir William Howe. We know not what plots are hatching."

" He has never kept secret that he receives letters from his friends in the city," said Margaret, in a low tone.

" No; and his friends, André and De Lancey, and Shipton and Greyson, were here not so many weeks ago. 'Tis natural to write to them."

" I fear me, the vigilant skirmishing parties of the American army make visits of that kind dangerous just now," said Henry, with a trace of sarcasm. " If André or Musgrave or Shipton were to intrude now, they might find themselves in the hands of McLane or Lee."

" Intrude? Choose your words, my son. Of a

verity, 'twas at Peggy's wish that Captain André came."

"Well, well," said Henry, sharply, "I like not this exchange of letters. Now that the British are no longer in Germantown, well you know that patriot soldiers oft have come hither from White Marsh. They will also come from Valley Forge; well you know that patriots meet them here from other parts, to devise ways of furthering the cause of liberty. As you know, this has long been a trysting-place. Now he has the run of the house, see you not what chance Captain Peyton has to do our cause great harm?"

Margaret began walking up and down rapidly. She spoke in quick, bitter tones: "Yes, see you not the chance I have to let forth this life-blood, which pulses quick and fast through my throbbing veins? See you not the chance I have to take your sword and plunge it in my father's heart? But I restrain my hand."

She reached the fire.

"See you not the chance I have to seize one of those firebrands, touch curtain, wainscoting, with the destructive flame, and bring these stately walls — "

Henry went to her, and seized her hands.

"Margaret, hush!"

Charles Murray's voice grew strained in his excitement.

"You owe your life to him. He not only brought you in from the highway, but he stayed by you all that terrible night — fought death by your couch — fought it defiantly inch by inch. And when your sister finally came, there was naught for her, nor for any of us to do, but to accept from Captain

Peyton's hands the gift of your life. You owe it to him that you are here with us now, my son."

Margaret turned with an impulsive, grateful gesture to her father.

Henry Murray grew excited.

" Who struck me down? Those troopers were on the other road. Of a verity, 'twas some one who had heard of those letters, who wished to take them to Howe, — some one in Howe's confidence, who struck me, and threw me on the — "

Henry stopped at sight of the look in Margaret's eyes.

" Henry! You mean not *that*."

" No, daughter, he doth not mean it. Of a truth, he spoke but lightly."

Henry Murray frowned. Then put his hand up to his head.

Annette had come into the room, and heard the last words. Now she same nearer.

" Doctor Worthington says that had Captain Peyton's horse been fit that October morn, he, too, would have joined in the hot pursuit."

" Hush, girl, and quote not Doctor Worthington so oft," said Charles Murray, sharply.

Annette answered, somewhat petulantly: " Doctor Worthington is a most courteous gentleman, and full of wit, and has a fine address. This long winter were many times but dull, came he not here to play cards with us of an evening, and to sing and tell us the gossip gathered in his frequent visits to the city."

" Doctor Worthington will be here to-day, without fail. Methinks sometimes he is here all the time. How fare his other patients, oft 'tis a marvel to me."

Annette took a few dancing steps about the room.

"Oh! when will we be able to get to the city again? We might all enjoy a minuet."

But Henry watched her with grave, preoccupied eyes.

"One of my anxieties is Washington's contemplated visit. From behind the secret panel can be heard all that is uttered in this room," he said, gloomily.

"We will take heed what we say here, my son, and when the General comes — "

Mr. Murray's voice grew husky with emotion. Then Annette spoke again: "I told Doctor Worthington that the General once slept here one night. 'How easily he could have been taken,' quoth he. Then he added that many a Tory would be right glad to get the guineas which Mr. Howe would pay, could the General be lured hither. Mr. Howe would send out a force; and what a triumph it would be thought to take the calm-eyed Virginian into custody!"

"Yes, it be the opinion of many round about that, with the capture of Washington, prosperity would come to the land. He has many enemies among the Tories of Pennsylvania. As for the British, many a man would think it a stake worth playing for. With Washington a prisoner, where would be the strength of his cause? The other generals are mere puppets. The Congress is made up of fools. See you, father, the drift of my thought?"

"I see it but too plainly, son."

"Think you not, father, that we should not seek to detain this British guest?"

"Certainly not. He may go whenever his health permits, but not before."

"When Washington slept here last September, he might easily have been taken. Another visit could scarce be kept from the knowledge of a guest here. And we expect him soon. . . . Of a surety Captain Peyton is well enough to go. Let him ride to the city in your calash. His very presence here is a menace."

Had Henry Murray looked at his sister's face, he might have hesitated; but he was absorbed, and paid no heed but to his own excited thoughts. The hot flush faded out of her cheeks. She grew white. Then she went over to her cloak and hood.

"Dinah will serve coffee when you wish," she said, quietly. "Annette, will you see that Doctor Worthington is not forgotten? Wait not for me, should I be late."

And she went out into the hall, and slowly betook herself up the stairs.

Annette had been wandering aimlessly about the room. Now, as she turned and saw that Margaret had gone, she smiled and said: "How blind she is that she will not see the devotion of that man!"

"What mean you, girl?" asked Mr. Murray, impatiently.

"Knew you not that the good Doctor loves the very ground she treads on? The poets have oft said that, but, at this moment, I can conjure up no more expressive term. Could you but see the passion in his eyes when he gazes at her! Ah! It must be sweet to be loved in that fashion."

She cast up her eyes in mock pathos. The gloom of her husband's suspicions and fears oppressed her. She must try to dispel it. She gave a somewhat nervous laugh.

"How I love a fine romance! But Margaret cheats me of it. She will not be romantic, not even for my sake. She will not see that, while Doctor Worthington's heart is, indeed, on fire with love for the patriot cause, it is, nevertheless, her approval that he hungers for. Ah, me! To be so blind, and to cheat me so!"

Just then Chloe appeared with some steaming cups of coffee and a dish of seed bread-cakes, which Dinah had just baked. They were a perfect colour.

With a cry of delight, Annette seized the dish from Chloe's hands. Chloe looked around anxiously for Margaret. Her plan was, indeed, getting "fusterated," and she saw no clear way out of her difficulties.

"I get her all safe in one place, an' met'inks I know what to do, and den de missy's off in anodder. I wish dat Jake had done dis bizziness hisself. My brain's too small to take care ob all dese matters."

"Chloe," said Henry Murray, "my sister said something of Doctor Worthington. Has he come yet?"

"Yes, Massa Harry, Doctah Worthington been heah some time now. T'ink he like some music berry much," answered Chloe, with a martyr-like expression on her round face. "Spec' he bettah come in heah an' get some coffee. He's toastin' sword an' coat 'fore de fire in de big room whar

de spinit-t'ing is. He wants to see Missy Margaret,
I spec' — but met'inks he'll hab to wait some yet."

Henry laid his cup down hastily. "Let us have
some music. Yes, yes! Come, father, come, Annette, my head troubles me much this morning. I
need to be soothed by your singing, sweetheart.
The spinet is waiting."

Mr. Murray got up slowly. Henry sprang to his
help. The two went out together.

"Send for Dorothea, Annette," her husband called
from the doorway. "I am in the mood for that
song of Palestrina's, and we need the violin."

But Annette did not seem disposed to obey at once.
Another wafer of seeded bread pleased her fancy;
and despite the lack of encouragement from Chloe,
she evidently had the wish to linger for a moment's
talk. Poor Chloe! How was she to get this troublesome family disposed to Captain Peyton's satisfaction? Would the exacting guest stay where he was
put; would he be content with the spinet and with
Annette's singing, and that strange wailing music
from the violin, while craving Margaret's companionship?

Annette went out into the hall, opened the rear
door a little way, and peered out. A blast of frosty
air swept through the house. Poor Chloe shivered.

"Oh! oh! Missus Annette, doan' open de door
for de sakes alive! I'se got de awful misery in
my knees dis mornin'. My berry bones froze. Dis
ole house so cole, so cole."

"Chloe, we will have to send you back to Virginia," said Annette, smiling at her affectionately,
as she closed the door.

Chloe laughed. "Not till de winter is ober,

missus. But you's gwine to sing, ain't you, honey?"

Annette nodded, then her face grew thoughtful. "Chloe, your mistress ought not to go into Philadelphia in this terrible cold."

" Dat's shuh, dat's shuh. Let ole Dinah be much concerned 'bout de poor condition ob our larder. Won't hurt ole Dinah. She can bake moah ob dese seed breadcake."

Annette smiled. "Yes, we fare right well with them."

"Dinah's ebber fussin' 'bout her cookin', an' makin' de missy t'ink mus' take dat long ride to de city. Pity 'bout ole Dinah. Pity she cawn't go herself, an' ride ober de rough stones, an' den she see how tired de missy an' my Jake git. But wot de use ob talkin' to my missy, when she t'ink Massa Murray or Massa Henry an' de Cappin need good t'ings. De missy say we scarce 'nuff in de house to las' us till de morrow — an' ef it storms on de morrow she couldn't go, pow'ful 'fraid she couldn't go. Massa Murray put his foot down plump hard, an' say, ' You not go 'tall to-day,' an' den Missy Margaret hab to do as de massa say. Massa Murray let de missy go jes' as long string as dat — den he pull de string tight, so, an' de missy come 'roun'."

CHAPTER XXVII.

"I find when I question my heart, — I find that my heart keeps turning to you."

MARGARET threw a piece of wood on the already blazing fire in the schoolroom. Through the windows the glorious sunlight streamed, — the snow and the ice in the garden sparkled with a dozen beautiful colours. Out into the hall through the door leading from the room which Chloe called "the spinit-room," there came the sound of a merry voice and bright, happy laughter.

Margaret went to the table and began to arrange the quills and ink-wells on it. The papers were in disorder — on one, Annette had evidently been trying a quill, for scattered over it were quaint lines and devices, definite words like "Cliveden," "Peg," "Henry," "Captain André," blending with sketches of a dog which had been left in Annette's city home, a pet for whom she daily mourned. Margaret carefully removed the paper to the mantelpiece; then turned to find herself face to face with Peyton.

He looked at her a moment in longing, tender scrutiny. Then he smiled joyfully as he held out his hand to her. He had seen the swift, glad look in her eyes.

245

"What joy to see you again!" he said. "Here! in this room where I saw you first. But I have waited so long, so long."

Her eyes were lowered in confusion. His voice had a strange thrill in it.

"Margaret! Margaret Murray! Look at me, love, look at me! . . . Ah! Margaret, you know my love for you. I feel you do. You have known it all these months. These long, weary months when I could not speak, could not tell you. . . . But now, I can wait no longer. I have been so patient. But Margaret, I can wait no more. I am not patient. . . . Margaret, tell me, will you let me love you? Ah, you cannot help that. But will you give me the right to say to all the world I love you? Can you have patience with a poor wrecked soldier like me, — the enemy of your country, the enemy of your beloved General? Tell me, dear, tell me! I can bear this suspense no longer. If you cannot love me, I am going away from this house to-day."

She started violently and put out her hand as if to ward off a blow. He seized the hand impetuously. She sank in the chair near the table; and she would not look up again to meet his eyes.

"I have loved you from the very moment I saw you, that day that the troopers came with Musgrave, that day you were starting out for Washington's camp. I knew not you were going there. And how I longed to go with you on your ride. I wanted to shield you, to take care of you."

Margaret's head went down on the table. He bent over her, and kissed her hair. "And then you trusted your brother to me so sweetly, so nobly! I felt like going down on my knees then to you

and saying, ' Thank you, thank you for your trust.
I am a man with a heart to feel, a soul to love.'
And my soul went out to you then, Margaret. . . .
You little know how I felt to see you riding off
into unknown perils.   And when there was nothing more to do for your brother, and after that
beautiful hour with you before the dawn, I rode
back to Germantown, I felt I might never see you
again.   The world was desolate and lonely.   It
was more desolate and lonely, dear, than it had
ever been before."

There was a pause.   Then he went on:

" What was it, Margaret, that had come to me
— to me, a rough soldier, away from home and
country, in a strange land?   A vision of home,
and of rest; a vision of peace and comfort, of holy
joy."

Margaret stretched out her hand impulsively
towards him.   He seized it and held it tight.

" Then came the battle. . . . When I fell that
terrible day, my first thought was of you.   I felt
I would die there in the dust and the blood, the
smoke and the fog, — die without seeing you again,
and you would never know how I loved you.   Then
I was carried into your house, and I felt your care
and your sympathy.   I, who had longed to take
care of you; I, who was so strong, was stricken
down to be cared for by you. . . . I feared me
I would die and you would never know how I
loved you; and yet in the midst of all the suffering and the noise and the horror, there was a pure
and holy joy in my heart.   I was with you, even
if I died."

The laughter and merry talk in the next room

had ceased. The notes of the spinet had been heard, then Annette's voice singing. But now the merry songs she sang changed to the one soft and plaintive, and the sobbing, thrilling accompaniment was played by Dorothea's violin. It went straight to Peyton's heart. He paused till the song was done.

> "Love were not mine, and it were all unblest,
> Full of doubt and turmoil, and a wild unrest;
> Were it not of Heaven, strong, unchanging, true —
> Tender, strong, unchanging: thus my heart loves you.

> "Love were mine own, and life were fair and blest,
> Could you trust me wholly and be thus at rest;
> Think me true and faithful, strong unchanging, true —
> Tender, strong, unchanging: thus my heart loves you.

> "Love were mine own, and life were fair and blest,
> Could I give it shelter and be thus at rest, —
> Give it tender shelter, keep it strong and true:
> Tender, strong, unchanging: thus my heart loves you."

"Tender, strong, unchanging," repeated Peyton, softly, as the last notes died away into silence.

Margaret sprang up suddenly and went and stood by the fire. There was agitation in her face. "But — but," she began, brokenly. Peyton put out his hand as if to stop her. There was appeal in his look.

"I know all you would say, dear love," he whispered. Then he stopped. A sudden mood of discouragement swept over him. He had been fighting that mood for weeks. Only this morning had he conquered it enough to summon courage to tell Margaret Murray how much he loved her. Once with her again that love had surged through his heart with an impetuous rush of passionate emotion. He had forgotten himself and spoken compelling, impetuous words. But now all the old self-

distrust assailed him, all the difficulties, the obstacles, the thought of which had made success seem
utterly impossible. Then the bravery of the true
soldier once more asserted itself. He spoke again,
— low and broken at first came the words. But
he gained confidence as he went on.

"I know that I am not worthy of you, Margaret. I can never hope to be. But there are other
difficulties, that may in your mind be obstacles.
Pray Heaven they may not be. . . . Think not for
one moment, dear love, that I see not all these
difficulties. They almost make me now afraid to
speak. All through these months of illness I have
been suffering both happiness and pain of soul. I
have seen how you feel about General Washington;
and I belong among his enemies. I have seen how
your heart is bound up in the success of his army,
and it is the duty of my friends to do everything
to frustrate him and make him fail. O Margaret,
my soul has been torn and tossed on a troubled
sea. . . . But this morning, Margaret, your father
said that which comforted me. He came into my
room quite early to see if 'twere best I venture
down-stairs to-day. 'Of a verity,' he said, ' 'twill
be warmer to-morrow, and 'twere better to wait.'
Then he spoke of many things, mainly of your Washington and the truth of his cause. Then he talked
of the suffering at Valley Forge, as though I could
sympathise, and he said, dear, that he constantly
forgot that I was a British soldier. He helped me,
Margaret. He took away some of the trouble and
the darkness of my mind. He made me hope that
you could love me for myself, and could also sometimes forget. It gave me the feeling that perchance

I could speak to you at last. Oh, how hard it would be to keep silent! Look up, dear, tell me, can you trust me? Tell me, will you love me? And when I am well enough, go with me to dear old England, — your old home, Margaret, your England as well as mine. Look up, Margaret. Let me see your face."

He bent over her and gently lifted her face. Then he saw that her eyes were quite full of tears.

"If you cannot love me, I must leave you, dear."

Margaret put out her hand with a restraining gesture.

"General Howe has written for me, Margaret. A letter came to-day. He says he needs me about many things."

"You cannot go. You must stay here — with — me. It would kill you to go."

A great joy illumined his face. But she put out her hand to keep him back.

"Wait! I cannot think."

He spoke impetuously.

"Love is the holiest duty. Marry me, Margaret, let us go to England together."

She was silent, and he continued, softly: "'Tis your England, your England, as well as mine. Oh! you already know some of its loveliness. And my home at Castereagh. Oh! that I could take you there. . . . Yes! 'tis your country as well as mine. Why, I have heard William Pitt say often that the Americans are the true children of England."

Margaret smiled through her tears.

"And England scolds her children right well and acts as if they were of little worth but to be put into a dark closet till they become good."

He smiled at her; then said, wistfully:

"O Margaret, I know all the difficulties — my soul is heavy because of them. Think not for one moment, that I see not that this love will bring you both happiness and pain. But listen to your heart, tell me what it says."

With shy and tender grace, Margaret put out her hands to him; her face was wistful, pleading. He seized her hands as she spoke. His glowing eyes were fixed upon hers.

"I find when I question my heart, that — in spite of all the difficulties — my heart keeps turning to you."

"Margaret, dear!"

What a joyous ring came into his voice; but she was still holding him off.

"Wait!"

"No! I wait no longer."

He threw his arm around her and took her to the big chair before the fire.

The firelight danced and flamed. The sunshine fell across the floor in broad masses of glory.

CHAPTER XXVIII.

"He fights against Heaven who takes not love into his soul."

"MARGARET," said Peyton, after a pause, "Margaret, I feel to-day as if my mother were so near me, and she has been in heaven almost a year. O Margaret, I wish she could see you; and you! how you would love her!" His voice faltered.

Her heart gave a great throb of sympathy for him; but she did not speak. Then he continued, softly:

"All this morning I have been thinking of her, and blended with this love for you has been this tenderness for her. . . . She died in my arms, Margaret. We had gone with her to Italy with the hope that the soft air would help her. Bob and I had gone. My father was too much occupied in the House to leave just then. This country of yours, Margaret, was very troublesome, and all England was aroused. My father scarce knew how ill she was. But Bob and I knew. She died one bright morning in Florence. . . . She was beautiful, Margaret, and — and I loved her."

There was another pause; and Annette's clear, sweet voice, singing songs grave and gay, frolicsome and tender, was an accompaniment to Peyton's and Margaret's thoughts.

"I went home," he said at last, "but it was home no longer. All England seemed changed. . . . O Margaret! I wish you could have seen and known my mother!"

And just then Annette's voice took up her favourite refrain, and the sob of the violin was heard again:

"Love were not mine, and it were all unblest,
  Full of doubt and turmoil, and a wild unrest;
  Were it not of Heaven, strong, unchanging, true —
  Tender, strong, unchanging: thus my heart loves you.

"Love were mine own, and life were fair and blest,
  Could you trust me wholly and be thus at rest;
  Think me true and faithful, strong, unchanging, true —
  Tender, strong, unchanging: thus my heart loves you.

"Love were mine own, and life were fair and blest,
  Could I give it shelter and be thus at rest, —
  Give it tender shelter, keep it strong and true:
  Tender, strong, unchanging: thus my heart loves you."

The song broke off. There were sounds of distant voices and laughter. All at once there were heard soft footsteps near the door. Margaret sprang up — smoothed her hair, and went swiftly to the other side of the fire. But it was only Chloe, all smiles and out of breath with pleasurable excitement. She put her head inside the door, and said, in a loud whisper:

"Hurry, Massa Cappin! I 'spec' you's 'bout through wid you bizziness. Dey's comin' soon. Massa Murray's tired and done gone up-stairs. I'se done my best to keep um dare — made de fire bright, as bright, forsooth, as dis fire. I'se gibben dem moah coffee. But dat spruce doctah keeps lookin' restless and sayin' he mus' be ridin' 'way. I spec' he's gwine to come back heah. Dar's his cloak on dat chair. Hurry, Massa Cappin. I'll keep um dare long's I can. But dey'll come soon, shuh 'nuff."

Chloe withdrew.

The lovely flush on Margaret's face deepened. She spoke hurriedly.

"We can keep it from them? I am in no mood for — for — "

"As you will, dear. But not long. I feel as if I had conquered a kingdom. Ah! Margaret, I am rich and happy. I cannot keep it secret. The whole world will know."

He went to her and seized her hand, looking down deep into her eyes.

"Your father, Margaret?"

Her eyes grew even softer, tenderer. What could keep him from bending down and kissing them?

"Yes! yes! my father. We will go and seek him."

"Wait one minute. I must write one word to Shipton. Of a surety you will let me tell him?"

Margaret smiled. She understood his wish to keep her longer. Strange happening! She herself had much sympathy with that wish.

"Come, dear, show me how to write better with my left hand. Then there is Howe's letter. Perchance you will write that for me?"

"Perchance, an it be not too long an one."

"Trust me for that — come."

Hand in hand they went to the table. Peyton took up a quill and began to write. He made awkward work of it. They both laughed.

"There! I writ that with mine own hand. It is wondrously well done. Now read: 'Dear Bob.' Think you not that is as well done as with my right hand?"

"I have never seen your right handwriting, remember."

"True, love."

He threw down the quill and reached for her hand. For a moment they both forgot quills, writing, and all the world besides. Then Margaret gave him a whimsical smile.

"You have but one hand for use now. Go back to your writing, I pray you. I fear me we cannot be alone much longer."

"Yes, yes, I will be ready soon. Now look!"

He leaned on the table, and for a moment or two wrote hurriedly.

"There! that looks well. Of a truth 'twill please Bob mightily." He turned around to her and laughed again, as he caught the amused expression in her eyes.

"It behooves you to be more enthusiastic, my dear Lady Disdain. Believe me, it was harder to write than it would be to storm a fort. Now read and see what I have written. . . . Obey me, dear. By my troth, 'tis not too soon to begin obedience."

Sitting down by the table, he spread out the paper upon it. Then he looked up tenderly into her face. Margaret took up the paper hesitatingly. There was an eloquent pause as she read. Then she glanced down. As she caught the look in his eyes, she lowered hers in confusion.

"Read it, love. 'Tis only to Bob — my friend —

that I could say these words. But they are from my heart."

But she held the paper without looking at it.

"Read on!" said Peyton.

"I cannot."

Then into her eyes there came a swift, mischievous look.

"Of a truth, 'tis too much praise of me. I approve it not."

"Ah! you read it, you read it!"

"Yes! yes! But — come! I fear me it will be many a day ere you write well."

"Methought you were kinder. But I shall practise. Some day I will make you envious. Meanwhile will you write to General Howe for me? And take it to the city when you go?"

"Yes, if the letter be short and to the point."

"How could it be to the point?"

She gave him an eloquent, glowing look.

"That you will stay here at Cliveden till you are wholly recovered from your wounds. It will be long — long" — her voice almost broke with emotion — "long — ere — there is — cause for you to be needed by — your friends."

He started up and threw his arm passionately around her.

"Margaret, a truce to those thoughts. We will think of our love and of each other. Come — let us go to your father."

But she buried her face on his breast and sobbed.

"You would not want me to — "

"No! No! Honour is more than love. I could not ask you to disturb your soul's fair peace."

Peyton gently stroked her hair.

" Perchance our way may become clear to us before there is cause for me to go, or before I am well enough to go."

She was silent. He held her tighter.

" From all you tell me of Washington, he must indeed be a noble man, a man of charm and of strength of character, a man to draw to him the hearts of men, — a man to form a nation, to save its integrity, to give it laws, to show it the right path. Heaven preserve your hero. My whole soul revolts against England's drawing the sword against such a man. And yet, Margaret, the allegiance America owes England. It is in rebellion against its King. It has a duty to its King."

She looked up. Her eyes were full of tears, and there was a sad curve to the sweet lips.

" One must do his duty. Duty is more than love. May God show us more clearly by and by what duty really is. Meanwhile — "

He took the words from her as she paused.

" Meanwhile, let us love each other and be happy."

" Yes! yes! come. We will go and seek my father."

She disengaged herself gently. Then flew to the table and seized the papers upon it. But one fell from off the other side and she did not see it. Peyton walked slowly towards the fire and then turned to watch her. His face was full of happiness. He threw back his head proudly. Then they heard in the distance Henry Murray singing the refrain of Annette's song:

" Love were not mine and it were all unblest,
    Full of doubt and turmoil, and a wild unrest;

Were it not of Heaven, strong, unchanging, true —
Tender, strong, unchanging: thus my heart loves you."

The violin gave out a few throbbing notes, then voice and violin were silent. They heard the player's light step as she went up the stairway. They heard Henry Murray's heavy step near the parlour door. Then his voice, saying:

"I will be with you presently, Worthington." Then the door was shut, and they heard Henry go into the dining-room.

"Come! Come!" cried Margaret, rushing to Peyton and handing him his cane. "Come! Come! I hope we can get to the spiral stairs before they come out and see us. I will help you up the stairs. In faith, we must not be too late."

Laughing like children, they hastened across the hall.

CHAPTER XXIX.

"It would be death for him to go yet. Believe me, he has a proper and courteous sense of his position here."

THAT morning, as Doctor Worthington had ridden to the stables and given his horse in Jake's charge, the honest fellow's face had beamed with pride and joy.

"Massa Cappin done gone outen his room at last," he said, chuckling. "I helped him, t'ank de Lord."

But Jake saw in the Doctor's face no sympathy for his joy. "Damme!" Worthington exclaimed, roughly. "What was Mr. Murray thinking of, to allow this without my permission? 'Tis far too cold for the venture."

Jake's face clouded. "Massa Murray nor de missy nor nobody know 'bout it. We planned it a s'prise. De Cappin knowed 'twas all right ting to do. He's mighty tired stayin' in dat room so long whar' he cawn't see Missus Annette or de missy scarce a minnit. 'Spec' he's kin' o' achin' to see de missy, though he'd not be de man to say so in de public meetin'. But ebberybody could see dat wid half an eye."

The Doctor looked at Jake and frowned. Then a dark flush came into his face, which stayed there

259

till some time after Chloe had conducted him into the room in which Captain Peyton was resting.

Jake's words had struck Doctor Worthington with sudden and overwhelming force. Here was a man who might possibly thwart his plans. The thought was as distasteful as it was unexpected. This captain, with his interesting pallor, his honest dark eyes, must be reckoned with. All the Doctor's latent obstinacy and jealousy of disposition sprang into sudden life. But caution, as usual, soon became dominant. Anger, vehemence, jealousy — all these emotions must be concealed. He must work quietly, secretly.

It was obvious that the first thing to be done was to get the dangerous Captain away from Cliveden as soon as possible. His presence there might prove a hindrance not only to the plans in regard to Margaret Murray, but also — well, the good Doctor scarce spoke of that other plan even to himself.

But ere he sought to bring all his influence to get the dangerous Captain away from Cliveden, he would test this man. He would seek his aid in his enterprises. If happily he won this aid, then he would have a hold on him which would be of great service should any emergency arise. If he were thwarted or treated with contempt or neglect, then perchance the opportunity for revenge would offer itself. If it did not, then perchance the opportunity could be created. Doctor Worthington was fruitful in expedients. Then he himself must delay no longer. He must woo this maiden in right vehement fashion, — woo and win her. He had delayed this wooing, not so much because of self-distrust, for he had little doubt that he could win Mistress Margaret to his will; but he had meditatively enjoyed the sense of uncertainty, of joyful anticipation, of dallying with happiness, instead of stretching out his hand to take it from a beneficent, compliant fate.

But he must wait no longer. That fact was very clear.

Why had Margaret not appeared to welcome him? Where was she all this time that they had been taking that excellent coffee and singing that excellent music? Doctor Worthington grew restive. He would go into that room off the hall where he had left his cloak. Perhaps she was there. . . . But he found the room quite empty.

As he was on his way to the fireplace, he espied the piece of paper Margaret had let fall. It was covered with Peyton's awkward attempts at writing with his clumsy, unpractised hand. Doctor Worthington's face was crafty and meditative as he put the paper carefully in his pocket.

"Methought my sister was here," said Henry Murray, at the door. Worthington turned to him a tranquil, serene face.

"No! I see less of your sister than my heart wishes, Murray."

Henry Murray looked at him sharply as he came further into the room.

"Yes, Murray, you guess my secret." The tranquil, serene face grew pensive and had a show of melancholy. "But you will honour my confidence. I seem to make no progress with her. The time, methinks, is not yet ripe to win her. But by Jove! I will have her. I want her. I want her."

He spoke with increasing passion as he walked up and down. Henry Murray smiled and went and sat by the fire.

"How beautiful she looked yester-eve as she filled my saddle-bags with those packets for Valley Forge. Egad! I wanted to reach down my hand and toss her up on my horse, and we ride, ride away together. But she is not a girl to be won in that fashion. Zounds! I would she were!"

"Methinks she would do but scant justice to the love you bear her."

"But if she should favour the Captain?"

Henry Murray frowned.

"An enemy to our cause. Bah! she will never, if she once finds out."

Henry looked surprised and expectant.

"It may be my duty to tell her. Or stay! I will tell her brother. Then she would turn to me. The Captain once out of the way, it would be my task to comfort her. Yes! 'tis best that I tell her brother."

"You speak in riddles, Worthington."

The Doctor glanced cautiously round, then came nearer Henry Murray, putting his hand on one side of his mouth.

"Know you that Captain Peyton received this morning a message from Sir William Howe?"

Henry started back.

"How know you that?"

Worthington smiled blandly.

"I know it because a packet also came to me."

"You traitor!"

Worthington lifted his white hand in gentle protest.

" Nay, nay, not so hasty. The letter I received is fully at your service."

He took several papers from his pocket, Peyton's slip among them. He looked at them with slow precision.

" In truth, I must have it here." He placed the papers back; then took another from an inner pocket. No one but he knew 'twas merely the back of an old letter with no writing upon it. But it would serve! It would serve!

" As you well know," he said, gently, " I am but a humble surgeon, but well known round about by my services to the wounded of both armies. I have told both Washington and your sister (she and I have had many a quiet talk) that I can render the most efficient service to the patriot cause by not revealing my own sentiments. You see?"

Murray looked at him thoughtfully; then he said, slowly, after a pause:

" Yes, I see."

" Yes, we have spoken of it oft. . . . Sir William Howe therefore assumes that I am neutral, and can easily be tempted by British gold to do some service for him. You see?"

Murray made a motion to take the paper from Worthington's hand; but it was held away from him.

" Now this letter tells me that if I wish to get well rewarded, and will but serve his Majesty faithfully as I value my own neck and the safety and ultimate prosperity of my country, it bids me communicate with a prominent subject of his Majesty, a man of influence because of his social rank in England, and his wealth."

Worthington struck the paper with his fist.

" Murray, the letter has made me very angry, nevertheless, I may extract from it some good for our dear cause, and so shall keep silent over it. And before I tell you the name written in this letter, you must promise, too, to be silent, till I bid you speak. Thus only can we work together."

Worthington's voice had risen in his assumed passion. Now he lowered it, and once more glanced around cautiously.

" Show me the letter." Murray's voice was loud and authoritative.

" Nay, not so loud. The walls may have ears. This British captain — "

Murray recoiled. Worthington smiled.

" Of a verity, I know your feeling. He is your guest. But chance — the force of circumstance made him your guest — against your will, perchance. Common humanity would prompt you all to succour him. Zounds! I honour your motives, but here is that which absolves you from sentiment; but tell me, Murray. You promise silence, you will help me? Murray, were he to know that I had told you this, all hope of my helping Washington would be over. My neck would answer for it. . . . Methinks you yourself have had suspicion of the integrity of this British guest. You will help me?"

" Yes, yes," said Henry Murray, with a touch of impatience. " I promise silence, I will help you."

" The letter says I am to communicate with one Captain Peyton, the honoured guest of a house, past which men of both armies ride."

Murray's face darkened. Worthington continued:

" But there be many whispers that Washington sends secret emissaries thither, that he may be lured hither again."

Murray put his hand to his head.

" No more, Worthington, no more; give me the letter."

Worthington turned and listened.

" Wait, I hear footsteps near the door."

It was Annette. Worthington bowed, then hastened to the door by which she had entered and closed it softly, saying earnestly:

" This is the way I treat letters which are thus an insult to my manhood and to my patriotism."

He strode to the fire, and before Murray had guessed his intention, the paper was flung upon the glowing flames. It curled up its edges and grew black. The Doctor's air of indignation was well simulated. Murray stood frowning, perplexed. Then he turned to Worthington.

" He must not remain longer in this house."

" You purpose well, and wisely, Murray. Of a truth I were sorry to be the cause of his leaving, but I had not told you of all this did I not think his presence here a menace."

Doctor Worthington glanced at Annette's puzzled face. He bowed gracefully.

" Of a verity, madam, your husband will tell you, but he has promised to keep this matter secret till time furnishes cause for its explanation. By silence and watchfulness we may happily prevent conspiracy and treachery. Captain Peyton may leave you, but even then — "

" Yes, yes! I know," interrupted Murray, impatiently.

Worthington raised his hand deprecatingly. Annette noticed how fine was the lace around his wrists. The hand was so white — and yet there was a strength in it like iron.

There was a pause, then Worthington took up his cloak.

" Methinks I can tarry no longer to-day," he said, " but I had wish that I might see your sister. Then 'tis so exceeding cold outside I feel loath to leave your fireside."

And he gave Annette one of his most brilliant smiles. Then he stopped as if a sudden thought assailed his mind.

" Your pardon, Murray, but one thing more ere I ride to the village. Your sister is a brave horse-woman, but fear you not that some evil may e'er befall her on her frequent rides to the city markets? "

" She goes thither to-day," said Annette.

Henry placed a chair nearer the fire.

" There seems to be no choice in this matter, Worthington. Without her, even Jake could not pass the British lines. Were I to attempt it, I fear me I should have short shrift with the sentries."

Annette shuddered and drew nearer her husband. He put his hand over hers a moment.

" Ah! 'tis not that I mean, my friend. But what if the sentries suspected your sister might carry to you information she gets in the city — if they knew that you have access to Washington."

" Margaret would refuse to bring me information, even wished I for aught. She is under oath. Should any miscreant dare to — "

But Worthington's smooth voice cut short Henry Murray's vehemence.

" 'Tis only my anxious affection puts these unquiet thoughts into my brain. I had dreamed that perchance I might arrange to ride to the city with your sister could I but know the days she has to go. There are many dangers this side of the British lines, as you well know."

Annette gave him a swift, comprehensive glance.

" Yes; my father speaks oft of these perils. But Margaret insists they are but figments of our brains."

Henry Murray looked dreamily into the fire.

" I would I were well. My head pains me more than wont this morning."

A beautiful expression of tender solicitude irradiated Worthington's face. He came and stood at the back of Henry Murray's chair.

" Ah, you must have had a terrible blow from that knave who struck you down."

" Try to forget it all, dear. 'Tis too painful a remembrance."

But Henry Murray paid no heed to his wife's gentle protest. He continued in a meditative tone:

" I really saw not the man who did it; but I have a confused recollection of not toppling over at once. I struggled and fought. Then all at once, once, only once, I caught sight of his face as he turned to strike me. 'Twas only the side of it I saw. But it sometimes seems as if my imagination could piece out the whole picture and make it perfect."

" Nay, nay, Henry — speak no more of it. Come,

dear, we will go back to our music." Annette's voice was anxious.

" His face keeps coming up before me. I try to grasp it, but my mind seems hovering in the shadows. Such a strange feeling I have. In faith, 'tis as if I were trying to put my hand on my memory and it slips away from my grasp."

" Yes, I have had such experiences myself," said Worthington, soothingly. " Your nerves are all awry, Murray."

" It haunts me so. It is as if I were in the land of dreams, trying to clutch, clutch something which is forever evading my grasp. I come upon it, I stretch out my hand, and it fades away into shadows."

" Come, Henry, come back to the music-room. You liked that song, that last one. Come." There were tears in Annette's voice.

" Then again it comes before me. . . . Then again it is gone before I really seem to see it. But when it is the most vivid it seems to be like your face, Doctor Worthington."

Henry Murray turned around in his chair and looked at Worthington. Worthington laughed.

" What nonsense! My friend! you are visionary."

" I know it, but why is it that it seems to be you with whom I am struggling? I am struggling with something overpowering, gigantic, terribly vindictive. Why is it that it seems to be you, Worthington, why is it?"

" Easily accounted for," answered Worthington, quietly. " All these months you have seen my face very oft. During your delirium, when you recovered."

"Yes, yes," said Annette, earnestly. "You have seen more of him than of any one, unless it be of Sam or Jake."

"Yes, Murray, she has the right of it. Most natural thing in the world that the actual reality before you should be confused in your weak state with the visionary phantom of your disordered brain. Then, perchance, I look like some one you have seen."

Henry Murray turned back to the fire.

"'Tis not only the look, it is still more the voice. Not the voice you are speaking with now, but the voice you had when you flung that paper in the fire. The two voices are quite different, Worthington."

Worthington gave a nervous start behind Henry Murray; but he kept himself in good control.

"I cannot get rid of the voice," continued Murray, thoughtfully.

"You see, Murray, you are still very weak. You have been under a fearful strain, — fever and delirium."

Worthington's voice was sympathetic.

"Yes, and in that delirium I was struggling all the time with that fearful face, over precipices, down gorges — "

"Of course, of course! That is quite usual in fevers. And when you get over the fever, the visions in your delirium recur and recur. That is very common. Give a man good health and his nerves will be good, and he will see no troublesome visions. But you are waxing stronger every day,

Murray. In a month you will be riding across country even as far as Valley Forge."

" Thanks to you and your good care of him," said Annette, with a grateful look.

Henry Murray rose and stood with his back to the fire. The firelight shone full on Worthington's face. Was he conscious of Murray's scrutiny?

At that moment Margaret opened the door and came in. Worthington turned to her. His eyes shone. Annette, watchful for his romantic symptoms, thought that his hands trembled.

" Saw you a paper, Harry, which I had let fall on the floor yonder? "

Worthington came forward.

" Ah! Good morrow, Doctor Worthington. Your pardon. I had forgot we had not met before to-day."

Worthington bowed over her hand, and then carried it to his lips.

Henry Murray seemed not to have heard her question. He looked at her gravely, and then said, in a low tone:

" Margaret, I implore you not to think me brutally ungrateful; but 'tis impossible for us to harbour this British guest beyond the time 'tis safe for him to go. I have already given you abundant reasons for my caution. . . . Yes — Doctor Worthington is in my confidence. He will help us to be on especial guard while Captain Peyton tarries here."

Margaret looked at her brother in open-eyed astonishment. Then she drew herself up haughtily. There was a pause.

"Henry, take heed, take heed. I hear him coming," whispered Annette.

They all turned towards the door. And as Peyton came in slowly, they were struck by the expression of his face. There was happiness in it, and a proud dignity.

His head was thrown back. His shoulders were straight and firm. He reached Margaret and took her hand.

Henry Murray started back in astonishment. Doctor Worthington's face grew black.

"Gentlemen!" said Peyton, and there was a joyous ring to his voice. "Gentlemen, give me your congratulations. This is my betrothed wife, and with her father's full consent."

CHAPTER XXX.

" I am but a humble surgeon, yet well known round about
by my services to the wounded of both armies "

DOCTOR WORTHINGTON rode on to the
village with scarce a thought of the inn
where he would choose to have his dinner.
In truth, he was more disturbed of mind than he
had wish to be, or had thought himself capable
of being. All the smouldering passion of the past
weeks and months now seemed bursting into bright
flame. Its fire was a torturing pain; and yet the
man's pride helped him; his egotism consoled him
with the thought that perchance the case were not
so hopeless as it seemed. There were chances that
he might yet come off victor.

He drew rein at Ye Roebuck Inn, only to find
that dinner would not be served that day, because
the landlord had been obliged to go to the city
for supplies. It being market day, British troops
would sally forth to protect the farmers bringing
their loaded wagons to the market stalls. Many
villagers entered the city in the wake of these soldiers.

Some time had passed now since the coach had
been running that once had gone from Germantown
to the George Inn on Second Street in the city.
Travellers were few, because of the troublous

272

times, the difficulty of getting passes through the
lines, and the still greater difficulty of getting out
again. But this morning it had been noised abroad
through the village that the coach would start from
the King of Prussia Inn and would happily have
a prosperous journey. Four travellers who had
arrived from Reading the night before had been
so benumbed by the biting frost that had made
riding almost perilous that they had decided to
sell their horses, or, failing that, to leave them
in the village, and had persuaded the landlord to
bring out the old coach to take them to the finish
of their journey. A crowd of villagers, largely
made up of erstwhile stocking weavers, now, alas!
without work to relieve their poverty, surrounded
the coach as Doctor Worthington rode up to the
inn. This excitement was most grateful to them.
The horses had not yet been put in. The fortunate travellers were yet enjoying the good dinner
in the common room, where a bright fire was
burning.

Doctor Worthington was not in the mood to
tarry here long. He had intention to dine hastily,
then ride across the Schuylkill. If weather and
mood favoured, he might perchance ride as far
as Valley Forge. As he entered the big common
room of the inn, his quick, alert eye saw that
not far from the travellers seated at the table was
the man who had befriended him on that day the
British left Germantown. He did not feel disposed
to accost him; but Rodney Bingham sprang to
his feet and came swiftly towards him, smiling gen-
ially.

" Egad, sir ! We meet again at last. Methought

you had gone the way of some of your unfortunate patients, and bidden this earth a last farewell."

Doctor Worthington could not resist the charm of Rodney's smile. He smiled in return.

"No! I am still above ground, thanks to my good sense and the skill of my physic. A thousand pardons, sir, that I failed to come that night. After your kindness to me the least I could do was to keep my word."

"I failed to come also, so we are quits. 'Twas a rough night, and I ventured not out into the storm."

"Had I known your home, I would have writ an excuse. But I detain you. Go you not with the coach that leaves within the half-hour?"

"I am not so fortunate. I have no pass. I would indeed like the comfort of seeing Penn's beloved city once more ere I die. But I fear me, these British guests are fixtures there."

"Perchance I could serve you if you wish to go. I am but a humble surgeon, yet well known for my services to both armies. Come with me sometime to the city — that is, if I can be assured of the innocence of your intention."

Rodney laughed. "Methinks I could do little harm, even were I so disposed. But I bear these British no grudge. But you, sir, you have excellent opportunity to gain intelligence which you might carry to either camp at will." Rodney lowered his voice. "Methinks General Washington has need of trusty spies. Doubtless General Howe, also."

How much did this troublesome stranger know?
A crafty look came into Worthington's eyes.

"I have no time for aught but my profession.
Besides, a man of honour would scorn to be a spy.
'Tis my fate to have access to both camps — but
I take little interest in politics. My work absorbs
me. But come, sir, I beg your company to dinner.
But I know not even your name."

"Kelper, sir, Kelper. I am owner of lands here
in the country, but the war has of course made
havoc of my resources. I live but humbly. At
one time 'twas my whim to be a hermit. I stayed
five days in a cave."

Worthington laughed. "Methinks I was told
of a philosopher who had such sport."

"'Twas when the British occupied Germantown.
But I soon tired of my whim. My temperament
is not for solitude."

For an hour the two men ate and drank and
smoked together. Bingham did his best to find
out whether this brilliant physician were Tory or
Whig. If Whig, he wanted his help, he was sore
in need of help that morning; if Tory, he would
have to be watched. But, with consummate skill,
Worthington fenced with all of Bingham's hints
and questions. When they parted, neither of the
men had advanced to a better understanding of the
other.

CHAPTER XXXI.

" And therefore he felt glad, dear Margaret, that you have had the courage to look love in the face and feel its power and its glory."

THE days sped by on golden wings.

How much there was to say to each other! So long as they were both in love, and talked together by the hour, it mattered little what they talked of, — that which interested her the most or him.

But they soon found that they were interested in the same things, only they had points of difference in their opinion of them. What zest there was in discovering these points of difference. Each day brought this freshness of discovery.

After the first flush of their enthusiasm was past, they settled down to the discussion of almost every question that would engage the attention of a thoughtful man or a deep-hearted girl, who looked at life earnestly, and were not forgetful of the responsibilities and obligations imposed by the advantages of circumstance and position which had blessed them both.

They talked of Europe, of the Italy they both loved, of the relations between France and England, and, of course, about the problems connected with America. Then they would not have been lovers if they had not talked of books and poetry, and read many poets together, though they lingered longest over Shakespeare. They would "explain things," and would wander far into the paths opened out by that wonderful searcher of the human heart.

There was a freshness of appreciation about Margaret, which was a perpetual delight to Captain Peyton; while she, in turn, was stimulated by his maturer mind, his larger experiences of life. Neither of them had been strangers to high thoughts, — their souls had always dwelt in a large place; but now even wider vistas were opened to their eager vision; they awakened in each other thoughts and emotions which they knew were better and went deeper than ever before.

Often and often he had to speak of his England, of the old castle where he had spent his childhood; then of his life at Eton and at Oxford; his life in the army, and finally of his plans for Parliament. Many graphic pictures of the gay life of London gave sparkle and zest to his talk.

She had to tell him of her days in old Virginia. Then of the happinesses of her life with her mother, when the house was filled with gaiety and cheer and brightness, the first shadow coming when her father's misfortune overwhelmed him. Then they spoke often of the tragedies and the terrors of last October, — the October when she had first met him! Cliveden, desolated, suffering Cliveden, but, oh, how dear a place! It would always be their first home.

Thus their thoughts would go back into the past; then forward into the future; tremblingly sounding the depths of joy; glancing at possible griefs, yet feeling strong to bear any fate, if that fate could but be met together.

And the long days were short; the lonely, cheerless days were bright and sweet and beautiful. To these happy lovers, the clock had ceased to strike.

When the roughly written letter came to Shipton, which told of his friend's happiness, the lad's heart swelled within him, and he longed to gallop the miles which separated them. But expeditions across country were perilous just now. There was no special cause for getting from the commander-in-chief permission to form an escort. Shipton had no wish to risk the lives of his men for the sake of mere sentiment; besides, his friends and fellow officers were mainly concerned in making the dull winter gay with feasting, gaming, and devising plays at the old Southwark Theatre for the entertainment of the fair maidens of the placid city of Penn. Even were escorts numerous and easily obtained, and Light-Horse Harry and Allen McLane and their American troopers not ready to swoop down upon chance Englishmen outside of the city lines, Sophie and Peggy Chew would not have looked with much favour upon a long sleigh-ride in such bitter cold. Besides, Mistress Peggy confided to the admiring André: " Your friend, Arthur Peyton, is right happy at Cliveden. He has no need of you, nor of your Lieutenant, forsooth. Methinks he finds scant comfort in society, other than that of my friend Margaret." And Captain André would answer: " And where in the world could such beauty and adorableness be found to comfort him, save — save — " And the affectionate Captain would sigh and give her a languishing glance, which might mean everything — or — nothing.

" 'Tis no wonder hast fallen in love with Captain

Peyton, my dear," she said one day, when Margaret, accompanied by Jake and Sam, had ridden in to the city markets, and had halted for a brief time at the hospitable home on South Third Street to warm benumbed fingers at the big fires, and to carry thither brief letters, written by Captain Peyton to André and Shipton, — letters which Mistress Chew begged to deliver.

" Of a truth, I shall see them both at the Assembly at the City Tavern this evening. I have promised your Lieutenant to be his partner at a harmless game.

" Yes," she continued, looking at Margaret, mischievously, " 'tis no wonder my fair friend is captured at last by this dashing stranger. . . . Yes, my love, I mean it true. He has a clear eye and a straight glance. I have seen him but when, as the Lieutenant says, he was but half a man, — wounded, ill, thin, and with scarce a trace of colour. Look not so grave, my love. . . . But your happiness is safe, Margaret. In faith, he will not fail you when the pinch comes. So many people fail you when you need them most. Then your Captain has a future before him. The Lieutenant has told me of how he is trusted by Lord Chatham and Mr. Burke. And Mr. Howe here shows the need of the stimulus of men like him, men of energy and action. Yes, my love, he reminds me of John Eager Howard.[1] Methinks you have remembrance of him. He was with his Maryland regiment at the big fight near Cliveden. . . . Yes, my love, your Captain can

---

[1] Peggy Chew married Col. John Eager Howard. The wedding ceremony took place at Cliveden in 1787. Washington was present.

be trusted. He will not fail you when the pinch comes. Look to it well, Margaret, that you fail not to give him your trust — always, always, Margaret. If you once doubted him, and he were to know it, he is not the man to sue twice for your faith. Your happiness would be wrecked, Margaret. Guard your happiness well, my love. 'Tis a frail and transient thing, not to be trifled with."

A silence fell between the two friends, then Mistress Chew continued:

" Methought Captain Peyton had been in the city long ere this; but Doctor Worthington informed me yester-eve that he gains not strength, that it may be weeks yet ere it be safe for him to venture out into the cold air."

" Yes," answered Margaret, with a swift look of pain in her eyes, " that is the only grief of it all. Were he but well." Then she added: " But Doctor Worthington is so kind, so kind!"

" Wherefore so kind?" asked her friend, with a sidelong glance.

" I know not. But he is at Cliveden near every day, devising some relief for Henry's headaches, seeing that — that Arthur is not imprudent, entertaining Annette, and giving father many a spicy news gathered in the city and the neighbourhood round about.

Peggy laughed mischievously.

" And what does the careful philanthropist for my fair friend, Margaret Murray?"

But just then Jake appeared to " tell de missy dat de hosses could take de ride home."

" Are the panniers filled as full as can be?" asked Mistress Chew.

"Yes, missy, met'inks so. Sam's is so full he hab pow'ful trubble gettin' on his hoss. We got to mahket early. De farmers hab pow'ful hard time gettin' in deir tings dis cole wedder — de chickens mos' froze. Mistress Pemberton come 'long, an' feel bad dat we got some fine tings she wanted." And chuckling to himself, Jake went out to wait for his mistress.

"Madam Pemberton feels the lack of her coach that was pressed for Mr. Howe's use," said Peggy, turning to Margaret.

Margaret smiled. "If 'twere not that my tongue is tied, I should say, Peg, that methinks many people of Philadelphia would feel the presence of these British most irksome."

"But your tongue is tied, my love. You cannot say it."

"No, Peg, I cannot. But the thought will force itself that we Americans are not loyal to Washington and his army who are fighting for us at so much sacrifice and suffering at Valley Forge, when we make so much of these British, — give them dinners, fêtes, applaud and caress them."

Mistress Chew laughed merrily.

"How many dinners give you to Captain Peyton, Margaret?"

Margaret smiled in return, but she did not answer.

"We enjoy these dinners and fêtes right well, my love. Captain André and De Lancey and Lieutenant Shipton and others of their friends make the winter pleasant; and when they go, we shall miss them sore. . . . You have heard that Captain André, of late, is in the Binghams' town house?"

" Yes, one of Annette's friends wrote her of the circumstance."

" Is the Bingham house in the country shut up? "

" I know not."

" We have heard naught of Rodney for an age. Dear old Rodney! I miss him. A letter came once, saying he was at Lancaster, where the Congress stays. Know you aught of him, Margaret? "

And Margaret was thankful enough that she could answer truthfully : " I have not seen Rodney Bingham for many a day. Nor heard from him. Henry and I spoke of him but this morning. We were hoping he was well."

" Perchance he has joined the army. Oh! that reminds me, Margaret. There was much excitement in town yesterday. A spy had been found, who had been hiding for three or four days in the bell-tower of Christ Church. You remember that the big bell was taken away to Trenton when 'twas heard that the British were coming. There was ample room in the tower for that poor spy. He had been there in comfort. A rough bed had been made with cloaks. There were remains of food found. But he was dragged out, and was being taken to Walnut Street Jail, when the mob became so great that a certain hue and cry was raised; and in all the bustle and commotion, the man got off, ran down to the river, threw himself into a boat, and was off ere he could be caught. Dolly Stark was riding up Front Street, and drew rein to let the crowd go by that was in pursuit, when she caught sight of the man's face. She says 'twas surprisingly like Rodney Bingham. Dolly Stark was ever fanciful, but she was right positive about this. She said the man's dress was strange, that his figure was not like Rodney's, but the face, the face was his. . . . What is the matter, Margaret? You are so pale, and your hand is trembling. . . . There! my love. I have tired you with all my talk."

CHAPTER XXXII.

"'Tis a beautiful world, Bob. Oh! that we men would not spoil it by our hates, our discords, our cruelty, our hard selfishness."

WHERE could she find Rodney? How could she give him help? She was in a fever of uncertainty and apprehension. She dared not take Peggy into her confidence; yet she felt she could not return home without first seeking to do something for the friend who was, perchance, in deadly peril, a fugitive, not knowing where to take refuge. She made no plan. She simply felt she must stay in the city. She wrote a hurried word to Captain Peyton and her father; then, to Mistress Chew's delight, she told her she would remain if shelter could be given her and Jake.

Sam, they would first accompany as far as the redoubt at the intersection of North Front Street and the Germantown Road. She would get him safely past the sentries. Then he could betake himself home. Mr. Murray's anxiety would be relieved; and then Margaret and Jake could choose their own time to return to Cliveden.

The streets in the neighbourhood of the redoubt were thronged with soldiers, both artillery and foot. While Margaret waited to have speech with one of the sentries, a troop of cavalry came into view down the Germantown Road, and there was a long delay ere she could show her pass, and explain the necessity of Sam, with his heavily laden panniers, getting through the lines. At last her task was done, and she and Jake rode slowly back along Front Street, till they came to Callowhill, where they turned. At the corner of Second Street, by the entrance of Mr. Noble's house, Jake spoke. " See de ten commandments cut in de stone gate-posts, missy. Dey keep de bad spirits away."

" They seem to have slight influence upon the British," Margaret answered. " Several officers are quartered there, I hear. I fear me our friend has little comfort."

"Dare's a big garret runnin' de whole length ob de house, missy. Pow'ful fine place under de eaves for a rebel to hide."

" But what use, Jake? No rebel could pass these formidable redoubts and fortifications. See how that abatis stretches across. They have felled all the beautiful trees. O Jake! that abatis is impassable. No one could possibly get out."

" Not so shuh ob dat, missy dear. Dare are holes in it. Spec' I could fine a place, big as I be. Doan' worry, missy, Massa Rodney got a head on his nec'. He's pow'ful clebber. He'll get through dat obstruction. No prevaricatin' dat he will."

As they passed Christ Church, Margaret looked up at the tower, and had a strange fancy that Rodney, despite having been caught there once, had returned to his hiding-place. If she could but go up and see!

At Pine Street, they turned again, and came near St. Peter's, meeting many soldiers by the way, though she paid no heed to their bold glances of interest and approval. But as she came to the Presbyterian church just beyond — now, alas! desecrated by the British, who were using it as a garrison — she got into a crowd of rough grenadiers, among them a number of officers. To her consternation, she recognised Captain Baines. She wheeled her horse quickly, and the next moment was trotting back over the rough pavement. To her relief she was not followed; but she did not take breath till she had reached the house at the junction of Little Dock and Second Streets. She had the feeling that perchance the woman who lived there might know something of Rodney.

Lydia Darrach was a well-known patriot, honoured by every Whig in town. Margaret knew that she had once been nurse in the Bingham family, and her husband had been teacher to the boys. It might happen that Rodney had applied to her for help in his desperate plight. She would stop and see her anyway.

Underneath the gallery running along the front of the house was the little shop now used as an office by the adjutant-general of the British army. Opposite was the house occupied by General Knyphausen. Margaret and Jake found themselves in a very nest of Britons and Hessians. It required some courage to dismount and open the door of the office; but do it she did. She preferred this task to the unpleasant one of sitting on her horse while Jake did the service for her. She was in no mood to endure the curious and the bold looks of these Hessians, that filled the windows and doorways of the big house opposite.

She passed with dignity through a crowd of soldiers and secretaries within the office, and she knocked at the door of an inner room. A loud and harsh voice answered her and bade her begone. She knocked again. The voice within was raised in anger. A soldier behind her laughed, but was promptly rebuked by another.

"Mistress Darrach is in one of her humours to-day," the soldier said. "You can do naught with her."

"I thank you, sir. But I will try again."

Meanwhile Jake had ridden close to the house, and, standing on his horse, reached up and knocked peremptorily with his whip on the edge of the balcony. At first there was no response. He knocked again. Then a step was heard on the balcony, and a head wrapped in a shawl leaned over. 'Twas Lydia herself.

"Begone! If you want the General, ye can find him in the shop beneath. Begone, I say. I want no black thieves around here. Begone, I say."

Margaret came out on to the street.

"Lydia, Lydia," she called, softly. "You know me?"

The woman shaded her eyes from the sun.

"Come down, Lydia, and let me in. I wish speech with you a moment. In faith, Lydia, you must welcome me right heartily."

The woman's face changed, as if by magic. With a glad cry, she hurried across the balcony, and a door above, opening into the house, was heard to slam violently.

Margaret reëntered the office, and in a moment the door of the inner room was opened to her.

"Come in, come in, Mistress Murray. I was but catchin' a cat-nap betimes, and I was angry at the noise. If I let in all the people that knock here, I would have my little sittin'-room packed as tight as a box of herrin'. 'Tis right glad I am to see ye. Sit there. And how is your father? An' ye are all alive after that big battle. Well, well, 'tis right glad I am."

"You have not been for flour again to Frankford, I hope," said Margaret, in a low tone. She had seen that the door behind her leading to the office was carefully shut.

The woman's sunburned face grew redder.

"Ah! who told ye of that? Be careful, Mistress Murray. We only whisper here."

The woman went to the door and placed her ear at the keyhole and listened. "'Tis all right," she whispered, softly. "They be all talkin' an' wonderin' who ye be mayhap. How knew ye of that?"

"My brother heard of it from Alexander Hamilton himself," whispered Margaret, laying her hand affectionately on the woman's arm. "But your secret has been well kept, dear Lydia. Wait till the British are gone from the city, then every patriot will hear of your exploit."

The woman smiled, as she whispered back: "Ye see, I listened at this very door. I heard these officers meet an' tell of a secret plan to attack the camp at Whitemarsh. In the middle of the night I got up an' dressed, an' started off with an empty bag to walk to Frankford for flour. I come back with the flour, but I'd told the Americans all I heard. When these rascals marched away to at-

tack the camp, they found my General all ready
with his guns. They gained naught, naught. I
heard how angry they was at their failure." Lydia
chuckled.

"A brave and noble deed, Lydia," whispered Margaret. "But your legs and your poor back must
have been so tired, dear."

"Ay, they was," answered the woman, simply.
"That flour weighed tons as I drew near Philadelphia, but I reckon we women might do something for the country when the boys are givin' their
lives. My son was killed at Brandywine, mistress."

"O Lydia, Lydia!" and Margaret put her arms
around the woman, and they both shed tears.

Then Margaret leaned over and whispered in the
other's ear. The woman started. "Yes, 'twas Mr.
Rodney. I took him food while he was hidin' in
the bell-tower."

"And where is he now, Lydia? Know you
that?"

"I dare not tell ye. Ye cannot help him."

"Oh! I can! I can!"

But Lydia shook her head obstinately. "He is
safe. Be assured of that. But he can't leave the
city yet. His work ain't done. He has secret commission from the General to do some work for Lafayette. The moon is wanin'. When a dark night
comes, he can get through the abatis at a point
where it ain't very thick. 'Tis on the Ridge Road
yonder. He knows. He knows. Ye can trust
him. I will care for him well."

A load was lifted from Margaret's heart.

She drew from her girdle her purse, and laid
upon the table all the gold pieces within it.

"At the market-houses this morning," she said, smiling, "I spent more than I would have, had I known. But, Lydia, give him these, and tell him that our thoughts and prayers are with him. And, Lydia, remember, that if aught ever happen that you hear of secret attacks on Valley Forge, and you plan to give Washington warning, you must not walk that long way. You must have a horse. Go to Mistress Chew. I will tell her that any moneys you may wish are at your command. Remember, Lydia. Hesitate not one moment. I do it, not for you, Lydia, but for the cause. Your devotion to the cause must make you willing to take it. You will, Lydia? Ah! you are kind. I thank you. Now, Lydia, good-bye. This evening I shall be at Mistress Chew's. If you have aught to let me know, or Rodney desires to send any message, I shall be there. Good-bye. Good-bye."

The shadows were lengthening as Margaret and Jake returned to Third Street.

After dinner, which was held at the fashionable hour, she watched Peggy bedeck herself for the Assembly.

"You must come with me, my love," said Mistress Chew. "The hair-dresser has skill and time to help you, and that pink brocade of Sophia's will fit you to a nicety."

But Margaret shook her head. "In faith, I wish my own gown, and my head-dress, and my own jewels, Peg. My first appearance among these dashing officers must not be in borrowed splendours, Peg. No, 'tis no use to urge me, dear. Then, I confess,

I feel right weary. These long rides are tiring, dear. And I must be up early in the morning. Here! Let me fasten those jewels in your hair. My Peg looks lovely, lovely. Dear heart, how beautiful you are!"

CHAPTER XXXIII.

"True, girl, but his chance is great to do our cause great harm."

THAT evening the Chew mansion on Third Street was quiet. In the absence of the Chief Justice, who had been banished to Virginia by the Congress, Madam Chew and her daughters were glad of the distractions and gaieties planned by the officers of his Majesty's army. Every Thursday night Mr. Smith's City Tavern was gay with bright lights, gorgeous gowns and handsome uniforms, laughter and merry voices. Captain André and his brother, Captain De Lancey, Major Stoddard, Colonel Tarleton, Lieutenant Shipton, Colonel Musgrave, Major Greyson, Captain Niggard, and many other of their friends, made themselves most agreeable to Margaret Shippen, Rebecca Franks, Dolly Stark, Mistress Auchmuty, Mistress Chew and her sisters, and many other fair maidens of the city of Penn.

After the departure of Madam Chew and her daughters, Margaret settled down by the library fire, and for a time got interested in one of the Letters that the mysterious Junius had recently published; but she soon grew very sleepy; and, curling up in Benjamin Chew's big armchair, she soon lost herself in dreams. How long she slept, she knew not, but she awoke to see a maid-servant standing beside her, who told her that a serving-man was in the dining-room, waiting to have speech with her.

Margaret dismissed the maid, and immediately betook herself to the dining-room. The man was standing near the sideboard, and the gleam of the candles burning upon it fell full on his face. A disfiguring scar stretched across his right cheek; his mouth was drawn to one side, giving an effect somewhat odd and hideous. When he spoke, his voice was husky and muffled, his accent common. His clothes were coarse and shabby, his attitude awkward, and his manner servile.

"I come from Mistress Darrach, lady. She bids me give you this."

He handed her a small slip of paper. The words were few, and written in the small, cramped characters common to the women of that time.

"This man will tell you all you wish. Have not speech with him in regard to the matter unless you are quite alone. Speak freely to him, after you see that no one listens at keyholes.   L. D."

Margaret went to the doors leading to the pantry, to the hall, and to the library. Saw that they were all closed securely, and that no one was within hearing. Then she returned to the man, and whispered, softly: "Will you tell me of Mr. Bingham? Is he safe? Is he well?"

"Yes, lady, he is."

"Are you acquaint with him?"

"Yes, lady, I know him well. I saw him only a short time agone. Ye are sure we can speak freely, lady? 'Tis of most importance that none of these servants hear us. Make sure that you do naught but whisper, lady."

"Yes, yes, I understand. Tell me of Mr. Bingham. And who are you?"

"Mistress Darrach's man, lady. I work for her. She's gettin' feeble now, an' needs help in her business. She is a Whig, an' so be I. I can hear a deal o' secrets given out by these officers when they are in their cups."

"Yes, I am glad; but what of Mr. Bingham?"

"He is a mean, deceitful man, lady. He deserves hanging, and these British may well bear him a grudge."

The man gave a low, amused laugh. Startled and alarmed, she looked up into his face. The queer twist of the mouth was gone, though the scar, of course, remained. But the expression of the eyes had changed.

"O Rodney! Rodney! You wretch, you wretch!"

Then they fell to talking, but very quietly and not for long.

"You see, Margaret, Washington keeps hearing reports that the British are to evacuate the city. But they go not. The reports deceive him. He has tried spy after spy, but they are most of them either fools or knaves. He has intention to fall upon the enemy's rear as soon as they start, and 'tis of the first importance that he know at least twenty-four hours before the move is really made. . . . Now, Margaret, the British, since this last thaw set in, have been committing depredations which make every patriot swear. They have not only been burning houses up country, — you heard about the attempt

on Stenton, and how finely they were fooled, — but
they have been sending expeditions up the Delaware,
destroying our shipping between here and Trenton.
Think, Margaret, we lost fifty-four vessels in one
day. Heaven grant to send freezing weather once
more. That makes the red devils stay in the city.
. . . Now, to restrain these depredations, Washington has intention to send Lafayette, with twenty-
one hundred chosen men, to a point near the enemy's
lines, that he may be a security to the camp at
Valley Forge, and a cover to the country between
the two rivers, that he may interrupt the communication with Philadelphia, and do general good service. This will be a secret expedition; but before
it can be undertaken, he must obtain trusty and
intelligent spies, who will advise him faithfully of
whatever may be passing in the city. I am using
the identical words, Margaret, the General used in
his letter of instructions to the Marquis. I destroyed
the letter, but I know it by heart. ' 'Tis of the
utmost importance,' he said, ' to obtain intelligence
of the motions and designs of the enemy.' My work,
Margaret, has been to find out and hire two or more
spies who are trusty. And to my grief, the task has
been difficult."

"But how obtained you access to the city,
Rodney?"

"As Mr. Kelper, of Germantown, I came with
Worthington."

"Worthington! Not Doctor Worthington?"

"Who else?"

"But 'tis his scheme to appear neutral. He will
not take sides."

"Nor will he. He knows naught of my political

opinions. I rode into the city with him one day. We halted at the Indian Queen Tavern. Then we parted. I have not seen him since. Methinks he would not know me now."

" Of a truth, no. You are greatly changed."

Bingham smiled.

" I would not trust that man too far. I have scant liking for him."

" Henry thinks him a true patriot, working in secret to help our cause."

" Tell Henry not to trust him too far. O Margaret, we can trust so few these perilous days. There is some one in Germantown, or in the region round about, who is working against us. There are so many proofs of this. I have no time to tell you of the matter now, for I must be going, and that right speedily. But as soon as I can get away from the city, I shall return to Germantown and ferret out the matter. I will find the man if life be granted me. I know not where to look, but find him I will! Some one is working against us, who discovers our secrets, betrays our expeditions, diverts from us the forage that belongs to us, induces many of the men to desert, and in a thousand ways deceives and does us injury. I owe that man a grudge. I will find him and track him down."

" Be careful, Rodney. Be careful. Run no risk of being caught, as you were yesterday."

" Who told you?"

" Peggy says that Dolly Stark saw you on Front Street, as you were getting away."

Bingham looked grave and anxious.

" I will be careful, Margaret. Thank you for the warning. Now ring that bell, Margaret, and when the maid appears, tell her to conduct me out, and bid me good-bye, as if Mistress Darrach had sent you a message by me, and you were sending one back. Yes — I see you understand. I have stayed long. Forgive me, Margaret. Oh! just one word. How is the Englishman?"

Margaret's face flushed. "He is recovering very, very slowly, Rodney. . . . 'Tis a grief to me, Rodney."

Bingham looked at her sharply. Something in her face answered his unspoken question.

"You are to marry him then?"

"Yes," she answered, simply.

"Then Heaven keep him for you, Margaret."

CHAPTER XXXIV.

"I felt your care and your sympathy. I, who had longed to take care of you, I, who was so strong, was stricken down to be cared for by you."

BUT as time went on, and he grew no stronger, there came sad, dark days when she would look at him and say, tearfully: "If you were but well! That is my heart's wish."

Then he would soothe and comfort her, and kiss away her tears.

And in her trouble, Margaret realised how strong was the bond of sympathy between her and her father. By the quick and subtle intuition of the heart, Mr. Murray knew of Margaret's griefs; but he said little until one day he came upon her as she was alone by the fire in her own room. The weather had been of great severity, — storms and intense cold. For a week she had not ventured to ride forth from home. The few stragglers on the road, the few Continental troopers who had halted at their door, had brought dismal tales of suffering. The shadow of Valley Forge made everything seem dark. Then Mr. Murray spoke of Peyton.

"How can you tell, dear father, when you cannot see him?"

"I feel, daughter, I feel. And my love for you makes me know. I can tell by your voice every morning when you first greet him. I can tell that you are more anxious."

" 'Tis so long, so long since he has been out in the air, father. If I feel of low spirit and shut in, because for a few days I could not gallop over the snow, how must he feel? Would I knew if 'twere best to take more risks. If 'twere but possible to have Doctor Shippen's advice."

" Doctor Worthington is of opinion that he ought not to venture."

" Yes, yes, he assures me it were dangerous. But at one time he had not this opinion."

" Doctor Worthington is right skilful."

" Yes, yes, and, of a truth, he has been more attentive than we have the right to look for."

" Henry has improved marvellously of late."

Margaret's face brightened. " Yes, he rode last week ten miles. And when the change comes, and this bitterness of cold abates, he hopes to ride to Valley Forge to see the General."

" Ah! could I but go with him! "

" You can, father, you can! We will get out the coach as soon as weather favours. You shall go! "

There was a joyous ring to Margaret's voice. But Mr. Murray shook his head.

" I could never ride over these rough roads and devious paths, even if the calash were lined with pillows and rode on fairy wheels."

" 'Tis possible you could not endure it," answered Margaret, thoughtfully. " But 'twere a pleasure for you, dear."

" I shall have to wait till he himself can come here. His last letter gave me much hope. We shall yet have him as our guest."

CHAPTER XXXV.

"The time will be short, but rich in counsel. My weary heart longs for a sight of your beloved face."

THE days and the weeks sped on, till finally there came a day in April when a troop of horse galloped up the garden road, and their leader flung himself hastily from the saddle. Margaret threw open the door.

"A letter, mistress. A letter for Mr. Charles Murray."

She took it eagerly, then bade the man betake himself and his escort to the stables.

"Warmth and refreshment for you all when the horses are bestowed," she said, with a smile which made him her slave at once.

"I pray you, go to the stables. I will send thither to you."

The soldier bowed. She shut the door, and going to the dining-room, found herself face to face with her father.

"'Tis from him? Of a surety, from him?"

"Yes, dear. The General writes a bold, strong hand. It shows character, force. Father, you remember it?"

"Quite well, daughter."

She saw that he was trembling with impatience for the letter, so she broke the seals and drew nearer

Mr. Murray. Had she but known that, behind the secret panel, there was lurking in the darkness some one who could hear every word through the thin board of the wainscoting, she would have touched the spring, and bidden him come forth into the light, — come forth to shame and scorn and disgrace.

She read in a low, but clear tone : —

" ' Valley Forge, April 20, 1778.

" ' Having cherished the profoundest sentiments of friendship and regard for you, I am most anxious to see you again before aught occur to cause me to leave this region. From our intelligence, there is reason to conclude that the enemy may perchance soon evacuate Philadelphia. In any event I shall break camp as soon as he starts, and shall fall in his rear. I had hoped that you could come to us in your calash ere this, but the last letter from your daughter drives that hope away. The Congress clamours for action from the army. God alone knows the conditions which have made it impossible to be aught but inactive. But should our intelligence prove truthful, then all this will soon be changed. There will be another big battle. Before it comes, I long to see you. There is an especial matter about which I crave your counsel. I will not write it because it is of a private nature, and concerns you and your family. As I am so near The Chew House, it seems prudent for me to visit you once more, and should we break camp, it must be soon. I am coming Friday eve, at five o'clock. If you know aught to stand in opposition to my visit, send, I pray you, a letter by the trusty messenger who carries this to you.

" ' I shall bring a strong guard, but it is best that my coming be kept secret. I shall depart before daybreak. The time will be short, but rich in counsel. My weary heart longs for a sight of your beloved face, for, if I go out into the darkness and the smoke and the dust of battle, I shall never see you again. I feel it to be so. Adieu, dear Charles.

" ' Your affectionate
" ' GEORGE WASHINGTON.' "

Margaret's voice faltered. " How beautiful it will be to see him again," she said, brokenly. " The mere look of his calm eyes strengthens my heart Of a verity, I will write that it is safe for him to come."

" Methinks 'twere best to dismiss the messenger with words spoken, not written, that the General will be warmly welcomed here Friday night. I like not written words that can so easily be seized by chance foraging and skirmishing parties. And yet, the General himself has not taken such precaution."

" Of a truth, 'tis best to do as you suggest, father, and Henry himself can convey a further word of welcome. Of late, Captain Peyton has lost all letters he has sent by the messengers bringing letters to him. His friends have received only the few that I myself have carried. And you know how seldom of late I have had occasion to ride to the city, therefore his friends have not received the half of what he has writ."

Mr. Murray's face grew grave. " 'Tis most unpleasant, daughter. Of a truth, I like it not. Why should the Americans suspect that he could find aught of importance to write to his friends? "

Margaret's face was also grave. "It looks, father, as if there were purpose in this seizure of the letters. If it happened a few times, but that it should happen all the time! It looks as if there were system in it. I cannot understand it, father. It looks as if this house were spied upon by the Americans. And we are true patriots, father. We are. We are."

And Mr. Murray kept repeating: "I like it not. I like it not."

CHAPTER XXXVI.

"Think not for one moment that I see not that this love will bring you both happiness and pain."

IT was the morning of the day on which the visit of the General was planned.

Margaret had hoped to discover sufficient provisions in Dinah's keeping to ensure a fitting entertainment for her guests; but, to her consternation, so little was discovered which would avail that she straightway resolved to ride to the city, and hurry back as soon as Selim could bring her. She gave a hurried order to Jake; then sent a message to Captain Peyton to prepare a hasty packet if he chose that she carry it, or he could send by the same messenger that the half-hour before had brought letters to him, bearing the seals of Sir William Howe.

Now she was on her way through the hall when she came upon her father and Annette. The big door stood slightly ajar, but a bright fire was burning on the hearth of the little room at the end of the hall. Margaret went to the door and closed it.

"Doctor Worthington has but now stepped out into the garden," said Annette. "He came to say that he was riding to the city and might, happily, be of service to you. When he learned that 'twas

304

your purpose to go thither also, he intimated that he would tarry here till you depart."

" 'Tis most kind and thoughtful methinks," said Charles Murray.

Annette smiled wilfully.

" Yes, and he has missed Henry even now, in spite of this early visit. And of a verity, 'twas his eager wish to see Henry and confer with him over special matters."

Margaret did not seem to understand the meaning of Annette's smiles.

" Has Henry ridden forth ? " asked Mr. Murray.

" Yes, he departed on Black Kit at early dawn," answered Annette.

Mr. Murray turned to Margaret. " You cannot tarry long in the city, daughter, else you will be not back in time to see the General when he first arrives."

" No, I will deliver Captain Peyton's letters as usual, go to the markets, see Peggy one moment perchance, and gallop back. . . . How thankful I am that we had not to send word for the General not to come ! "

" O daughter, yes ! 'Twould, in truth, be a bitter word."

Annette suddenly glanced over her shoulder, and said, in a half-whisper : " 'Twere terrible were there aught dangerous in the General's visit."

Margaret paused. She had started on her way to the staircase, now she turned back.

" How were it possible that aught should be known of it ? "

Ah ! if Margaret had but known that some one

whom she trusted was even then watching to betray, waiting to strike a treacherous blow!

"Think you there is danger from this visit, father?" she asked.

"I think but little, now that we have kept secret the fact from any one that we expect him. It matters not who knows it when he is once here. His guard will be a protection against any chance foraging or skirmishing party. And yet, even now, it is not well to speak to Captain Peyton of our expectation."

"Father, how could he betray us, even if he knew of it?"

"Henry has often said that the temptation were great to let the British know."

Margaret made no reply. Annette continued: "'Twere a great triumph to the man who would be the means of the General's capture. His name would go down into history. He would be immortal. A great triumph!"

"A triumph which Captain Peyton would scorn to have."

Annette did not reply. Margaret turned to her father and said, in a husky voice: "Father! He would not betray us."

Charles Murray was silent.

Margaret's voice became insistent: "Father!"

"True, child."

"Speak not in that way, father." She came nearer him. "Father! I will not permit you to think!"

"There! there! daughter, I will stop thinking. But the whole land seems so full of treachery these days. We know not half the time who our foes are, and I sit here so much of the time, and brood over the sorrows and uncertainties of the future."

"No one knows of this visit, not even the servants?" asked Annette.

"No one. Not even Doctor Worthington," answered Margaret.

"You have not told the Captain?" asked Mr. Murray.

"No."

"That is well."

"An open foe is not to be dreaded; it is he who stabs in the dark."

"True, child."

"Captain Peyton is an Englishman, a man of honour."

"True, daughter; we will say no more."

Margaret went over to the fire and looked into it with thoughtful eyes. Then she turned and said, earnestly: "Father, the time is coming when this country will be free. And away off in the future, England and we will be friends, — true, good friends. The discord and the strife will be forgotten. You and I will be but dust; but in the future, father, England and America will be together, and England and America together can defy the world."

She stopped in confusion when she caught sight of Annette's laughing face.

"What eloquence, forsooth. Margaret, you are learning your lesson well."

Margaret's face clouded.

"Of a verity, dear," Annette continued, with an affectionate look, "it grows late. I would 'twere not needful that you go. But Dinah will have that wherewith to cook and brew, or you, my love, will have neither peace not joy."

Margaret went to the window and looked out.

"Father, Jake has but now brought out Selim to be saddled. I have but scant time to prepare for my ride."

"Forget not your safeguard petticoat. The roads must be pool-strewn."

Margaret smiled. "These heavy rains have worked sad havoc with my roads. I take but scant comfort in the thought of my ride to-day."

And she went swiftly out into the hall and up the stairs.

"Of a truth, 'tis a comfort that Doctor Worthington will ride with her. I like not the aspect of the skies," said Annette, with a shiver, as she went nearer the fire.

"Where is he now?" asked Mr. Murray.

"He came unusual early, saying he was passing on his way to see old Dame Keibert, who has a distemper of a virulent order. When he learned that Margaret had intention to go to the city, he said he could easily wait and ride with her, as the roads were uncommon rough since the violent rains."

"And he has gone to the stables now?"

"Methinks so. That messenger who brought the letters to Captain Peyton tarries there to rest his horse from a hard ride. Doctor Worthington said something about conversing with him as he left me. But, father, Doctor Worthington has become here so familiar and intimate a guest that his comings and goings are oft unnoticed and unannounced. Of a verity, I took little heed of him. I have not yet ceased to marvel much why it is that Henry rode away so early."

" Before daybreak ? "

" Yes, I was not awake. When I awoke, I found a paper pinned to my pillow. It said merely: ' I ride to Valley Forge with Sam. We are well-mounted. Be not anxious, sweetheart.' What can it be, father ? "

" I know not, child. Was he not absent all yester-afternoon ? "

" Yes, he was riding about all day in the village, then along the old Ridge Road, then, methought he tarried till late in the evening at the solitary tavern where Doctor Worthington has been lodging the past few weeks."

" At Dame Van Slycke's ? "

" Yes, the house near that dense and lonely wood. I like it not, father, that Henry rides thither in that direction. The house had once a most gruesome reputation."

" 'Tis all a thing of the past, dear."

Annette's face grew very thoughtful and grave.

" He has of late grown very silent, and it has oft been a sore puzzle to me. I fear me that he has apprehension of some danger, or has part in some secret enterprise. . . . Father, I have not told Margaret, for I had no wish to make her burdens heavier. And I had no wish to trouble you; but I am most anxious, most anxious. Father, three days ago there came a letter from Rodney. The breaking up of the cold had permitted his return to Germantown. He wished Henry to meet him at the old trysting-place on the Wissahickon. Not far from it stands that solitary tavern of Dame Van Slycke's. The lonely wood is there. I am glad that he took Sam with him to-day, but yester-afternoon he went alone. . . . O father! when will this miserable, anxious time be past?"

CHAPTER XXXVII.

"O Margaret, my soul has been torn and tossed on a troubled sea."

ANNETTE turned, and found herself face to face with Peyton. She swept him a long, graceful curtsy. "Of a truth, sir, you startled me."

He bowed to her in the same manner, his hand on his heart.

"Madam, your humble servant."

She laughed. "Excellent, excellent, Captain Peyton."

He bent and kissed her hand. Then his glance fell on Charles Murray. His face grew grave and thoughtful.

Annette's eyes fell on the packet in his hand.

"Of a truth, sir," she said, laughingly, "you have been long writing those epistles. Methought 'twere a history of our perilous and eventful times."

"I have writ but short ones," he replied, going to the table and laying the packet upon it. Then he turned back to Charles Murray.

"Mr. Murray, I have but now received a special messenger from Sir William Howe. My cousin, Lord Carlisle, has arrived from England. He craves my presence in the city. The other peace commissioners will come later."

The look on Captain Peyton's face made all the laughter die out from Annette's. She went softly out from the room and closed the door behind her.

Peyton continued: " I can endure battles. I can fight. Ah, Mr. Murray, I feel this moment as if I could gallop up into the very teeth of glittering bayonets, storm forts, run my sword through any opposing force, but — it were all easier than — to — leave you and Margaret. It tears my heart in twain."

His voice grew tender and soft, and he went and laid his arm across Charles Murray's shoulder. Mr. Murray put up his hand and gently stroked the arm.

" I know not how she will receive the news of your departure," he said, with a break in his voice. " You have not told her? "

" No! no! I will wait till she returns. I will not mar her ride by my bad news. . . . Would she were not going to-day. Could we but have this last day together."

He began a restless walking up and down.

" I will leave her in comfort till she returns. General Howe thinks best to send me an escort made up of my friends. The roads are infested by American skirmishing parties and foragers. But it will not be here till about nine to-night."

Mr. Murray rose in excitement.

" It comes not to-night — not to-night! "

" So says Howe's messenger."

" It *must* not be to-night! To-morrow perchance, but not to-night. No! no! "

" It were no easier to-morrow."

" You must write General Howe not to send till

to-morrow, not till to-morrow. Here! here! Here is pen — paper."

His trembling hand was fumbling with the papers and quills on the table. Peyton came nearer.

" The night is best for a small escort," he said.

" Write, write for to-morrow night, then. It must not be to-night. Here! Write to Howe, write to Shipton. Margaret will take the letter. We have visitors here to-night. We want you here, but not your friends."

Peyton laughed. " Be it so, then."

He took up a quill, and wrote a few words with his left hand, speaking meanwhile.

" 'Tis no easy task for me to let her go to-day. Of a truth, my task has not been easy these last few weeks. I have, indeed, had a few rides on very warm days, but not far; comes the least chill in the air it seems best that I remain indoors."

" Yes, Margaret fears still for your health."

Peyton smiled. " She has had the right of it, I know; but 'tis hard for me not to care for her comfort, rather than have her troubling ever about me. But I must go to-morrow night, health or ill health, wind or no wind, rain or soft air. Go I must. I have much to say to Carlisle. He must not act; he must take no measure without consulting me. My influence may avert catastrophe. Methinks your Congress will not receive with patience the overtures of these peace commissioners from the King. These overtures come too late. I see that all too well. Heaven grant that Carlisle may show a measure of tact and discretion. All depends on that, Mr. Murray. The King has need of servants to show the tact and discretion he himself lacks.

My cousin will be popular, I have no doubt. . . . I have much to say to him. And I myself am hungry for news of my dear Lord Chatham. I must go to-morrow night."

"Ah! I know not how she will bear to have you go."

Peyton folded and sealed his letter, and placed it with the packet on the table. Then he turned impetuously.

"O Mr. Murray, come with me — you and she — both with me. Then — then — "

He paused in confusion.

"Complete your sentence, my friend. Then — then you will be married. Ah! Captain, I am not so selfish that I will stand in the way of my daughter's happiness. She is free to go, free, free."

"But you must go with us. You must go to England with us."

Mr. Murray raised his hand in protest.

"Mr. Murray, Margaret needs you far too much for me ever to wish to separate her from you."

He looked at the sad face of the man before him. His earnest words brought a warm flush to the pale cheeks.

"Margaret needs me? me? I need her, but — but — "

Peyton put his hand again on Mr. Murray's shoulder. "She needs you. She depends upon you. Ah, Mr. Murray, think not for one moment that I hope to come between you, — to separate you. My wife must be happy, and without her father my wife could not be happy."

With an uncontrollable sob, the older man buried his face on the shoulder of the other. Then he said, brokenly: "You are kind, my friend, kind indeed, but I much fear me — "

"I speak truth, Mr. Murray. I have Margaret's word for it. . . . As for myself, Mr. Murray, you know not how you and your home have become wound around my heart. England, the old castle in Kent, my old home, — they all seem the dream and the shadow. This is the reality. . . . Mr. Murray — "

The Captain face flushed like a schoolboy's. His voice faltered.

"Mr. Murray, may I return to you after I have been to the city and seen my cousin? May I? May I come for you and Margaret? Will you go back with me?"

"Hush! she is coming."

The father's quick ear had caught the sound of Margaret's step in the hall above. As she came down the stairway, he stole quietly away. Peyton met her at the foot of the stairs. He glanced at her riding-hat and gown; then grasped her hand eagerly.

"I received your message. So you are really going, after all. I fear me the rain is not yet past."

"But the clouds are breaking. See that patch of blue over there?" She pointed out through the window. But he kept his eyes upon her.

"Will not the roads be well-nigh impassable? They are drenched. Go not. Stay with me."

Margaret smiled. "You will be very hungry to-morrow, were I not to go."

"To-morrow!"

"And very cross and ill."

"Never cross, dear, never with you."

" Wait, we will see."

Hand in hand they crossed the hall to the little room at the end.   She sank into a chair.   He moved aside his packet of letters and the papers and quills, and leaned against the table.

" Why not tell Chloe what you need? "

Margaret laughed.   " Would not Chloe enjoy the wump, wump of Selim or Tempest over the stones and through the mud?   She would suffer ' de awful misery ' in her lame joints for a week.   Why, Arthur, there is much wrong with your judgment this morning."

He smiled in return.

" I know there is.   I have no judgment where you are concerned."

" Of all the compliments I ever received, this one is the most beautiful."

" Well, you know what I mean."

Peyton glanced cautiously around, then went and threw his arm around her.

" I have you fast.   You cannot go.   I shall keep you all day."

" If you do, you will be hungry to-morrow."

" You said that before.   Say something else."

" What shall I say? "

" Draw on your imagination."

" I have no imagination where you are concerned."

" You no imagination, and I no judgment.   What kind of people are we, then, Margaret? "

" We are — we are — "

" Well, dear, what are we? "

" Well, Arthur, tell me — what are we? "

"I have decided the matter clearly in my own mind."

He left her, and walked slowly to the fire and turned.

"Come here, Arthur."

"Not till you tell me."

She looked at him mischievously. Then a sweet, tender look came into her face. She held out her hands. He sprang forward and grasped them.

"Oh, you know it, dear. You know I love you."

There was a pause. Then he spoke.

"Margaret, what was your feeling before I saw and loved you?"

"I had no existence."

Then they both laughed.

"You were in a state of waiting. You were waiting for me."

"Yes, and when you came, my heart seemed to know you at once. Of a truth, I knew not at the time that it was love's recognition. But now — but now I know!"

"'Twas the same with me. Amidst all those wretched troopers, all the noise and turmoil, you stole into my heart, into a quiet, serene place, — away, away, where the quietness and peace rested me."

She leaned her head on his arm, and closed her eyes.

"Then quicker than thought, there flashed through my mind a vision of my lost mother. It was vivid, overwhelmingly vivid. I saw her and you together — together in the depths of my heart. And there you have dwelt ever since with her."

At that moment the redoubtable Clem cluttered to the door.

"Missy, Jake sen' me to tell dat he pow'ful sorry he cawn't be ready half-hour yet. Suffin' wrong wid Selim's hoofs."

Clem spoke to Margaret, but his eyes were fastened on Peyton's face. Peyton's smile won most generous response, then Clem cluttered away noisily.

"Selim is most considerate," said Peyton. "Happily his hoofs will take an hour to repair. . . . Stay here to-day, and to-morrow I will go to the city with you."

"'Twere not safe for you to go without an armed escort. Where there is no danger for me, there is much for you. An important personage like you, dear, would be a worthy prize for some of my countrymen, were you to be found on the open road. Besides, Doctor Worthington is of the opinion that it is needful that you wait a few weeks more."

"We will leave your careful surgeon out of it, an it please you."

"Why, Arthur! What is it?"

"No matter; but a truce to all surgeons, useful as they are. Come! Let us go to the city together. You can be at Peggy Chew's. I can visit you there. We can join in a few of the festivities. André writes that a spectacle is planned when Howe leaves, which will be a delight to all lovers of novelties. Wait till to-morrow, and we will go together. I would love to show my future wife to all those grand dames of the city."

Margaret smiled.

"I much fear me that my gowns have become

somewhat old-fashioned from disuse. I would cut but a sorry figure among all the grand folk."

" You would be the sweetest — "

She lifted up a hand to stop him. " Nay, nay, love. . . . Tell me! Like you Captain André? "

" He is my friend. He is frank and genial. Why, to show his spirit, I remember well hearing him praise the virtues and the patriotism of that heroic youth, Nathan Hale."

" The spy! "

Her face changed.

" You like not spies, even if they be of your own political opinion? "

" It were unbecoming in me to say aught against that noble youth, Nathan Hale. His deed was needed, and he did it gladly — with sublime heroism. He deserves a lasting place in the memory of his countrymen. But — "

" But what? "

Margaret laughed nervously.

" Well, I should not wish to get very near a spy. I like not the feeling. There is no comfort in it."

" Oft is she nearer one than she imagines," was Peyton's swift thought. Aloud he said: " We will join in the Mischianza, if fortune favour, though it may be weeks yet ere the preparations are complete. Think you not that you can be there, that you would enjoy it? "

There was an anxious tone in his voice. He was catching at every hope of seeing her after the parting, which was to come on the morrow. His heart was not only heavy because of that; but he had a vague feeling of foreboding, of coming disaster. What was it? Why could he not shake off this strange depression? why not grasp the full sweetness of the present?

Margaret little dreamed of what was in his mind.

" The Mischianza they are planning? " she asked, briskly. " Oh! that must be of what Peggy spake when I saw her last. Enjoy it? Of a truth I would. Now, Arthur, think you not I love fine clothes and balls and routs? Never have you seen me in much beyond my riding costume and my safe-guard petticoat for rainy days. But I assure you I am most fond of beautiful things. I have many fine gowns in my wardrobe."

Peyton smiled at her tenderly. " We will go. We will go together. I will be your knight. André has writ me that he will be the knight of Mistress Chew. He is designing a marvellous costume for her. What will you wear, Margaret? Something to be a setting to your gold hair, to the dark blue of your eyes — to the — "

But she raised her hand again in gentle protest, then spoke with a trace of gravity.

" At first, when the war broke out and there was such lack of ammunition, not lead enough for the bullets, — well, I gave up wearing new gowns. I had no leaden statue of the King to melt up, such as they had at Bowling Green, New York, but I did all I could to save money to buy powder and bullets. I even took out the weights from the big clock in the hall."

He threw his arm around her eagerly. " You san-guinary, bloodthirsty, patriotic mortal! And be-think yourself what havoc those bullets made. Of a verity, some of them are sticking in the wood-work of your own home here! "

Her whole expression changed. She shrank into the depths of the arm-chair. Then covered her eyes. He spoke with quick contrition.

"I am sorry I said that. I should do all I can to make you forget these awful scenes of war."

"It seems as if I could never forget. No one can pass through such scenes as I saw, when the dead and wounded were gathered up from the garden here, and be the same again. The iron has entered into one's soul."

There was a pause; then she turned and looked earnestly at him.

"Oh! what a desolate place it was, and even now, Arthur! Look there! See the marks of the bullets in the side of the portico. And you know how the front doors had to be taken down, they were so riddled with musket-balls. And one big door fills the space now. Great pieces are torn off the house in different places. The statuary is all broken; poor Mercury's winged helmet gone! I know not when we can set about the repairs. Father gives almost all his money to the poor army. Only this morning he and I were consulting if we could spare six hundred pounds to give to General Washington when he comes — "

She broke off suddenly in confusion.

"When he comes? Where?" asked Peyton.

Margaret spoke with increasing confusion.

"Why, when he comes to Philadelphia, of course. Think you the British are always to stay there? We will have the city soon again. Never fear!"

She gently took his hand and placed it on the arm of the chair. But before she could rise, he had his arm around her again.

"What means this undue haste? Selim is not yet ready. You cannot go. I shall keep you here as long as I will.."

"Arthur, you are a tyrant! I had not thought it possible of you. Ah! but when I bethink myself, you are an Englishman, and therefore —"

"And therefore born to rule."

"But America wishes not to be ruled. She rebels."

"She is lovely in her rebellion, but very obstinate and wilful. Some means must be devised to keep her from wandering."

"No Englishman is wise or strong enough to keep an American from doing her duty."

But Captain Peyton soon proved to her that she was wrong. This Englishman seemed to have much power over this American maiden, and the minutes flew by unheeded. But at last, with a sigh of half content and half regret, she rose and said: "Arthur, I am sorry, but time waits not. It flies on and on. I must go, or Dinah will have naught to cook and brew."

Peyton put out his hand to her.

"Stay with me just a little longer. Why hasten, dear? I need you this morning. I am lonely when you go away."

"Dear!"

Her tone was soft; and, as he looked down deep into her eyes, he knew how his heart loved her.

"Ah, that trooper! Has he taken your letters?"

"No; you are my trusty messenger. I have writ but a few words to Bob, and one or two to Howe. The packet is there on the table. But will you but stay at home to-day, I send them by the trooper gladly. Stay! What care we for what Dinah cooks and brews? Let her gather simples by the wayside. Put her on Selim, and let her gallop afar, then the world will grow bright once more. And Clem, dear little Clem, will stand on his head all the day, he will be so happy."

"Poor Clem would have naught to eat."

"He would not need food while standing on his head. . . . Yes, Dinah is a tyrant. She is so self-centred, and, being one of the heavy ones of this earth, she considers herself of far too much importance. I like Chloe and Keziah and Clem much better. Ah, Clem is the boy for me. Of a surety. Clem has no liking for Dinah."

"You are mistaken, sir. Clem has a bigger appetite than even you. Poor Dinah!"

"Yes, poor misguided Dinah. But we will have to forgive the tyrant, and swear fresh allegiance."

Peyton's tone changed suddenly. He spoke vehemently.

"'Tis my place to go with you. I ought to go with you."

"Be good to me, and be careful a little longer. Ah, Arthur, be good to me! The wind outside is very chill. I hope that to-morrow we can ride out together."

"To-morrow!"

"Yes, 'tis sure to be milder."

"And we can ride to the city together. Wait then, Margaret."

For answer, she buried her face on his shoulder. Her plumed hat came in his way. He tossed it on a chair.

But the next moment she reached hastily for it.
There were footsteps coming nearer.

Peyton went over to the fire.

Then the door was opened softly, and Doctor
Worthington appeared.

After greeting him, Margaret asked if he knew
if Jake were almost ready.

"Yes, Mistress Murray. He begs your indulgence only a few moments now. I have your permission to ride with you?"

Doctor Worthington was most gracious and
considerate.

He looked at her with a smile on his lips, but
a deep, hungry longing in his heart.

"How can I wait with patience?" he would often
say to himself. "How can I endure this waiting?
Oh, to win her! to have her my own! My own!
My own!"

Margaret went to the table, and took up the
packet of letters. Doctor Worthington reached for
it, and took it from her hand.

"Your whip?"

"It is with Jake."

Peyton's face had become set and stern. Worthington glanced at him with a trace of anxiety.

"Your permission, Captain, that I take charge
of Mistress Murray. My way lies with hers, and
her father has pleasure that I, as well as Jake, escort
her. Sam is away with her brother. It were not
well for *you* to go out in this chill wind."

Peyton bowed. Margaret gave him a smile.

"There! You see I am right, Arthur."

He smiled in return. Neither of them perceived
the anxiety in Worthington's eyes, nor the look of

relief in them, as Tom appeared at the door. Tom bowed awkwardly.

"Massa Peyton, dat trooper would berry much like to confer wid you a few minnits befoh he rides away. He's in de dining-room, please, Massa Peyton, or will be soon's you's dare. Dinah done gone feed him up, an' he's ridin' furder 'long de post-road, now his hoss all right."

Tom glanced at Worthington furtively. The Doctor gave him an almost imperceptible gesture of dismissal. He went and held the door open for Captain Peyton to withdraw.

"Tom," said Margaret, hastily, "be at Captain Peyton's orders, should he chance to wish any attendance."

"Yes, missy. . . . I spec' Jake be 'roun' to de portico in berry few minnits."

With another furtive glance at Worthington, the servant followed Captain Peyton, and softly closed the door behind him.

Worthington, with the packet of letters held lightly in his hand, walked to the fire, and stood looking into it. Then he turned hastily. He and Margaret were alone together.

CHAPTER XXXVIII.

"Now is our time to strike the blow."

WHAT happened during his short absence, Captain Peyton had no means of knowing; but had he seen Margaret just before his reëntrance, he would scarce have recognised the tender-hearted girl he loved. She held letters in her hand, which she was wildly tearing into small pieces. She threw them upon the table, then began walking up and down, her eyes flashing, her hands tightly clenched. In every gesture, every expression of her face were evident mental unrest, painful agitation.

"I implore you not so to distress yourself," said Doctor Worthington, gently. "Be calm. What else was to be expected from an enemy like him? The temptation was too great."

Margaret's face grew drawn and white.

"Be calm — I implore you. . . . You will be ill."

She silenced him by an imperative gesture.

"I beg you will leave me."

"You ride not to the city?"

"The city?" Margaret spoke as if her mind were far off. "What are you saying? No! I ride not thither to-day. . . . I beg you will leave me, Doctor Worthington."

"Your pardon, but what of the General?"

She looked at him in bewilderment; then she understood.

"I must hasten to Valley Forge."

"Ah, that is wise! That is best. But 'tis needful that we ride in haste. Even then, I fear me, I fear me."

With trembling, uncertain fingers, she gathered the fragments of the letters she had been tearing. They formed a heap on the table.

"There he will find them. He will know. He will know why we have gone."

But Worthington sprang forward and swept his hand through the heap. Some fragments fell on the floor. He stamped on them brutally, then threw them into the fire.

"No! no! 'Tis best that he know naught till we return. He must not know we are to warn the General. He would escape. He must not know."

Margaret began walking up and down again, restlessly. It seemed as if in her agony of mind she had forgotten Worthington's presence. He spoke several times, but she paid no heed. Finally, he spoke vehemently.

"'Tis not likely he will come back here. That trooper has much to say to him; but should he chance to come, be calm, Mistress Murray, be calm. Let him not know that which you have learned. Be warned; be prudent. He *must* not know that you purpose to ride to warn the General. Be prudent, I beg of you. We must protect the cause of liberty against such treachery, — protect it, even if we break our own hearts. Come! Let us hasten. Remember the General's danger. Come!"

She shook her head. He grew impatient.

" Mistress Murray, of what are you thinking? You must come, or else I fear me our journey will be in vain. Be brave. Summon your strength. I will bring the horses. Come at once. Remember the General's danger. I insist upon going with you. You are not fit to go alone."

She turned from him wearily, as if too preoccupied even to resist. With an anxious face, he hurried to her and put out his hand, as if to support her. But with a strong effort she rallied and drew herself up with a sweet and pathetic dignity which was most appealing.

" I thank you, sir. I am quite well, quite well. Get the horses. I will be with you at once."

He turned away, and went hurriedly out the front door.

CHAPTER XXXIX.

"Think you not that many of these Tories play a dangerous game?"

THE trooper was not to be found in the dining-room, and Tom was bidden to go and seek him. It was a sorry sight that finally met Peyton's eyes, — a man dazed and heavy with drink, unfit to ride further, or even to return to the city, — unfit to understand aught that Peyton spoke, — anxious only to sleep — to sleep.

"Well that Margaret is to take my letters," thought Peyton, ruefully. "The escort would be here for me to-night, were she not entrusted with the word to defer the expedition to the morrow." Then he bade Tom guide the man to his own quarters, that he might happily be soon put in better plight.

A mug of warmed wine by the kitchen fire, that had been all. But it had been peculiar wine, and it had sent the hot blood surging and tossing through his excited brain. Then had come a mad desire for sleep, an overpowering haze, a benumbing of all the faculties of thought and of speech. Peyton's indignation would have been merged into surprise and pity had he known that, in obedience to Doctor Worthington, it had been Tom himself that had put the trooper in this plight. His condition would happily serve to keep Peyton engaged till Margaret should depart. There would be no chance of Margaret meeting Peyton again. But there had been a miscalculation. Peyton made shorter work of his interview with the trooper than Doctor Worthington had planned, and Margaret, alas! did not start as quickly as the clever Doctor felt sure she would.

Margaret must be surely gone! No need to hasten back to catch one more merry, tender glance from her dear eyes. Yes, he had heard the horses dash out from the stables, and their hoofs had been stamping on the gravel in front of the portico. But he would go back into the hall, and look out the front window, that, perchance, he might catch sight of her riding away. To his surprise, he saw the horses there, and Jake doing his best to restrain the fiery, impatient Selim. Clem held Tempest. Yes, and there was Doctor Worthington, with his horse's bridle in his hand.

Peyton hastened to the door leading to the little room at the end of the hall, and opened it softly. Yes, she was there by the window. There came glad welcome into his face.

" What joy to see you again! " he exclaimed, fervently. " I had thought you gone. And now I am to have one more farewell before you start."

But she did not turn to greet him. What was the meaning of this strange look on her face? What change had come over her?

As he drew nearer, she moved away, and yet there was a fixed look in her eyes, as if she did not see him. He paused in bewilderment, then started towards her again. As he reached her side, she shrank back from him.

"Come not near me," she whispered, in a harsh, strained tone. "I cannot bear it!"

"Margaret! love! you are ill."

His tone was tender, appealing, — but he made no further move nearer her.

"My love! what has happened?"

She pointed to the fragments of paper on table and floor.

"A mischance has happened to your packet, Captain Peyton."

But he had eyes for naught but her.

"My letters? It matters not, dear."

He stood and looked at her in increasing wonder.

"Tell me, love! Tell me what it is."

Margaret resumed her restless pacing up and down.

"Oh, I cannot bear it! I cannot bear it!" she moaned.

"What is it, love? What is it?"

Her only answer was a trembling gesture towards the table.

Slowly, thoughtfully, he went to it, and took up several of the pieces of paper upon it. He stooped and caught a few of the fluttering fragments on the floor.

"My own letter!" he exclaimed. "My own letter in shreds! Torn, soiled, the edges burned. Margaret, who has done this? Who would take the liberty of tearing or burning my own letter? Tell me the meaning of all this."

"Think you, you could write thus, and *I know it,* and *not* destroy the letter?"

"But, Margaret, I would have told you; but I wished to keep the mischief from you as long as

possible. I wished not to have this last day together spoiled by any shadow of evil. The grief
of parting will come soon enough, love."

Margaret was now by the front window, looking
out with unseeing eyes. Her hands kept clasping
and unclasping, as if her suffering were beyond
control. When he made an effort to grasp her
hands, she shook him off.

"Come not near me!" she repeated, huskily.
Then she turned fiercely upon him. "Why could
you not let me dream my dream? Why awaken me
with such bitter cruelty? Oh, I cannot, cannot
bear it!"

"Margaret, love! I understand not your meaning."

There came terrible anger in her voice and look.

"You tell me that you understand not. Oh!
why deceive me so?"

"Deceive you, Margaret? Deceive *you, you?*
There was no deception, no thought of that, love.
Why, I told your father."

"My father!" The scorn in her face made his
heart almost stop beating.

She went to the fire, then almost immediately
back to the window. In his astonishment and surprise, he could find thought of naught to say but
the repeated entreaty, "Tell me, love, tell me!"

"Add not falsehood to your other sins, Captain
Peyton. I cannot bear much more."

He drew himself up with a proud, noble dignity,
which, had she been not blinded by suffering and
passion, would have won her admiration.

"Falsehood?" His voice was husky.

"Yes; is it not enough to betray the house that

has sheltered you; to strike a blow in the dark at the girl who once thought she loved you? It is the basest treachery."

Her scorn was as blows on his ragged nerves.

"Yes! You could exalt honour. You could say you had the same opinion as I of a man who worms himself into the confidence of friends who trust him, who accepts their hospitality, and then betrays them. You could praise the great General, and say you could not bear to draw your sword against him. No! you would not dare, you coward! But you strike a blow at his back, — a mean, cowardly, contemptible blow. And then you have the audacity to tell me you understand not what I mean. Oh! there are no words to describe such contemptible conduct as yours. No words!"

Peyton attempted to speak, but she silenced him with a scornful gesture. Then she continued, vehemently: "You at least might have left the house whose hospitality has been showered upon you."

"I was going on the morrow. My cousin has come from England, and wishes me in the city. Howe had intention to send me an escort to-night. I hoped to keep the cruel tidings from you as long as possible. But that is why I felt so your being gone from me the entire day. Our last day together."

Margaret's face darkened.

"Yes! You struck your blow, and then were going to flee, ere your treachery was discovered. But I thank God I found it out in time!"

Peyton started violently.

"Margaret, you are beside yourself. I cannot understand the meaning of your strange and cruel words; but I tell you, on my word of honour, I have never by word or deed betrayed your trust."

" Your honour! "

" Yes, that at least is left me, since I have lost your love."

" You have not lost what you never had, Captain Peyton. I never loved you, Captain Peyton. I never loved you."

He looked at her a moment in pained surprise. Then he sank into a chair, and covered his eyes with his hand.

" O Margaret, were all your loving words false? O Margaret, were you jesting with me? You — whom I thought the truest, the loveliest woman in all the world! "

" No! I was not jesting. I would not jest of aught so sacred as love. But I was deceived. I fancied I loved you, but how mistaken I was! how fearfully mistaken! "

The scorn died out of her face and it grew very sad, and the sweet lips quivered. She leaned against the side of the window. Peyton started up. He spoke with authority and vehemence.

" It is due to me that I, at least, be told what has happened."

" You wish me to put in words your treachery? Ask your own heart. It will answer you."

Peyton's voice grew stern.

" I assure you, Mistress Murray, I cannot understand what treachery you mean. I see you believe me not. Were you a man, my sword would answer you for this mistrust. Take then, the word of an honest soldier and an English gentleman."

Margaret's face softened. She leaned against the

back of a chair. Her voice trembled so that he could scarce hear her.

" Without the proof of my own eyes, I would never have believed this of you. I would have upheld your honour and your loyalty against the whole world. Not even my own father could have convinced me. I would have believed you in the midst of any calumny. No one, not even your King, or your father, could have made me lose my faith in you. Indeed, you know not what influences against you I have been fighting all these weeks. But now — but now — "

Sobs choked her.

" Where is Worthington? Where is your brother? " exclaimed Peyton, wildly. " Some great mistake has happened. I must see Worthington. He must help me. He must. Where is your brother? "

All at once she gathered herself together and started for the door.

" It were well to avoid meeting my brother, Captain Peyton; but should you see my father before you leave this house, inform him that I have ridden forth. But it will be very late ere I return, for I ride to Valley Forge."

She got to the door. But he intercepted her.

" I demand an answer. I will not be denied an answer. It is my right. I demand you to tell me the meaning of your words before you go."

He seized her hands. Sudden passion swept over her.

" You dare to stop me! You fear my going to Valley Forge? You fear I would betray you? You would stop me from going? Stop me if you dare! "

He spoke sternly, almost roughly.

"I demand the meaning of your words. I *will* know."

She struggled in his grasp.

"You coward! You *are* a brave soldier to use your strength against a woman."

With a cry of pain, he let go her hands, and threw himself at her feet. But she pushed him away impetuously. He cried after her, but she paid no heed. She hastened out the big front door, which closed behind her with a heavy clang. Then could be heard horses' hoofs on the gravel road outside. He went back to the table, and sank in a chair, and buried his face in his hands.

CHAPTER XL.

"Why could you not let me dream my dream? Why awaken me so cruelly?"

OH, that wild ride! Would Margaret ever forget it? For they chose not the easiest route: down the Germantown Road to the Market Square, then along School House Lane to the Ridge Road, where School House Lane ended, then across Wissahickon Creek, and up the Ridge Road a little way to the point nearest the river, where a narrow lane ran down to the ferry. They thought to save time by cutting across directly to the Swedes Ford; and thus their course was on crooked, rough paths, through woods and across fields, over stones and hillocks, through holes and mud. Worthington oft rode ahead, and oft Margaret's horse and that of Jake galloped neck to neck. There was a delay at the ford, for the river was swelled by the late melting of the heavy snow of the severe winter. Only once did Margaret speak, and that was to say:

"Can we but get there before he starts!"

And Worthington made reply:

"I fear me he is already on the way. Our late discovery of the mischief and your delay in setting out may work sad havoc with your wish."

In his secret heart, Worthington knew the use-

lessness of her errand. He felt sure that the General
and his troop had reached the ferry near School
House Lane ere he and Margaret had left Cliveden.
In the tavern at the "cross-roads," there would be
concealed a large force of the enemy. The General
was even now on his way to Philadelphia, captured
by the British, — a prisoner at last!

But it was Worthington's wish that at this critical
time Margaret should be away from home; besides,
he was too wise to oppose her in her present mood.
Then it was his purpose to be of comfort to her,
to soothe her, to make himself a stay and a support
to her in her desperate grief.

As they approached the ford, Worthington called
Margaret's attention to the earthworks the Americans had thrown up to keep the British from getting across Swedes Ford. She looked where he
pointed; but she paid little heed to his words.

Then when they began to descend the long hill
that sloped northwards, and he found breath again
to speak, he talked of the picturesqueness of the
country through which they were speeding, and of
the beauty of the valley, which would soon be revealed to them.

"You have probably heard how William Penn,
when he had been exploring the valley creek, lost
his way on the hill to the south? He was in despair,
hungry and tired. When a man is hungry and tired,
he is apt to be in despair. He named that hill Mount
Misery. But when he came to the mountain opposite, and found that he knew where he was, his mood
changed. Despair was gone. He became happy,
and so he called the mountain Mount Joy.

"Mount Joy is beautiful now in the sunlight.

See how beautiful it is, Mistress Murray. We shall soon be near the outer fortifications of the camp. Brave men, brave patriots, how hard they worked to build this city of huts, this city formed of the demolished forests! . . . But could a better place be chosen for such a camp? How well guarded is the little valley by these glorious hills that shut it in. And you will enjoy looking at the waters of the creek as they sparkle in the sunshine; and with the dark shadows in them from the hills."

Doctor Worthington's eloquence cost him some effort. 'Twas not his habit to sentimentalise over shadows and hills and the beauty of the sunlight upon them. But ere they reached the outer posts of the camp, he saw that all his efforts were unavailing. Margaret paid him no heed. She was distraught, absorbed, — his tender solicitude and care made no impression. She did not even reply to him when he ventured to speak. So, in gloomy silence, they entered the city of huts, and galloped up to the house of the Quaker, Isaac Potts, where Washington had his headquarters.

It was Alexander Hamilton himself who met them at the door. His face lit up with pleasure and surprise.

"Mistress Murray! Of a truth, you are welcome."

She went directly into the house, but could scarcely speak for trembling.

"Tell me, has General Washington started for Germantown? He must not go. There is danger, — an ambush, a surprise."

The room they had entered was small, and showed poverty in all its furnishings. Two narrow-paned windows in front, between them a plain settee. A big clock, that no longer ticked out the seconds, stood in the left corner. The weights had long ago been taken to make bullets, and they had not been replaced. Two rough chairs were in the centre of the room near a table, littered, as usual, with papers and quills and ink-wells. The seat beneath the left window was also filled with papers. A musket leaned against the right wall near the stove; a sword lay on the floor near the window-seat. That was all. The place was silent and deserted. It looked forlorn and dreary to Margaret's tired eyes.

Worthington threw his hat on a chair, then gently took Margaret's whip from her stiffened fingers. He turned to Hamilton.

" Mistress Murray is much fatigued from her furious ride hither. I could not persuade her 'twould be useless."

" What mean you, sir? " Hamilton asked, sharply. " Wherefore useless? "

" His Excellency would have needed to have left here long before Mistress Murray started from home. As I understand her, he was to have been at Cliveden now."

" His Excellency is safe here," said Hamilton, as he placed Margaret in a chair by the table. " He is in the log-cabin at the rear. He will be back here presently."

Worthington walked quickly to a window and looked out. He had difficulty in concealing his surprise.

" My dear Mistress Murray," said Hamilton, gently, " what has happened? "

'Twas plain to see that Margaret was deeply

moved. She looked up into his sincere, searching eyes. Her face flushed.

" We have had a guest at our home since that awful battle."

" Yes, mistress, I know."

She continued in snatches.

" We had thought — we had thought it quite safe for you to visit my father, else we should have sent word, according to General Washington's request. But this morning, I was starting for the city — "

She broke off suddenly and turned away. And in the narrow doorway stood Washington.

" Margaret, Margaret Murray," he said.

His calm face had a soft and tender look upon it. He came and laid his hand gently on her shoulder. The months since she had seen him seemed bridged over. It was as if it were but yesterday that she had parted from him. And yet those weary months at Valley Forge had left their impress on that noble face.

" There has been treachery in our house," said Margaret, faintly. " 'Tis scarce safe for you to visit us. I came to warn you and prevent your going."

Washington and Hamilton exchanged significant glances. Then Washington put Worthington's hat on the floor, and drew up the chair nearer Margaret.

CHAPTER XLI.

"Oh! It is worse even than I thought."

AFTER she had, in a measure, conquered her emotion, she told her story.

"Oft have I been forced to go to the city to provide for my household. We were stripped of everything early in the winter by the foraging parties — "

"Yes," said Hamilton, "and we know of all your generous gifts to our camp."

Washington raised his hand.

"Continue, dear lady."

"I ride to the markets—sometimes to my friends, the family of Benjamin Chew, a loyalist, as you know. Oft have I carried letters thither, which our guest, Captain Peyton, has written to friends. His friends find the letters there. And twice have I brought back answers. This morning 'twas my purpose to go to the city in haste, that I might be back in time to greet you; but I bade our guest prepare his packet as usual."

She paused a moment to steady her voice, and then continued:

"I was about to depart, but was standing by the fire, talking to Doctor Worthington, who had something interesting to tell me of an Assembly at the City Tavern the previous evening. He had walked through the minuet with one of my friends, and she had sent me messages which he wished to deliver ere they slipped remembrance. He was holding Captain Peyton's packet in his hand as he talked with me. He held it lightly, and grew animated in his talk, when, by a mischance, the packet fell from his hand into the hot ashes on the hearth. He sprang to rescue it from the flames, and succeeded in a measure; but an outer paper, which Captain Peyton had used to wrap around the other letters, had taken fire, and, after Doctor Worthington had stamped out the flames, its contents were exposed to view. I looked at it sharply to see if aught could be done to make its condition more favourable, without troubling Captain Peyton to direct another wrapper, when I saw suddenly something therein written which was terrible."

She paused, unable to proceed. An orderly appeared at the door and motioned to Hamilton. Hamilton went out with him. Doctor Worthington came and stood where he could watch Margaret. She struggled a moment for composure, then continued:

"The few words my eyes involuntarily caught showed to both Doctor Worthington and myself the necessity of examining the whole letter. The outer paper had been addressed to Lieutenant Shipton; but there was a letter inside addressed to Sir William Howe. It informed him that naught had occurred to prevent your visit to-night, and that the plans for your capture, arranged in a previous letter, which had been taken by post-horse to Philadelphia three or four days before, could be safely carried out. You would arrive at a certain place at a certain time. A large troop of British could be sent to surprise your guard, and take you in triumph to Philadelphia. . . . I had scant time to reach here. I feared me you would have already started."

" Let me see the letter," said Washington, sternly.

" No! no! It burned and stung me. I tore it into small shreds. I could not keep it. No! no!"

She covered her eyes with her hands. Before her mental vision there came Peyton's face, as it looked when he had picked up the fragments of that torn letter.

Washington began slowly pacing up and down. Outside could be heard the impatient stamping of Selim's hoofs, and Jake's soft voice, as he soothed him. Then Jake could be heard taking the horses to the rear. Not far away Baron Steuben was drilling troops, and his loud, peremptory voice came to them every now and then, as it was raised to give forth a good, round foreign oath. In the distance were bugle-calls, roll of drums. As in a dream, Margaret listened to Washington's next words.

" This explains a hurried word from your brother at early morn. He rode into camp post-haste, saying our plans were known in Philadelphia, and that a large force of British troops had intention to intercept us at the tavern near where School House Lane strikes the Ridge Road, just beyond where the Wissahickon flows into the Schuylkill."

Margaret started from her chair. Her eyes were fixed in astonishment on Washington's face.

" My brother! How knew he aught of this?"

" He stopped not to explain, but immediately galloped off. . . . Had I not received his timely warning, we would have been at the cross-roads even before you started from home."

Well was it for Doctor Worthington that the General could not see into his heart, see the surprise and disappointment there. But the Doctor successfully concealed his emotions, and whispered softly to Margaret: "Of a truth, that is what I told you."

Washington resumed gravely: "Your communication is no surprise to me. I have been long aware that injury was being done by this guest of yours. The knowledge came by degrees. Letters were seized which he wrote to his friend, one in cipher. Some were to Captain André. You yourself wrote some of them. They were all signed. Then several letters were seized. They were unsigned, but were in the same handwriting. I need not weary you with explanations. But these letters involve affairs of great moment. There was a letter to Lord George Germain, another to Lord Carlisle, two or more to William Pitt. These were signed and seem harmless. 'Tis the unsigned letters that have shown the mischief. Everything seems to point to The Chew House, from which all the plotting comes. It is possible that Captain Peyton may employ a tool. Shut in as he has been, it seems scarce possible that he could work unaided. Has he had visitors at your home of late, who might bring to him intelligence of our movements?"

"Oh! it is worse even than I thought," said Margaret, under her breath. Worthington caught her words. A momentary gleam of satisfaction came into his eyes, but neither Margaret nor the General were concerned with him just now.

"Only this morning I issued orders for the arrest of this man, if he can be found outside of the British lines."

"What man?" asked Margaret, wildly.

"This Captain Peyton. He was desperately wounded at the battle of Germantown, for a long time laid aside from active service. He has been allowed to remain undisturbed, as is right and fitting. But when a man, in his retirement and illness, deliberately plots and seeks to do us deadly injury, then forbearance is at an end, and according to all the laws of war we have a right to protect ourselves."

Margaret shuddered. Had the General but known how she was suffering, he might have forborne, but he recked not of it.

"If the court martial happily have opportunity to try him, it will fare ill with him, Mistress Murray. He has been your guest, else I would not weary you with this detail. He has done many other treacherous things. We have reason to suppose that he was the cause of the danger to the Marquis de Lafayette the other day, of which you have perchance heard. The Marquis escaped, but if the designs of that spy had not been discovered, our friend were now a prisoner, and we were so much the weaker for the loss of twenty-one hundred chosen men."

Margaret remembered what Rodney Bingham had told her of the importance of the work that had been entrusted to the Marquis. Then those secret plans had been discovered! Mischief had indeed been wrought. But how could Captain Peyton have found out about the matter? Who had visited him?

What tool could he have employed? Ah, those messengers who had brought his letters! They had seemed to her so harmless.

" And if this — this — this spy be found guilty in the court martial? " asked Margaret, in a stifled voice.

And now Worthington ventured to speak. His tone was gentle, deprecating.

" My dear Mistress Murray, the fate of spies is soon determined. What was done with that noble youth, Nathan Hale? "

Margaret's emotion mastered her. She buried her face on the table and sobbed. Washington leaned over her and said, gently:

" My dear child, I beg you will not so distress yourself."

Washington turned towards Hamilton, who appeared at the door. They spoke a moment together, then the General went out hastily. The door closed behind him.

Hamilton went to the windows and began to close them. Worthington sprang to his aid. It had been gradually growing very dark outside. Thunder was muttering in the distance. Flashes of lightning lit up the shrubbery and trees.

" I cannot, cannot let him die! " moaned Margaret to herself. " I must hasten back to warn him. He would not have left yet. He will be there. They will seize him! I must tell him to flee. And then — how strange it is that I cannot conquer this love. In spite of all that he has done, I love him. Oh! how my heart aches with this love for him! And yet, I told him I never loved him. I must save him. Oh, how I love him! I must go at once. Whatever

I may think of his treachery, I cannot bear that any
one else should do him harm. I must tell him to
flee, and then we will never see each other again!"

Margaret hastily tossed her hair back, and rose.
Her face was very sad and worn, but she had regained composure. She must act now, — act with
energy and promptness. In the dreary future there
would be enough time to give heed to grief.

She turned to Hamilton.

"Mr. Hamilton, may I trouble you to send for
my servant? I must return to my father."

Why did she ignore Worthington? Had she forgotten his presence? But he was not a man to be
ignored.

"We are to have a big storm," he said, coming
to her side. "'Tis scarce wise to brook it. 'Twere
best that I bid Jake bestow the horses."

"I must return to my father," she repeated,
firmly.

"Mistress, your pardon, but bethink yourself of
the roads, of the horses, frightened perchance because of the storm. Your father, Margaret, would
wish that I took better care of you than to encourage
you to venture."

Margaret! He had never before presumed to
address her thus. He whispered the name linger-
ingly, passionately.

But she was too preoccupied to pay much heed
to his speech.

Her desperate wish was to get away from this
place, away from him, from Hamilton, even from
Washington. She wished to be alone. She wished
to ride, ride, ride, fast and furiously, to ride home

and be with her father. He would understand! He
would suffer with her. He would help!

"'Tis not as if there were need to risk aught in
such a storm," the soft, insinuating voice continued.
"Your father will thank us for our caution."

But Margaret shook her head.

"I have already trespassed here too long. I will
trouble you to summon my servant."

Worthington smiled at Hamilton.

"'Tis plain to see that Mistress Murray has no
thought of the claim you have upon her testimony
and upon mine."

She looked at Hamilton in bewilderment, as if
asking the meaning of Doctor Worthington's words.
Hamilton's face flushed.

"I had not thought you wished to depart so soon,
Mistress Murray," he said.

And as she still questioned him with her eyes,
he added: "I must request you to wait till his Excellency comes back."

"He cannot permit you to go," explained Worthington. "That rests with his Excellency."

Margaret drew herself up haughtily.

"Will you be kind enough to inform me why?
I fear not this approaching storm."

Hamilton pointed to papers on the table. His
face flushed hotly. He wished not to say what he
had to say.

"As you insist, Mistress Murray, it is my painful
duty to tell you that these letters show us that you
are in a measure implicated in these affairs. You
have written letters for Captain Peyton. You have
carried them into Philadelphia."

Margaret stood motionless and looked at him in

amazement. Her eyes were wide open, her look one
of consternation, as he went on:

"We have here a letter written by you to Sir
Robert Shipton. It is at the captain's dictation, and
in it are certain ciphers. Is not this your handwriting?"

He took a paper from the table and held it out
to her. She did not seem to see it.

"Be kind enough to tell me if you wrote this,
Mistress Murray?"

She took the letter, and held it a moment, not
looking at it. Then she drew her hand wearily
across her eyes.

"It is worse than I could even think," she said
to herself. "He not only deceived me, but he made
me his tool. He hesitated not to involve me! Oh,
it is not to be forgiven! And yet I cannot have
him die. I must get back. I must warn him. I
will show him the secret panel."

Aloud she said, after making desperate effort to
fix her attention upon the paper: "Yes, yes, I
wrote that. I remember it well. It was to his
dictation ere he learned to write with his left hand."

"Has he lost his right?"

"No, it is fast recovering."

"If he is captured!" said Margaret, wildly, to
herself.

"Remember you how he dictated the cipher?"
asked Worthington, drawing near.

"He said he and his friend had a cipher they
had used for amusement while Lieutenant Shipton
was at Eton."

"A clever ruse, Mistress Murray," said Worthington, with a trace of sarcasm.

" Could you possibly be deceived? "

The thunder was heard louder. The room grew still darker. Hamilton tossed the table into, if possible, greater disorder, and then went over to the window-seat. Lifting the papers lying on the cushion, a cavity beneath might have been seen, in which the General kept his valuable documents. Hamilton took care that Doctor Worthington did not notice this secret hiding-place. He quickly took a paper from it, then replaced the cushion.

" Here is a letter written to Sir William Howe. Naught of importance, but is it in your writing? "

Margaret turned and took the paper from his hand, and bent down to examine it in the dim light.

" Yes, Mr. Hamilton."

" Then here is a letter in regard to that infamous proposal of the Tories of Philadelphia, that General Washington be offered a large sum as the price of his fidelity. You have heard of Mistress Elizabeth Ferguson's part in that proposal. You have heard also how General Washington answered the insult? General Reed told Elizabeth Ferguson that not *all* the money of *all* the Kings of England could induce Washington to swear allegiance to King George, and be unfaithful to his trust. . . . Well, this letter, telling Captain Peyton of this offer of the Tories, is evidently written to Captain Peyton by one of his friends in Philadelphia. His reply stands here. I confess it shows good sense, and does him credit. . . . But the other letters are the ones significant and dangerous. He is evidently a man high in favour with men in England. It looks as if he were a secret agent of the British government, sent out here to spy and work mischief, and corrupt the unwary. But, Mistress Murray, permit me to ask if you know Captain Peyton's handwriting without mistake?"

"Yes," she answered faintly.

Hamilton lit the candles on the table. Their light gleamed fitfully on Margaret's agitated face.

"Then tell me if this is his?"

She looked intently at the paper.

"Yes," she answered, faintly.

"Are you sure?"

"Yes, Mr. Hamilton."

"Then there is no doubt of his guilt. May he be caught before he can do any more mischief."

"And if he is caught?"

"Mistress Murray, his letters here and your own words condemn him."

Margaret clutched a chair.

"O God! my own words!" . . .

"But you would wait. . . . You would let him see his friend, and Captain André, and his cousin, Lord Carlisle, who has but arrived from England to confer with Congress in regard to the peace proposals. Of a truth, you would not forbid their meeting. You would wait, you would wait."

Margaret's voice was hoarse and strained.

Worthington stepped nearer. He showed excitement.

"Did the British wait when they caught Nathan Hale?" he cried. "Did Howe let him see his father or his sister? Even his letters to them were destroyed! He was denied a Bible and the aid of a clergyman. Mistress Murray, expect you that General Washington is to be the one to show all the magnanimity and mercy?"

Hamilton's eyes flashed with indignation. His rich, musical voice grew stern and cold.

"Doctor Worthington, I fear me that you forget — "

"Damme, Hamilton," Worthington interrupted, hastily, "this tale that you and his Excellency tell of this spy's dastardly work stirs my gall. Your pardon, that in my zeal for the good of our cause I overstep the bounds of self-control. But bethink yourself, Hamilton, what had happened had his designs not failed."

Worthington strode to the window and looked out moodily.

Margaret mastered her emotion, and reached for her whip.

"Mr. Hamilton, I must return to my father."

"Your pardon; but I have no power to let you go."

"I consider it unnecessary to deny your charge, Mr. Hamilton. Nor will I sue for permission to go. Have the goodness to order my horses."

Hamilton's wonderful eyes softened.

"My dear Mistress Murray, you understand me not fully. There is no charge against *you*."

Margaret's hauteur changed to passionate indignation.

"General Washington would trust me. Oh, this is unbearable!"

The flush on Hamilton's face deepened.

"Mistress Murray, it would not pleasure us to have you remain against your will. Your pardon. I had no thought of wounding you. I will speak with his Excellency. I will be but a moment."

As Hamilton opened the door, a flash of lightning lit up the passageway beyond. Then came loud peals of thunder.

" I like not to have you ride across country in such a storm," said Worthington, coming over to Margaret. " Stay here in safety, I pray you. I am thinking but of you." His manner grew tender and caressing.

She turned away impatiently. " I beg you to leave me, Doctor Worthington."

" Leave you, Margaret? No! I am here but to protect you. Your lover has wronged you, deceived you, showed himself utterly unworthy of your esteem. My heart is torn with compassion for you. Knew you only how much I — "

But Margaret hastily interrupted him:

" Jake and I have had many a desperate ride together. He is trusty."

" It will come out in the court martial that you can give valuable testimony. It might cause comment were it known that you had been here and had been allowed to return home ere any investigation had been made. It were far better to remain. We must protect the cause of liberty against such treachery."

Margaret kept her eyes fixed on the door.

" Oh, there seems to be no doubt of his capture! Oh, if I may but get there in time to warn him!" she kept repeating to herself.

" 'Tis scarce possible that you would have to remain long. The troopers sent by Washington will soon be back from Cliveden. Captain Peyton will be unwarned. He would not know that his treachery had been discovered. We left, you know, while he was busied with that interview with Howe's messenger. The troopers will hurry back. Methinks we need not wait long. Have patience, Mistress Murray. We must all make sacrifice of personal preferences, that the cause of liberty may not be hindered."

Doctor Worthington's further words, welcome or unwelcome as they might chance to be, were cut short by the reëntrance of the General and of Alexander Hamilton.

CHAPTER XLII.

"How slowly the time goes when the heart is on fire with grief and with pain. But when one is happy — then the minutes fly. Their wings are gold. The clock never strikes."

"YOU understand it not fully, dear Margaret," the General said, as he came in. "One object of my visit to your father was in regard to those letters which have been known to come from your home. It may be best for you to remain here a short time. My wife and Mistress Knox are here. You will be made comfortable, and we are to have a big storm. It will be not wise to brook it, Margaret."

Margaret showed increasing agitation, but the calm voice continued:

"If the troopers who have started for The Chew House find Captain Peyton there, then they will return at once with him. 'Twould not take long for you to verify the assertions in regard to these incriminating letters. If you are willing to stay — "

Margaret gave a suppressed cry, and flung herself at the General's feet. "O sir, let me go to my father. Let me go. I must. I told him not I was coming here. He will be ill from anxiety. O General Washington, grant my wish. Let me go. I will return. I will return this very night. Only let me once see my father. I give you my

356

oath I will come back. You told me once you
trusted me as your daughter. I promise to return.
You may then do with me what you will. . . . O
General Washington, that I should have to plead
thus with you!"

Washington raised her gently. "My dear child,
be calm. Have it as you will. I had no thought
of imposing burdens on you. Return home. But
wait — my wife longs to see you but a moment.
Come with me."

They went out together.

Hamilton began to arrange the papers on the
table. Then he spoke.

"We were glad had we her testimony. 'Twould
save time."

"But you know how perfectly she has vouched
for Peyton's handwriting," answered Worthington,
eagerly. "Naught can contradict that."

"No. It is enough."

"Were it better that you have written testimony
to show to the other members of the court martial?"

Hamilton looked thoughtful.

"It might be well."

"Or I could give you my written testimony as
to Mistress Murray's words."

"We will get the General's opinion of this when
he and Mistress Murray come back."

"There seems to be little doubt of Captain Peyton's capture."

"No. The troopers must have reached The Chew
House soon after the time you left. You think he
had no warning?"

"He could not have. They may already have
brought him to the outer posts. You will work

quickly, sir, I know. This Englishman is wily.
Forget not how the British treated Nathan Hale."

Hamilton's face grew grave and stern. "'Tis
no need, Worthington, to remind me of that. I
loved Hale. He was my friend."

"This man's rank ought to make no difference
in the speed of his fate from that of a common spy
caught in a treacherous act and hanged in the morning."

"No, it ought not," said Hamilton, thoughtfully.

"I fear me, should you delay, he might slip
through your fingers. He has powerful friends."

"No friends, however powerful, ought to weigh
against what is just and right. The case might
furnish a precedent, and therefore his Excellency
would wish to do his duty, come what will."

"Yes, yes, and the British ought to look for
naught but a speedy termination to this case in
accordance with the precedent they themselves furnished."

"They could not criticise us when they think
of the haste with which they dealt with Nathan
Hale."

"And their refusal to let him communicate with
his friends."

"Has Mistress Murray shown special interest
in this guest? Methinks she is deeply moved by
his danger and his treachery."

Worthington stroked his chin.

"A mere passing fancy, a mere passing fancy.
She will soon get over it. Such fancies last not
when respect and trust once die. Mistress Murray

is not one to cherish the memory of a man for whom she has lost respect."

And then they fell to talking of other matters; for of late Hamilton's distrust of this popular physician had sensibly diminished. In truth, his services to the patriot cause had been in words rather than in tangible deeds; though indeed he had once succeeded in diverting to the patriot camp certain provisions which it was generally supposed had been destined for the British; sometimes he had brought news from the city — not of much practical worth, but his service indicated his wish to be of use; in fact, he had in many instances shown himself to be the friend of liberty, rather than what he in good truth was, — one of her most relentless, unscrupulous enemies.

To Alexander Hamilton's credit be it recorded that no secrets were revealed in this talk with Doctor Worthington — nothing of value was learned with which to regale the ears of Howe. Alexander Hamilton trusted few men. He made few mistakes. And he never betrayed the confidence of his General.

The thunder kept increasing, the lightning became more frequent and dazzling. Then came a sudden sound of rain.

" Egad! how dark it is," said Worthington, going to the window and peering out impatiently. " The roads were devilish before. This will not improve them. Women are capricious creatures. 'Tis against reason that Mistress Murray should wish to return home."

He stopped and listened intently.

" Hark! what is that? Hoofs, as I live."

Hamilton rushed to the window and threw it open.

" 'Tis Mistress Murray riding full gallop."

" Damnation! Bid her wait till I can join her."

He made a dash for his hat and cloak, rushed to the door, and came face to face with Jake. He started back in astonishment.

" Zounds, man, where is your mistress? "

" De missy done gone back home on de bes' hoss. De General sen' orderly wid her. I follow her soon."

Worthington pushed Jake rudely aside, and flung himself out into the storm.

CHAPTER XLIII.

"Mistress Murray, his letters here and your own words condemn him."

THE weary day wore on. Henry was still absent, the hour came and passed that Margaret should have returned. Finally the violence of the storm abated; but a steady rain set in. The darkness deepened. Night came, — without cheer, and cold.

Chloe piled the logs high, but neither Mr. Murray nor Annette took comfort. A restlessness and vague dread took possession of them. They sat together or walked about, sometimes speaking, more often silent and thoughtful.

"If the rain came ere she finished marketing she surely would ride to the Chews and tarry over night," said Mr. Murray once, as Annette paused by the spinning-wheel, and gave it a nervous whirl.

"If she had but ridden Prince instead of Selim! Selim never could abide thunder and lightning," was the somewhat querulous answer.

"In truth, the General will not come. I feel he will not, though storm and wind will not keep him."

Annette came and shivered before the fire.

"The poor Captain will be drenched unless happily

he has reached the city ere the rain fell in such torrents."

Mr. Murray sighed.

"I liked not to have him go in such sorrow. I urged him to wait till Henry's return. But words availed not. He seemed most anxious to find Doctor Worthington."

"Why should he wish to see him? And knew he not that Doctor Worthington rode to Philadelphia with Margaret? He must have known. Why, father, I saw them mount and ride away together. Of a truth, Captain Peyton must have seen."

Mr. Murray sighed again. "I know not. But I came through the hall about the half-hour after her departure, and found him by the table, his face hidden in his hands. In a broken, choked voice he told me he would leave so soon as Brown Bess could be saddled. He refused explanation beyond the simple word that he and Margaret had decided 'twere best he go to-day, rather than on the morrow. Why, I know not. But he spoke of Worthington in a strange manner. It has set me to thinking, Annette. When I heard him depart on Brown Bess, the way he took was not to the city. He said he would go in search of Worthington."

"Then he knew not that Doctor Worthington rode with Margaret."

An hour later, the two took up their conversation where they had left it. Mr. Murray spoke again of Doctor Worthington; and Annette, with a wise shake of her pretty head, made answer:

"Ah! the Captain has guessed his secret."

"What secret?"

Annette took up a strand of flax.

" His love for Margaret."

Charles Murray made an impatient gesture.

" Why, father! Had you but seen, you would have known that the Doctor is consumed with jealousy."

" Humph ! "

Annette laughed.

" Hast never heard of the green-eyed monster? Well, the monster has attacked the Doctor in a virulent form, and he has no physic in his saddle-bags which can cure him. He loves Margaret, or thinks he does. 'Tis all the same thing. Margaret thinks she loves Captain Peyton, but rest assured the handsome Doctor hopes to secure her some day."

" Margaret's heart is not a weather-vane, changing at every chance wind."

" Indeed, not. Margaret loves once, and loves not twice. That I know; but saw you ever a man who was not full of vanity? The vanity sticks out all over him, shines in his eyes, shows in his voice. Physicians are especially afflicted. Doctor Worthington has not lost hope."

Annette paused; then continued, thoughtfully:

" Could you but have seen his face this morning when he told me 'twas his purpose to escort Margaret to the city. I smiled, and said, ' Take good care of Margaret, Doctor Worthington. Her lover cannot escort her, forsooth.' He looked pensive, put his hand on his heart. ' Ah, madam, 'tis a pity,' quoth he. I laughed again, saying, ' Ah, 'tis a pity she has not a strong lover to brave wind and rain, as you can, my strong Viking.' Ah, father, his face, his face, could you but have seen it, — wrathful, sorrowful, wistful, revengeful, envious, — all the qualities of love and of hate seemed painted on it."

Annette's own face grew grave and anxious. "Father! I liked not what I saw. It gave me strange, unquieting thoughts. If Margaret would but return! Would Henry were here!"

And for the twentieth time that day Mr. Murray sighed.

At last Annette asked Dorothea to come, and for an hour the throbbing and yearning and sobbing of that wonderful music seemed to fit in with the mood of the listeners and with the wildness of the storm.

There was sorrow, enthralling sweetness of melody, and deep tragedy in that music, — the tragedy that forms the chief part of life, — for life that has in it the sweetness of love, has also its pain. Love is the companion of tears. The human heart, so deep, so sensitive, can feel the tragedy of love even more than its immortal joy.

Once during the day, despite her anxiety and restlessness, Annette had a moment of quiet merriment, when she came across Chloe and saw that her pleasant, kindly face wore a peculiar look of happiness.

"Of a truth, good Chloe, 'tis my wish to know what makes your contentment."

"How you t'ink I'se happy, missus?"

"Have I not the right of it, Chloe?"

"Yes, missus, I'se berry happy — my heart's jes' a-burstin'. I could sing, sing all de day. Oh! missus, Jake done gone an' got de courage. He's brave an' warrior-like after all, missus He done gone

an' asked me, an' I have 'cepted his attentions,
missus. It's all owin' to you, now — an' Jake 'pre-
ciates it, now, don't he now? He 'lows he nebber
been abul to git bravery 'cept you tell him how to
git it."

Annette laughed merrily.

" Such a big man, Chloe, so big and strong, and
yet to tremble before you, such a harmless thing as
you."

Chloe laughed in reply.

" He big an' strong, shuh 'nuff; but his heart,
de heart ob a little chile."

Annette's face grew soft and tender. " Such
men, good Chloe, are the treasures of the world,
better than all the gold and all the glory." Then
she added:

" I am very glad, Chloe, and I will bespeak Mr.
Murray to give you a fine wedding, forsooth."

" Oh, t'ank you, missus, t'ank you." Chloe's
eyes glowed.

" Of a verity, the bewitchment is passed, good
Chloe."

" No, I am bewitched moah dan ebber, missus."

Another change from the monotony of the long,
weary day, came when a troop of horse from Valley Forge clattered up to the door and made peremptory demand for Captain Peyton. To Charles Murray's anxious inquiry as to the cause of this unexpected demand, there came no satisfying reply. The
trooper in command had orders, he said, to convey the British captain under guard to his Excellency's headquarters, for what purpose he knew not.

The troopers remained for neither rest nor refreshment, but rode swiftly away.

And the rain fell steadily, the darkness deepened, and two anxious hearts waited.

At last Mr. Murray's quick ear caught the familiar sound of Selim's hoofs. He summoned Annette in haste. She rushed to the big doorway and threw back the heavy bar.

Margaret came in hastily. Doctor Worthington waited but a moment till Clem ran up to take away the smoking horses.

Margaret went direct to her father.

"Where is Captain Peyton?" she asked, in a tone which showed great nervous tension. "I must see him at once. Where is he?"

Mr. Murray stood silent in perplexity.

"O father! Torture me not! Tell me where he is!"

"He has left us, daughter. He took Brown Bess and rode away."

Then Doctor Worthington hastened in. He closed the door, shook the rain from his hat and cloak, and threw them across the settee. With a smiling, satisfied face, he came to the schoolroom fire. Its glow came out into the hall and lightened the heavy shadows.

"The troopers came not for Captain Peyton?" Margaret asked.

"The troopers came, but Captain Peyton was already gone."

Doctor Worthington's smile vanished. He gave the fire an impatient poke; then turned to listen.

Annette said, softly:

"He must have reached the city by this time, dear. He must be safe, now, with his friends."

Margaret looked at her as if she did not hear.

"I rode Selim till he nearly dropped," she said, in a stifled voice. "I hoped to get here in time to warn Captain Peyton and tell him to flee."

"Why should he flee? He has been here for months without fear."

Margaret could not answer.

"What is it, dear? Why should he leave us thus? What has happened?"

Across one of the chairs an army cloak was lying. It had been worn by Captain Peyton in the battle of Germantown, and was around him when he fell. Oft had it been in use during the winter. Annette now took it up and held it in her hand.

"Colonel Hamilton has overwhelming proofs of his treachery. He will be condemned as soon as found," Margaret managed to whisper. She began to shiver, and went nearer the fire. Her steps were unsteady. Annette gently helped her into a chair, then threw the cloak around her.

"The troopers will search for him," continued Margaret, in a hard, strained tone. "They may even now have found him. They will take him to Valley Forge. They will not show mercy to a spy."

"It is that?" exclaimed Charles Murray, in astonishment.

"That is why you sent him away? O Margaret!"

Margaret did not reply.

"Margaret, I cannot believe it," said Charles Murray, with an emphatic shake of his head.

Then Annette said, earnestly:

"Margaret, it is impossible. There is some terrible mistake. I will not, cannot believe it."

"Nor could I, had I not seen the proofs with my own eyes," Margaret answered, wearily. "But I will tell you of it all to-morrow. I can bear no more to-night."

She looked at the fire a moment, then turned and put her arms on the back of her chair. Then she reached back and drew the folds of the cloak around her. She buried her face in it. Sobs — sobs without tears — shook her from head to foot. Taking up a fold of the cloak, she kissed it passionately. Annette watched her anxiously.

"Grieve not, dear. He has had time to reach the city twice over."

"I left Jake in the camp," whispered Margaret. "If he hear anything, he will immediately bring me word."

"And if Jake comes not soon, quite soon, dear, you will know that Captain Peyton is safe within the British lines."

Annette turned and looked at Worthington. He composed his face to a becoming gravity and brought her a chair. She sat down. He leaned on the back of it and watched Margaret with hungry, passionate eyes.

"Then you went not to the city, daughter?" asked Mr. Murray, after a pause. And Margaret answered, faintly:

"I bade him tell you that I would ride to Valley Forge."

"He told me naught except that he must leave us, that you no longer wished him here."

"And he was not strong enough to go," said Annette, querulously.

Margaret rose slowly. The cloak was still around her, and her hands grasped it nervously.

"Good night, father."

" Good night, my child."

Annette started forward.

" Can I do aught for you, Margaret? "

Margaret shook her head, and with unsteady steps, went out into the hall and slowly up the stairs.

Annette watched her anxiously, then turned to Charles Murray.

" It is a mystery how she found out this treachery," she said.

" Yes, but she is in no state to be questioned. We must abide in patience till the morning. Doctor Worthington? "

" Yes, Mr. Murray, at your service."

" Can you tell me aught of this matter? "

" 'Tis a miserable matter, Mr. Murray, and perchance Margaret had the wish to tell you herself. But she discovered that Captain Peyton had written, in letters, of General Washington's visit, and expected to betray him to the enemy."

" How came he to know of the General's visit? " asked Mr. Murray, sharply.

" That remains a mystery, sir. But find out he did, and used his knowledge basely. And this we know from Colonel Hamilton and also from the General that your guest has been plotting mischief for weeks past. His letters, seized by American scouters and skirmishers, have betrayed him."

Mr. Murray gave a startled exclamation, then asked, abruptly:

" Doctor Worthington, have you seen my son today? "

" No, Mr. Murray. I rode with Margaret to Valley Forge. She seemed distraught, excited, beside herself. I knew not what might befall. I could not risk her being alone with Jake, and coming home she started with an orderly — but I soon overtook her; and at the ford across the river bade him return to camp. Ah! I never saw such riding. She rode Selim till methought the fiends were after us."

While speaking, the Doctor walked slowly up and down. He was friendly, suave, solicitous.

"Hush! Some one is coming," exclaimed Mr. Murray.

Annette rushed to the big doorway.

"'Tis Henry! 'Tis he at last!" and with trembling fingers she flung the door open.

Henry Murray came in hastily. He checked Annette's impulse.

"Off, love! I'm as wet as a muskrat. Touch me not."

"Where have you been all day? Harry! we have been most anxious and distraught."

"I have been looking for Worthington all over the village and across country. Ah!" As he perceived Worthington his face darkened. He threw down his wet cloak, then returned to the big door and threw its heavy bar in place; went swiftly to the windows and threw their bars across. Then with his hand on his sword, he strode down to Worthington.

"Yes, Murray, I am here," Worthington said, smiling, though he looked somewhat startled. He came well out into the hall. "I regret that you have had all this trouble. But I came here soon after you left. I have taken good care of your sister amid unexpected perils. But it is time I went, now you are safe here. By my faith, 'tis later than I dreamed."

Henry Murray's face grew sterner and darker. His voice rang out clear and cold:

"You stay here till the morrow. You are my prisoner."

With a bound Worthington sprang forward and confronted Henry Murray. His face was pale. Then it took on a cautious, guarded expression. He whispered, hoarsely:

"What the devil is your meaning, Murray?"

"There is no use in your acting a part any longer, Worthington. You need not deny or argue or stand on your dignity. I know all your tricks, your treachery, and your villainy. You go with me to-morrow to Valley Forge."

An angry light shone in Worthington's eyes. Then he smiled indulgently.

"You are beside yourself. The delirium has mounted again to your brain."

Henry Murray smiled sarcastically.

"I am in my right senses, Doctor Worthington, and you know it. You contemptible traitor!"

Worthington ripped out his sword fiercely. Then he controlled himself with a violent effort. His sword fell to his side.

"I will not fight with a sick man," he said, quietly. "You are not responsible."

Again Henry Murray smiled.

"You're a gamester, Worthington, and a desperate one. You have played your stake and lost."

"By Gad! You are beside yourself. Come, now, Murray, tell me your meaning or my patience will be gone."

He tried to resume his usual airy manner. But it was a failure. His eyes grew restless, anxious.

"You know well what I mean, you traitor. On guard, Worthington. I may kill you. I know not what I shall do. But fight you I will."

"Murray, I warn you. I am one of the best swordsmen in these parts. Think twice. Compose yourself."

Worthington's tone was the perfection of manly courtesy and friendly care. He glanced for approval at Annette. But her eyes were fixed in astonishment and apprehension on her husband.

"Worthington, on guard!"

Henry Murray's tone was commanding.

"Your sword, your sword, you traitor."

Worthington's self-control was at an end.

"I will not suffer such insults," he exclaimed, and his face was distorted with rage.

With a wild, exultant cry, Henry Murray sprang towards him.

"That face, that face! I have it at last. I know you! I know you at last!"

Annette gave a startled scream. Was it possible? Could it be true?

They fought well, swaying from side to side, parrying and thrusting. The fight was long and desperate, and for a time to the disadvantage of Murray. The shock of the discovery that this was the man who had injured him so wofully and well-nigh been the cause of his death, excited and unnerved him. But gradually he gained composure. Worthington soon saw that his opponent was of relentless purpose, and that he possessed a skill

and delicacy in sword-play of which he himself
was not master.

Finally, a deft thrust of Murray's sword wounded
Worthington in the arm. His sword flew from
his hand. He sank into a chair, and said, breathlessly:

"You know me at last, then, Murray. Oft have
I regretted that day's deed."

Henry Murray made a gesture of disgust.

"But it was in the interests of my country. 'Twas
necessary that those letters should not reach Washington. I was sent by Howe to recover them. You
stood in the way of my purpose. But I was serving
my country."

Murray laid his sword on a chair and said, scorn-
fully:

"You have no country, you traitor."

"I am no traitor. It is you who are the traitor
and the rebel. I am a loyal subject of his Majesty."

The scorn and honest indignation which Henry
Murray felt overwhelmed him beyond control. His
voice grew loud and menacing.

"You were born here in America, and in her
great struggle for liberty you refuse to serve her.
You have no country, you contemptible Tory!"

Worthington rose and made a wild dash for his
sword. But Murray kicked it aside with his foot.
Murray continued, relentlessly:

"And you serve the English because you think
America is not going to have her liberty; and you
hope when she is forced to give up the struggle,
you will get fat pay and big rewards. But America
is not going to give up."

Worthington's face grew dark and ugly. The merciless voice went on:

"You *will* not live to see it, and 'tis possible I *may* not live to see it. But there will be those of your kind who will live to see this country free. What will they do, Worthington? Go to Canada? As for America, bah! she wants not these loyalists."

Annette went to her husband and touched his arm.

"O Henry! see that wound! Help him! Talk no more."

But he was too absorbed to heed her.

"Remember, Worthington, England is fighting against her own blood in this war. It was her best blood that left her. She isn't fighting against the French or the Spanish or the Turk or the Indian. She is fighting against her best blood. She therefore cannot prevail."

"O Henry, talk of it not now. 'Tis not the time. Will you not help him? He suffers. Talk no more."

Though she shrank from the baleful look in Doctor Worthington's eyes, Annette was moved by compassion for the man she had so long regarded as a friend. Henry Murray went on:

"You Tories will not feel at home here when the great day of liberty comes. Where will you go? What will you all do, Worthington?"

But Worthington refused his enemy the satisfaction of a reply. With a defiant, contemptuous glance, he turned away and seizing his cloak tore a strip from it. Ere Annette could render aid, he had with his uninjured hand wound the cloth around his wounded arm. Then he sank into a chair. But Henry Murray's quick eye had noted that his seat was chosen near the door, and that he had glanced furtively over his shoulder as if he meditated escape, should occasion happily serve.

CHAPTER XLIV

"Life that has in it the sweetness of love has also its pain. Love is the companion of tears."

UP-STAIRS in her lonely room, Margaret Murray was fighting with despair. During those desperate and perilous rides in the storm she had been upheld by the definite purpose, first to save her General, and then the lover who had deceived her; but now there was naught to do but to suffer. And the very strength and depth of her nature made this suffering a terrible thing.

She felt crushed to the earth, as if some invisible force were opposing her, — a cruel, relentless force. No power of resistance seemed left to her. She would never be able to rise.

And that great loneliness of soul that comes with an overwhelming grief almost appalled her. In all her life she had never felt so utterly alone. The passionate enthusiasm, the power for deep feeling which had made possible that happiness which had been glorifying all her days now made this loneliness thus appalling. Deep natures always have to pay a heavy price for their joy.

Margaret Murray had had visions and dreamed dreams, — of loyalty and constancy and high honour, of devotion to that which is worthy and beautiful. The dreams had been but phantoms, after all. They had faded. Nothing was left. Even the memory of them was a bitterness.

If he had but died in that awful battle! Then, memory would not have had this bitterness. She would have sorrowed for him, but she would have had exceeding comfort, too. She would have kept in her heart the unfading remembrance of his brave and worthy life, its high purposes and ideals, the sweetness, the beauty of his character and mind, its truth, its honour, its tenderness and strength.

But now there seemed to be no comfort anywhere. Everything was gone.

Margaret paid no heed to the time she sat there in the chill and darkness of her fireless room.

Suddenly she was roused by the sound of swift footsteps. Then her strained eyes caught the gleam of a candle.

" Margaret! Where are you? Methought I could never find you. Come quickly. Delay not."

" What is it ? "

" O Margaret! I cannot stay to tell you. I know not all, but come. Henry and Doctor Worthington have fought. In truth, I know not all. But come! come by the spiral staircase. The torch is burning in the passageway."

There was a cadence of joy in Annette's incoherent, breathless words which made Margaret's heart beat.

CHAPTER XLV.

"No! No! It burned and stung me. I tore it into small shreds. I could not keep it. No! No!"

AS Annette, hurrying on before, opened the door into the big hall, Margaret heard her brother's clear, distinct voice saying:

"But you are not only a Tory, Worthington, but you are a dastardly spy. And you are too cowardly to take the full risk of your perfidy. You liked the feel of your head between your shoulders. You wanted to put another head in the noose."

Margaret paused in wonder on the threshold.

"'Tis not the truth!" shouted Worthington, with a sharp cry.

Henry Murray answered, sternly: "You know it is the truth. A court-martial will soon make that clear to all."

And then he turned and saw Margaret.

"Margaret," he said, as he pointed to Worthington, "there is the man who has wrought us all mischief. He has been long in the pay of the British and has been working to betray our cause. He has not known that one of our friends has been watching him. He warned me of our danger, and I have been gathering proof during the last two days. I have found that this knave has even worked to cut off the forage from our camp, and thus induce the men to desert. He sought to have the Marquis and his men entrapped the other day. He has sought to find out all the secrets of this house. He has been behind the secret panel — "

"No! No!" cried Worthington, with a passionate look at Margaret. But Henry, not heeding the interruption, continued:

"Yes, he has called himself our friend, a patriot, the friend of our General; and he has not scrupled to betray our confidence. He has listened to talk not intended for his ears — "

"You have no proof, no proof. Bah! Murray, 'tis easy to assert these terrible crimes. But you have no proof."

There was a remnant of the suave Doctor's old manner manifest now. He looked at Margaret; and he almost smiled.

But her face was perplexed and full of pain.

"I have no time to tell you of all his trickery," continued Henry, "but when I tell you that he — "

He stopped at sight of the passionate protest in Worthington's eyes.

"Murray! you tell her that at your peril. Damme! My patience is at an end. Beware! You tell her that at your peril."

Murray smiled sarcastically.

"One further word, Margaret, and I am done. 'Tis he, Margaret, that attacked me last October; and 'tis he who knew of the General's visit planned to-night, and he sent word to Howe to capture him at the cross-roads near the ferry."

Worthington started from his chair.

"'Tis a lie, a damnable lie!" he cried, hoarsely.

" Mistress Murray knows well who is responsible for that."

Margaret had been standing spellbound in the doorway. Now her worn, sad face flushed, and the effect of Worthington's eyes fixed upon her was almost painful. It was as if a heavy mask had fallen from him, and his face revealed the true nature of the soul of the man beneath. The revelation was astounding. She shrank in almost horror from it. Going swiftly over to her father, she placed herself within the shelter of his arm. Then she turned to look at Worthington once more.

" You have wronged Captain Peyton," whispered Mr. Murray. " He is no spy."

Henry caught the words and turned impetuously. " What is that you are saying? Peyton a spy? Margaret — what know you of this wretched business? "

Margaret spoke as if questioning herself.

" Ah! I see! He is Captain Peyton's tool of whom Washington spoke."

" Washington? When saw you Washington? Margaret, what is it? "

And now Worthington made one last effort. He would throw his last card — win or lose by it. He was indeed a gamester and a desperate one.

" Murray," he said, blandly, " your sister and I have been to Valley Forge and have discovered that the man who has been your honoured guest and been permitted to betroth your sister, is known in his true character by Hamilton and Washington. Long have I known that you were risking much by giving him shelter; in faith, I warned you once; but I could say little, for my own vows to Howe restrained me; but an accident to-day happily revealed to her the true facts of this matter."

He pointed to Margaret with a gleam of triumph in his eyes. Henry Murray stamped his foot impatiently.

"No! No!" he cried. "No! No! Captain Peyton is no spy."

"The proof is with Hamilton; and Mistress Murray has herself vouched for its truth and verity."

"What proof? Out with your words, man, or —"

Worthington cast a furtive glance at Murray, then a cynical smile distorted his face.

"This worthy Captain is the confidant of Howe; a tool of the King's ministers. Many a grim secret have they shared together. He is a man of wealth, and I am poor. He is devoted to the King. Four days agone he gave me one hundred pounds for the information that Washington was expected here to-night."

"You take back that lie, or you will never live to utter another," cried Henry Murray, breathlessly.

But Worthington felt himself master.

"The proof is in letters which are at Valley Forge — Mistress Murray knows this well. She has herself asserted that they are written by her lover."

"Margaret!" said Henry Murray, solemnly. "You have been deceived and wronged. This fellow has forged Captain Peyton's handwriting. There is a letter here in my pocket which he writ and I saw him. Had I not seen him with my own eyes it were hard to persuade me that the Captain himself had not writ it with his own hand."

A great light dawned in Margaret's face. She started forward impulsively. Peyton's cloak fell partly from her shoulders.

"Tell me, Doctor Worthington. Is this true? You wrote the letter to General Howe which you let fall on the hearth? Tell me! Tell me at once!"

Worthington was silent. Henry Murray lifted his sword threateningly.

"Answer her at once, you cowardly traitor, or you will rue it."

There was entreaty in Margaret's voice.

"Oh! keep me not in suspense. Tell me at once. Tell me!"

"Tell her what you have done," said Henry, sternly.

Worthington spoke doggedly.

"I have naught to tell."

"There is no use in keeping up your game longer, Worthington. You must tell her, or, egad! I'll run you through," and Henry put his sword at Worthington's breast.

"Tell her yourself and go to hell!"

Worthington's eyes gleamed, and he looked at Margaret with growing passion. Then his eyes fell on the sword touching his breast. A glance at the face of the man holding the sword made him start back hastily. Then with an impatient gesture, he muttered:

"I writ the letter, Mistress Murray. Captain Peyton knew naught of this business."

Doctor Worthington had played his last card. He had lost.

Over Margaret's heart there swept a storm of passionate joy and yet more passionate regret. And there was tenderness in her voice because of her thoughts of Peyton.

"Oh! what could be your motive to seek to ruin him? He never did aught to harm you."

The smouldering passion in Worthington's eyes burst into a flame. Passion mastered him beyond control.

"You ask me for a motive? You!"

She looked at him in wonder as he came quite near to her.

"He wrought me a most deadly injury. . . . I hate him! I hate him! I will kill him some day. He won your love. I want you. I want you myself. Oft have I been about to ride off with you. I waited too long. I love you. Come!"

He put out his arms eagerly. She shrank away from him, and covered her eyes.

"Oh! this is too much," she moaned.

With a sudden movement, Worthington seized Peyton's cloak from her shoulders.

"He is past hope. I need fear him now no more than this."

He hurled the cloak on the floor and trampled on it brutally.

"By to-morrow's sun he will have been court-martialled. Hamilton will work quickly. Ere word could be got to him, your lover will have been condemned. Then what will avail, even if he be guiltless?"

Henry Murray looked at Margaret in surprise.

"What means he, Margaret? Where is Peyton? Is he not here?"

"Henry! tell me! Sent you not word to Washington that Captain Peyton has had no concern in this matter?"

"Margaret, how could I know that Washington suspected him? 'Tis only late last eve I found that this knave has been forging Peyton's writing. Before daybreak, I rode post-haste to camp to warn the General; then off, hunting, searching for this fellow. I feared me he would get wind of my warning and be off beyond my reach."

"O Henry!" exclaimed Annette, hiding her face in her hands. Henry looked at her dubiously.

"Then Peyton is not here? He is in danger? Speak, girl."

"Father," said Margaret, "I must go at once."

Charles Murray put out his hand to her.

"He has had time to reach the British lines twice over."

"Yes! Yes!" A look of agony convulsed her face. "But he might not care to hasten."

At that moment was heard the clatter of hoofs on the garden road. Henry Murray hastened to the big door and began to lift the heavy bar. He took no note of Worthington. The opportunity was not to be neglected. Worthington drew his knife from his belt and sprang forward. Then Margaret saw. Before the knife could be plunged in Henry's back, she had hurled it out of Worthington's hand. He and Margaret stood a moment confronting each other. There was a look of scorn in her face he had never thought to see. His eyes gleamed strangely, then they were lowered in confusion. She picked up the knife, and threw it towards the window. It shattered one of the panes and fell in the garden beyond. Henry Murray

turned at the noise and looked at her in surprise.
Through the open door rushed Jake. He darted
to Margaret and threw himself at her feet. She
stood with her hand on her heart.

"O missy! I seen him. T'ink, missy! He was
in de camp not long after you was dare. He was
took beyond the Schuylkill by some of Light-Hoss
Harry's troopers, as dey was roamin' 'roun' in search
of t'ings for de camp. Dey took him to a hut in
de outer posts, an' sent in word to headquarters,
cos dey thought him jes' not an extraordinary prisoner. I nosed around and seen Captain Lee come
out headquarters after dark and give orders to some
sojers to go and fetch de prisoner and bring him
'mediately to Colonel Hamilton. I followed de
sojers; cos, missy, I some way felt in my heart
dat de prisoner be my dear Cappin, and, missy, it
was. I seen him come out de hut with sojers all
around him, his hands boun'. I give him a look,
missy, and he doan' eben gib me a smile, missy,
way he used to. T'ink, missy, my dear Cappin
widout a smile for me. I rushed for my hoss, an'
come gallopin' fas' as his ole legs bring me."

Margaret had remained motionless while Jake
told his tale. He told it with groans and tears.
As he got on his feet she said, hoarsely:

"Saddle Prince at once. Hasten! You can ride
Tempest."

"Oh! missy, de shrubbery and garden is full ob
redcoats."

Charles Murray uttered an exclamation. A
gleam of triumph crossed Worthington's face. Annette and Henry both exclaimed:

"Redcoats!"

" Yes — dey rode slowly and I come 'long fas', cos I's in such a hurry to git heah. Dey was peaceable, and passed no word to me. 'Twas too dark to see how many dey was."

" It is the escort sent by Howe for Captain Peyton," said Charles Murray. " I asked him to write that they come not till the morrow; but Margaret carried not the letter. They will not harm you, daughter; but it is late, and the roads are dangerous. Send a message by Sam, or Tom, or Jake."

" Father! " said Margaret, with a sharp note of pain in her voice.

" Doctor Worthington seeks but to alarm and frighten you, my girl. . . . Your judgment will tell you this when you stop to think. Captain Peyton is no mere common spy. He is an Englishman of rank, well-known. Even after condemning him by court martial, they would wait. They would have much to consider. There is cause for no undue haste. And Margaret, have no fear. Doctor Worthington has sought but to alarm and frighten you."

" You are mistaken, sir," said Worthington, fiercely. " Hamilton assured me that they *would* work speedily, that the way Nathan Hale had been treated would make a precedent to follow. Not even Captain Peyton's powerful friends nor his influence would avail, His fate would be no more merciful than that of a common spy, caught in a treacherous act and hanged in the morning."

" Heed him not, Margaret. He seeks but to frighten you, my girl."

" But to have him under this suspicion, this calumny. To have his hands bound, to suffer Hamilton's questions, to endure Lee's scorn!"

"And to be told that you yourself believe him guilty — that your testimony has had weight in his condemnation," exclaimed Worthington, brutally.

"Hush, hush!" cried Annette, with an indignant look at Worthington.

"'Tis better that you go at once, my girl," said Mr. Murray. "Make all speed."

"I will go, so soon as I have made this fellow here secure," said Henry. "Or stay! I will take him with me, under guard of Jake."

But Worthington caught his words. Margaret, preoccupied as she was, failed not to note the crafty look in his face. She put out her hand to her brother with a quick expression of anxious emotion.

"Harry, I cannot wait." Then she added, in a low tone: "'Twere impossible for you to ride past those redcoats with him. He would make appeal to them. They would come quickly to his aid. 'Twould fare ill with you, Harry. See, that is of what he is thinking. He would not scruple to betray you."

"Of a truth, she has the right of it, Henry," whispered Annette. "'Tis best that you remain."

Henry paused irresolutely.

"'Tis sore against my will that you take this ride, Margaret," he said.

But she gave him a sweet, brave smile; and grasping Peyton's cloak, she hurried to the door of the passageway.

Through it she sped, then out the door, across

the lawn, sodden and rain-soaked, till she came to the stables where a solitary light gleamed. Her purpose was to be of help to Jake and also mount her horse and gain the road without being seen by the soldiers in front.

She found Sam busied with the horse brought in by Henry Murray. Jake's horse was outside, panting and steaming; and Tom, in obedience to a peremptory call, had just emerged from the servants' quarters and lantern in hand was stumbling along the path. Close behind him towered the tall form of Howe's messenger, who had recovered from his stupor and was thinking he must betake himself back to the city.

Margaret found Jake just leading Prince from his warm stall. With quick but trembling fingers she helped him on with the saddle.

" Jake," she whispered, faintly, " I have much to say to the General; but 'tis possible that I cannot ride so fast as you. Should I fall behind or aught occur to stop me, you will ride on fast and tell the General to wait till I come, ere he go on with the proceedings against Captain Peyton."

" You not feel well, missy? T'ink you better go, missy? "

" I must, Jake, I must go. I have much to say to the General. But, Jake, you must understand me and obey. Nothing, nothing must tempt you to disobey me. You have never failed me yet, Jake, my Jake. You will remember now. You will obey me. Should anything occur to make me fall behind, you must ride on. Even should danger threaten me, you must ride on. You understand? "

" Yes, missy. Jake will tell de Gen'ral all right. My dear Cappin mus' be set free till you come an' 'splain t'ings. Nebber you feah."

" 'Tis not, it cannot be as that — that man says, that they would not wait. You would get there in time to save his life, Jake."

" Yes, missy, nebber you feah. My Cappin not a man like dat. Dey not dare to do him harm till dey shuh. But t'ink we bettah take Tom 'long wid us."

" No, Jake. 'Twould be but a hindrance to have any one but you. . . . Now make haste with Tempest."

Margaret was forced to wait but a few moments. The rain had ceased. The moon was struggling forth from behind a drifting mass of storm-cloud; but the mass of cloud soon grew dense, — and it was lost once more.

The cold, damp wind came sobbing. There was wildness, unrest, throbbing misery in the air.

The spaces of the wide country, the desolation of the roads, impressed Margaret as they never had before. She had never before thought these wide spaces of sky and earth so desolate, so pitiless in their loneliness. The grief, the dread, the regret in her heart, cried out for relief.

She craved warmth, shelter, comradeship. And she knew that without him there would never again be warmth or comfort in all the world.

CHAPTER XLVI.

"Yes! the house had once a most gruesome reputation."

THE old Ridge Road that ran from Philadelphia was as crooked and devious as any
road that once had been an Indian trail
could be made: — near the Schuylkill at certain
points, then diverging widely. Just beyond where
School House Lane ended, it came the closest to
the river, — so close that only a short lane ran from
it down to the ferry. 'Twas near this lane that
the Wissahickon flowed into the Schuylkill.

At the intersection of this lane and the Ridge
Road there stood a solitary public-house, kept for
years by Dame Van Slycke.

Travellers from Reading stopped here for rest
and refreshment. Troopers and foraging parties
from Valley Forge, whether they crossed at Swedes
or Matson's fords, or at the ferry here, could not
resist the charms of this inn. Skirmishing and
foraging parties from the city made it their rendez-
vous. Thus it happened that this " Cross-Roads Tavern " was one of the most popular of the many inns
round about Philadelphia.

Many a stray shilling found its way into the
broad palm of the hostess because of her famous
ale which was said to be of the finest brew. But
the travellers by stage and private coach, on whom

she had once depended, had been few since the
British were in possession of the city. To increase
her scanty stock of coin, the good dame had of
late taken a permanent lodger; and in three of
her best rooms Doctor Worthington had been es-
tablished for two months. He found the place
most convenient for the prosecution of his peculiar
work. From skirmishing and foraging parties of
both armies and from many a chance wayfarer
or horseman he picked up valuable information;
and by subtle, clever, disguising talk, he oft gained
from the dame herself that which she had no
thought of giving.

But the situation of the inn was after all
its chief claim to his favour: he was not far
from Valley Forge; he could reach the city
quickly by means of the Ridge Road; and a short
gallop along School House Lane to the Market
Square of Germantown, then a mere mile up
to the gate of Cliveden, would bring him to her
who was each day and hour becoming more and
more the ruling passion of his heart.

Near the house there was a dense wood, running
back to the fastnesses and mysterious defiles of
the Wissahickon. The people of the country round
about told many gruesome tales of the robber horde
that once made this woods its hiding-place, and from
the caves and rocks on the Wissahickon sallied
forth to surprise and molest unwary travellers after
they had left the shelter of the inn. There had
been rumours, too, that old Van Slycke had been
in league with these outlaws; and that two or
three lodgers in his house had met their death by
mysterious means. One body had been found in

Van Deering's mill not far away. And to the old deserted monastery above another body must have been carried at night; for next morning it was found there when search was being made for a missing traveller.

Ere his own death, however, Van Slycke had lived down this unfavourable reputation, and his wife now enjoyed a fair share of popularity with the people round about. If she knew aught that had been dark and sinful in her husband's life, she kept the matter closely hidden in her own breast.

The servants of the house were not many; and they were probably no better or no worse than the average serving-folk of the time. It was possible that their standard of ethics would vary with the temptation of gold; and certain conditions always caused a variation in their politics. If British officers of rank, or British troopers of prowess, ate or drank at the inn, these serving-folk were plainly Tory in sentiment. When Light-Horse Harry or Allen McLane stopped for refreshment during their frequent excursions across country, they found all the folk staunch patriots. In truth, it mattered little to them what king they had — King George III. or Washington; for in their narrow minds there was no thought but that Washington was aiming to make himself King of America, — good luck to him if he did.

The hostess was compelled to wink at these sudden changes of opinion. And there was one man in her employ whom she secretly feared. He was a lusty German, of great physical strength, but with a shifty, indirect glance that caused distrust. He had principal charge of the cellars and tap-rooms.

Many travellers when they first arrived called him " landlord," and the title pleased him. It was possible that at some future time he might aspire to the ownership of the property. He was plainly avaricious even now. Dame Van Slycke would have been glad to be quit of him; but no fitting excuse offered for his dismissal, and she feared consequences.

The inn was of peculiar construction, practically two houses separated by a courtyard, but at the rear joined by a narrow corridor which ran from the second story of one wing to the second story of the other. The courtyard was underneath this corridor, and at the rear expanded into a large space, bounded on one side by the dense wood, and at the other by the stables and sheds for market-wagons.

A traveller coming up by the Ridge Road had practically two inns at his choice, for each wing had its own portico, tap-room, dining-room, and kitchen. In the days long ago, when old Van Slycke was still breathing the spicy breath that came from the adjacent forest, respectable guests could be entertained in one portion of the house and imagine themselves the sole occupants of the place; while guests of questionable repute could carouse in the other wing, and not be seen or heard. When the doors leading to the corridor above were locked, as oft they were, there was no communication between the wings except from outside.

These two wings were much alike, except that one was larger than the other, and stood higher up on " the ridge." It ran a considerable distance further back. Its courtyard in the rear was therefore smaller; and the trees of the forest came nearly to the windows of the rooms in the rear.

The east window of the room on the ground floor looked out upon a portion of the courtyard enclosed by a high wall. The side towards the forest was deemed sufficiently protected by the dense growth of the trees. No one in the tavern seemed to know that amid this density of foliage there was a crevice in the rocks, concealed by tangled undergrowth. No one in the tavern seemed to know that this crevice in the rocks was the entrance to a cave that widened gradually as it extended a long way back towards the Wissahickon fastnesses and bluffs.

Rodney Bingham was not far wrong when he assumed that he alone was master of the secret of this cave. It had been used by the men in league with old Van Slycke; but they were all dust now; and their secrets were buried with them in their narrow graves.

Doctor Worthington's rooms suited his needs well. They were on the ground floor in the rear of the wing nearest the forest. The first room was his surgery or office. Its windows opened on the courtyard underneath the corridor. Then came his bedroom, a large, pleasant room with two south windows.

The room beyond was for his private use. It was at the extreme end of the house, two windows looking south, one east, and this opened directly out upon the forest. In times of storm when the east wind blew, the branches of the trees were wont

to touch his window and make sounds like ghostly
fingers tapping on the panes.

In this room Doctor Worthington did his writing
and kept his private papers. Into this room occasionally were brought guests with whom he wished
to have secret conference. The high wall kept
curious listeners out of the courtyard beneath or
at side of the window — if curious listeners there
might chance to be. The forest was an impassable
and tangled mass of foliage.

CHAPTER XLVII.

"Oh! it is the basest treachery."

RODNEY BINGHAM remained in Philadelphia till the second week in April. As Lydia Darrach's serving-man he went over town on her errands; and when he saw that none of his old friends whom he chanced to meet recognised him in his new disguise, he gained confidence, and had many adventures.

The plans for the expedition of the Marquis de Lafayette were carried out faithfully. It was thought that they had been kept secret, that he could take his men across Swedes Ford and to the place appointed without any intelligence of his movements being carried to the enemy. That he was surprised and well-nigh entrapped by Sir Henry Clinton has now become a matter of history. Who had discovered these secret plans? Who had betrayed them? Clearly some one who was near the scene of action. Rodney Bingham set to work to solve the mystery.

That the British failed to entrap the gallant Frenchman was due to a discovery that Rodney Bingham made while he was performing the menial duty of sweeping the floor of the adjutant-general's office. He chose to do this work while the office was deserted except for the presence of one of the secretaries who was busied making copies of certain papers which he was examining. As Bingham came near the table by which the secretary was writing, he noticed that one of the papers was a rough plan. He must find out some way of examining it. Then, as if fate were in truth working for him, a horseman galloped up Second Street and halted at General Knyphausen's door. The secretary got up hastily, for he had a measure of curiosity like all men. Seeing the newcomer was an acquaintance and wishing speech with him, he went across the street.

He was gone only three minutes and a quarter by the clock, but that time was made good use of by Rodney Bingham. He had seen that the plan was of the entrenchments at Valley Forge, and the situation of the different brigades of the Continental forces. Another paper was a map of the roads to and from the fords across the Schuylkill, and of the course that Lafayette was to take from Valley Forge to the place appointed. These two plans were drawn by the same hand: a peculiar hand. Bingham determined to keep it vivid in his memory. The third paper, that which the secretary had been copying, was an order for the captains of different companies to have their men at Redoubt No. 6 at a certain hour. Then, under command of Sir Henry Clinton, they were to march up the Ridge Road to intercept the Marquis.

Soon after that, Lydia Darrach's serving-man was provided with a pass for him to cross the " upper ferry," in order to bring back flour from a gristmill about a mile beyond, on the other side of the Schuylkill.

His way to the ferry led him near the regiments stationed on the high grounds of Bush Hill and on both sides of Callowhill Street. He had good opportunity for inspection, but he discovered nothing of moment, except that the soldiers ordered to meet at the redoubt had not yet begun to move.

He was delayed several times, but his quick wit and ready tongue helped him; though he did not breathe freely till he was well across the ferry, and on his way to a place where he hoped to be able to buy a horse. This way did not lead him in the neighbourhood of that grist-mill; and if Mistress Darrach baked no bread that day for the benefit of the adjutant-general, 'twas clearly the fault of her vagrant serving-man.

Two days after that, Mr. Kelper appeared in Germantown and put up at the King of Prussia Inn. He did not visit his friends at Cliveden; for he soon found that Doctor Worthington was there an almost daily visitor, and he wished to find out certain things about Doctor Worthington without running the chance of meeting him.

But in less than a week, a little German boy was made happy by the gift of an English shilling. As compensation for the gift he was to take to the big house a letter, to be delivered to Henry Murray and to him alone. The letter was short.

" As soon as twilight falls, come to the same place as you met me the second of last October. Come alone, and burn even this unsigned letter. If you should be followed, throw the man off the scent."

Henry Murray rode to the tryst with a peculiar thrill of expectation and pleasure. Of late he had

had many anxious thoughts of his friend. Knowing Bingham's temperament, he had feared some mischief had sure befallen. The hiding in the tower of Christ Church had shown him that Rodney was capable of almost any foolhardy and venturesome scheme. And now to know that he was once more safely back in Germantown was joy indeed.

Henry Murray's surprise was almost a shock to him when he learned that his own vague suspicions in regard to Doctor Worthington were not only shared by his friend, but that proofs had been gathered both in Germantown and in the city.

" I have heard him talking to the young Lieutenant on Howe's staff. For a time Lieutenant Shipton helped Howe with his private correspondence. From what he said, I feel sure that Worthington is a paid spy of Howe's. And it seems that the fact is known only to Howe and to the Lieutenant. . . . Last night I got hold of something tangible. I will have to let you into my cave at last, Murray, for it will take both you and me to ferret out this mystery. Last night I lay beneath Worthington's window and for two hours had to wait. When he came he was not alone. The Crossroads Tavern had been full of noisy roisterers from the city, most of them Hessians who had been foraging. About twelve the hostess must have bade them begone, for the tavern got quiet all at once. After that, Worthington came into his room. I saw his window get light. You see, he is not careful of that window which opens on the forest. He never suspects that any one can be on that side. He is careful to close the shutters of the windows looking out on to the big courtyard; but

that east window he invariably leaves open for air.
. . . I saw him come to it, glance along the ground
and at the high wall; then go back to his writing-
table, apparently perfectly satisfied that he was secure. . . . Well, last night his companion was a
messenger of Howe's. I would not have suspected
this, had I not seen the fellow in Philadelphia at
Howe's headquarters. He is celebrated for his
dauntlessness, his quick grasp of chances. The troop
organised by Washington to scour this region and
seize all letters going into Philadelphia has failed
to catch him. He has eluded us all winter. To
spot him and run the fox to earth was one of my
tasks in the city. Well, when I saw him with
Worthington, I knew, as by a flash of intuition, that
I had at last my man. 'Twas Doctor Worthington
who had been doing all the mischief. What news
he himself could not give verbally to Howe, he
would send by this trusty messenger. We can only
be *sure* of this after we have captured that messenger, and after you have had a glance at Worthington's papers when you visit his rooms."

"Visit his rooms! What mean you, Rodney?"

"You see, Murray, 'tis impossible for me to
get into that room while Worthington is writing and
has his papers about. When he leaves the inn he
carefully locks them away. Then 'tis not to my
plan now that he recognise me for aught but the
harmless Mr. Kelper, who roams about the village,
or in the woods, or visits different taverns for the
sake of idle gossip. Mr. Kelper gets shabbier every
day, and oft frequents these taverns on the chance
of being treated to ale or wine by some good-
natured acquaintance. . . . Well, Murray, my plan

is this. To-morrow, as soon as twilight falls, you
are to meet me here. Then we will go to my cave
— go through it, emerge at the other end, and wait
till we see Worthington in his room. When we
see his window alight and him at work, I will go
around to the front of the tavern. The hostess is
well acquaint with Mr. Kelper — she always has
a bed well aired for him. I will go to the tavern
and insist on seeing Worthington; at once; quickly;
invent some fitting excuse; get him to leave his
papers hastily; though of course he will lock his
door. While I engage him thus, you are to climb
into his window and go through his papers. I
will give you a wee scrap of the plan I saw in the
adjutant-general's office. It has only two words
written upon it, but the handwriting is peculiar.
If it resembles Worthington's writing, then I shall
know my man. But wait till to-morrow night. Time
will show us how we are to manage this business.
You will understand it all then."

And by twelve o'clock the following night Henry
Murray did understand. And the understanding
brought with it a hot feeling of passionate indignation.

It was already dark when Henry Murray met
Rodney at the trysting-place on the Wissahickon.
The moon would not rise for at least an hour.

Once inside the cave, Rodney lit a torch which
he had ready.

"We can safely use it till we get near the end.
Then when I extinguish it, you must look where
I place it, so you can light it for your return jour-
ney. I shall likely not be with you, for it may be

necessary that Mr. Kelper stay at the inn. It all depends upon what luck we have on our first venture. . . . This is a wonderful place, Henry."

Crawling on their hands and knees at first, they were glad when they came to a portion of the rock where the space above them became much higher, and they could straighten up. But all too soon they were forced upon their knees once more, and obliged to go most carefully. Henry Murray scarce dared breathe; and long before they had reached the end of their circuitous and rugged journey, he begged Rodney to extinguish the torch.

"No one can possibly see us," answered Bingham. "There are no rifts or holes in the side walls for a long way, — and look up — see those firm boulders above our heads. Without our torch, we might get into mischief. See!"

And Henry Murray saw that the pathway before them was a mere narrow ledge with water on each side that seemed of great depth. Further on, they could hear the water foaming and splashing as if it fell over the rocks into a deep chasm beneath. The narrow ledge soon grew wider, and then became a solid floor of rock beneath their feet; the sound of the water was left behind. Ten minutes after that, Rodney said:

"I will put the torch here on this rocky shelf. Remember where it is."

They were immediately plunged in darkness. He grasped Murray's hand, and they stumbled on. Suddenly Murray felt the close, stagnant air of the cave change. A cold wind swept across his face. Then he heard the swish and moaning of trees. For a moment he could see the stars shining.

"We are in the midst of the forest," Rodney whispered. "On that side and above us there are rifts in the rock. But we are not yet out of the cave. The roof will slope more and more, and the holes in it become larger. Then just beyond, the rock will break off and end."

Then Henry Murray heard Bingham push aside leaves and tangled shrub-growths that grazed and scratched his face. All at once they came out into an open space.

"Crouch down. Keep quiet," Bingham whispered. "We are directly in front of his window now. It is dark. He has not yet come home. . . . We will lie here in the cave with only our heads out. 'Tis warmer so. Then if anything *should* happen, and we were pursued, we could easily get away without being caught. I have no expectation of being seen, however. And I fancy no one would be willing to pursue us into that blackness of darkness. . . . Now, Murray, my plan is this. If Worthington comes at all, and should do as he did last night, — sit writing and looking at his papers, I will give my arm a little cut, tie it to stop the bleeding, then steal around to the front entrance of this wing, and enter just as if I had arrived by the road. I will call for Doctor Worthington, make it a matter of urgent haste. If this succeeds, he will leave his papers lying there. . . . You climb in the window and look at everything you can in the time I give you. I will keep him engaged dressing my wound, till I can keep him no longer. Use your eyes well. Then I will order a bed from the hostess and sleep the sleep of the just, while you, poor fellow, are stumbling your way back through this cave. If you discover all we wish this first night, I will need to occupy that bed but once; but 'tis possible we will have to go through this process two or three nights. . . . When he dresses my wound, 'twill be in his surgery. His bedroom is between it and the room where he writes. You will hear him coming back. Then make a jump out the window. Go through the cave till you come to the torch. Light it without fear. No one can possibly see you. To-morrow about ten meet me on the Wissahickon. Now, methinks we understand each other, and we will trust to our quick wits and to the help of the Fates."

For more than two long hours they waited there, and as they waited they talked to each other softly and with care. They did not speak again of the business in hand, nor of the war, nor of the troubles of the time.

The silence of the night was around them; the mystery of the forest; the watching, patient stars were above their heads. And when they talked it was of the things that men seldom talk of to each other unless they have deep friendship for each other and confidence and sympathy. In all his after life, Henry Murray never forgot those quiet hours spent with his friend in that lonely place.

After a time they could hear noises in the distance as if guests were arriving in the adjoining portion of the inn. 'Twas not the habit of the hostess to inquire closely into the characters of her guests. Sometimes men came late at night and hurried away before daybreak as if fearful of being seen. As long as they paid their score, she asked no questions. Night was often her best time to gather coin.

But to-night it so chanced that these arriving guests were harmless travellers.

" 'Tis all to my liking," said Rodney, quietly, " for when the time comes for me to enter this wing, and I ask for Doctor Worthington's attendance, 'tis well that I get not into a band of roisterers, for it might not be easy for me to get away from them without having to drink more grog than my stomach has digestion for. Ah! See! See! "

Bingham's fingers closed over Henry Murray's. A window right before them became sharply defined from the dark, surrounding walls; and they saw plainly into a room growing brighter and brighter as candles were one by one lit upon the table in the centre.

Then Murray saw distinctly Doctor Worthington throw hat and cloak on a chair and come to the window. Murray could not get rid of the impression that he was seen, and he shrank closer back into the shadow; but the Doctor, after peering sharply down into the courtyard, turned back into the room. He laid some papers on the table; lit his pipe; smoked awhile, then began to read. And as he read, he made notes upon the margins of the papers.

" Now, Murray, I am going in a minute. . . . Remember. Ten o'clock to-morrow morning."

Their plan succeeded in a measure. . . . Rodney Bingham, with bleeding wrist, induced the hostess to call for Doctor Worthington. He came hastily

to the help of Mr. Kelper; but during his absence
Henry Murray discovered little.

The next night, they waited in the cave and nothing at all came of it. About ten, Doctor Worthington returned home, and after smoking a quiet pipe
by his window, he went off to bed.

The third night was momentous. The inn happened to be filled with British troopers, sent, as
Bingham and Murray discovered afterwards to be
in readiness to go into ambush the next morning
that they might attack Washington and his guard
as they would pass the tavern on their way to visit
Charles Murray at Cliveden.

Doctor Worthington was early in his rooms.
When Bingham and Murray arrived opposite his
window, it was already a blaze of light.

Mr. Kelper's wounded wrist had caused him
trouble that day. By a mischance the bandage
had become displaced and he had removed it.
'Twould be necessary to have a new one, if Doctor Worthington would be so kind. This all
took time, and it so happened that the genial
philosopher waxed talkative and besought the
Doctor's attention to some tales which were well
spiced with wit. Perhaps the Doctor would also
have a quiet smoke with him in the corner of
the tap-room near the chimney. To Mr. Kelper's
satisfaction, the good Doctor seemed glad to com-
ply. Worthington had carefully locked the door of
his private room, and he felt secure. In truth, no
fear of coming evil marred his peace of mind. All
his plans had been cleverly made. He had not only

strong hope but expectation that the morrow would bring their fulfilment: the great rebel would be in the hands of his enemies, and he himself would be the toast of the whole British army; his rival would be ruined; the maiden of his choice would after a time be brought to see that his love would be compensation for what she had lost. He had no fear of discovery in regard to the forged letters, — no one, not even Howe, knew of them. All traces of his work on these letters would to-night be destroyed. In truth, he had got them out to burn them when Mr. Kelper had so peremptorily called for help in his plight. Yes! he would burn even Howe's message to him which had come by the hand of one of these troopers carousing in the other part of the inn. It suited Doctor Worthington's prudent soul that no one but Howe should know of his share in the plan for Washington's capture till the full and glorious consummation of all his plotting. Then the whole world might know.

CHAPTER XLVIII.

"Think you he is here? Oh! ye have been nicely fooled by these rebels. They have played their game well. Your brilliant Captain is now a prisoner at Valley Forge, a noose is round his neck."

IN truth, it was a merry troop which had set out from Philadelphia — merry in spite of rain and bad roads. Once Colonel Musgrave grumbled; but he bethought himself that 'twas his own wish to ride to Cliveden, and that he himself had begged for the privilege of being one of the party Lieutenant Shipton had been bidden by General Howe to form as escort for the absent Captain Peyton. André was too occupied with social affairs to concern himself much with this expedition.

"Egad! I will be here to welcome Peyton," he laughed to Shipton, "and a right good welcome is in store for him. Tell him to limber up his legs for the dance, and catch no distemper because of these bad rains."

" 'Tis no weather for him," said Lieutenant Shipton. "I marvel much that Lord Carlisle waxes so impatient. 'Twere far better to wait till the storm passes."

" 'Tis hard for him to wait. It is long since he has seen Arthur. He has much to tell him of England and home, and his beloved Chatham. Arthur will not be comforted at the news of Chatham's illness. Carlisle has fears for his life."

The gentle-hearted André looked grave.

" 'Twill cut Peyton to the heart should Chatham die ere he have chance to sail for home."

" Carlisle says that 'tis scarce possible that Pitt can last much longer. The flame of his genius keeps him alive. Any excitement may bring great evil to him. He will never see Arthur again!"

" Come, come, boys, cheer up. Look not so glum, sirs."

'Twas Greyson who spoke. But Shipton's face did not brighten.

" 'Tis madness to bring Peyton out in such a storm," he said. " Appointment or no appointment, 'tis not best to ride across country to-night. Egad! Methinks I will go to Howe and ask permission that we wait till to-morrow night."

" No, no," said Captain Niggard. " Howe may have plans for another expedition to-morrow night. An attack on the rebels, perchance."

Expeditions of such a kind were so infrequently planned by the pleasure-loving, indolent Howe, that Niggard's remark provoked shouts and laughter.

None of these merry officers knew of the force that had already left the city, sent by General Howe to lie in wait for Washington. Howe had thought best to keep this plan secret. Should an accident befall, and the formidable rebel not be entrapped, 'twas best that few know of the attempt.

" How many troopers make up our escort?" asked Greyson, as he fastened on his sword.

" Near twenty," answered Musgrave, with a pleasant oath. " Would we might chance upon a party of rebels, and have a brush with them. 'Tis long since we gave the miscreants a touch of our steel."

And the gallant hero of the Battle of Germantown brought his eyebrows together in a heavy frown.

"Egad! boys. I have a proposal."

'Twas Greyson who spoke. The others paused in the buckling on of spurs, the arrangement of swords.

"Listen, boys. The shortest way to Cliveden is, of course, out Front Street to the second redoubt, then up country by the Germantown Road. But what a beastly road it is, full of holes and mud. Let us get an early start, long before dark, and take the Ridge Road. After passing the lines and once beyond the advance redoubt there, 'twill be a fine gallop up country. There is a wayside tavern this side of School House Lane. We can get supper there. Or we can go on further to the "Crossroads Tavern," just beyond where the Wissahickon flows into the Schuylkill. The ale there is of finest brew. Worthington has told me of it. If we choose, we can turn at School House Lane to the Market Square and up; or if we find we are not pressed for time and the wind isn't out of our beasts, we can keep on the Ridge Road till we come to the lane that leads off near the old Monastery. Then we could manage to get across the creek to that cross-road that will take us to Mount Airy, and so on down to Cliveden. What say you, merry gentlemen?"

Niggard laughed.

" 'Tis the road we ran on when his Lordship

heard the firing at Germantown. But we broke across the fields before we came to School House Lane, and thus got quickly to the help of Grey. We are sure to find some rebels on that road. The whole region around the Wissahickon swarms with them. Let us hurry and go."

"Should we meet any of the beggars, Musgrave, you can take command, an you will."

Musgrave smiled.

"Thank you, Greyson. 'Twould be a pleasure."

There were vexatious delays in starting; and they had only passed Redoubt No. 6 and not yet reached the advance-posts, when the storm broke. But they galloped on. But just before they got to School House Lane, the violence of the storm forced them to the nearest shelter, — a wayside farmhouse of sorry aspect without, but full of cheer within. The sight of magic English shillings made the farmer enthusiastic and full of energy. He piled up the logs and brought ale of good quality from his cellar.

There was so long a halt at this wayside farmhouse, that at last Lieutenant Shipton waxed impatient. With urgent manner he begged his companions bid farewell to the charms of blazing fires and foaming mugs; but the gallant Colonel, with a cheery oath, would order more ale and stretch out his legs with a sigh of content.

"Of a truth, the city with all its luxury has not furnished us with cheer like this. Naught like a good ride in the storm to make the appetite keen and worthy, and furnish zest to the good supper the landlord is providing. Would ye have us leave that supper untasted, boy? We need not to be at

Cliveden till nine or ten o'clock. And if the storm continue, we can leave the rebels untouched till we are on the home journey. Then let them beware! . . . And why, in sooth, be in such haste to wrest the Captain from the unwilling arms of his lady? My dear Sir Robert, methinks he will give us scant welcome when we do arrive. Look not glum, my dear Bob. I speak truth. Peyton has more preference to stay looking into the blue eyes of that brave maiden of many memories, than to ride with us in this beastly storm. Here, Greyson, here, Niggard, let us vote on it, boys. A vote, a vote."

But at last the farm was left behind and the garden gate of Cliveden reached just as Jake came dashing up the road.

He seemed in undue haste and passed them with scant ceremony. But the next moment, Shipton saw the big door of the house open and the glow of cheerful lights within. His heart gave a great throb. He would soon see his friend and grasp his hand.

The big door was not closed. It stood open as if inviting him; as if it had large hospitality, warm cheer, and good welcome.

CHAPTER XLIX.

"But Captain Peyton is an Englishman, a man of honour, a gentleman. A gentleman would not betray the heart that trusts him."

IN his sudden surprise, when Margaret threw Worthington's knife through the window, Henry Murray had neglected to close the door. Then his absorption in Jake's recital made him still forgetful of danger or the need of caution. He felt overwhelmed at the news of Peyton's capture, overwhelmed at the magnitude of the evil that Worthington's trickery had wrought. Margaret's vehement warning, also, gave him unquiet thoughts. He listened to her swift steps through the passageway, then went over to his father.

"Think you that Captain Peyton knew aught of these matters, and that was why he left?"

"I know not. I would you had taken me into your confidence, my son. Much of this unhappy mischief might have been prevented."

Henry looked troubled.

"Father, till last eve I had but bare suspicion on which to work. I had learned to doubt this fellow; but my suspicions could not be justified without proofs."

"I would you had told me," persisted Mr. Murray, plaintively.

" Father, I dared not. Had I taken any of you into my confidence to-day, Worthington might have escaped me. He is such a sly fox, he might have got wind of it. I wanted him to have no idea whatever of how closely he was watched. Father, I wished to take no risk of his escaping me. Had you and Annette and Margaret known, you could not have disguised your knowledge. Of a truth, the wily knave would have scented danger, and been off beyond my reach. Margaret, of all others, would have scarce been able to conceal her contempt."

" Are you sure you have perfect proof now? The rascal is slippery, and be sure he'll find a way out if any mortal can."

" He can't find a way out. I've woven a web around him, and he can't escape. But I am over-whelmed at this news of Arthur's capture. Of a verity, this trickery and treachery have been greater than even I thought possible."

" Hush! he may hear you," whispered Mr. Murray. " Egad! the door! I hear him moving towards it. Close it quickly."

Henry Murray sprang forward to lift the heavy bar and swing it in its place. But he was too late. In the doorway stood Shipton, his face smiling, his hand outstretched. Henry Murray started back in astonishment. Shipton came further in.

" Of a truth, Mr. Murray, 'tis glad I am to see you again. I saw your door ajar, and jumped quietly from my horse ere the others rode up. I wished to be the first to greet you all. Your pardon, if I startled you. Ah, madam! your servant."

Hat and hand on his heart, the youth smiled joyously, and went over where Annette was stand-

ing. But he stopped suddenly when, instead of the
sweeping curtsy he expected, she turned away and
burst into a passion of tears. He looked at Henry
Murray in bewilderment. There was an awkward
moment of silence; then the Lieutenant bowed to
Charles Murray gravely.

There was the sound of subdued voices outside
and the stamp of hoofs. Then Musgrave appeared
at the door, Niggard and Greyson not far behind.
Then came Captain De Lancey, Major Stoddard and
Colonel Tarleton.

Henry Murray was a man of the world, seldom
at a loss for words even in conditions awkward or
exciting. But now he seemed tongue-tied. What
to say, what to do, was the question. He could not
welcome these friends of Captain Peyton's, nor could
he refuse them hospitality. But how to explain
Captain Peyton's absence; how to impose silence
upon Worthington; how to keep this implacable
enemy from doing them all a deadly wrong! Henry
Murray was not kept long in suspense. Doctor
Worthington glanced in triumph at his puzzled face.
Then he turned to Musgrave and grasped his arm,
exclaiming, in a loud, vehement tone:

" Ye come well in time. Ye cannot bag the big
game; but I am a prisoner of the rebel here, who
threatens me both with tongue and sword. Gentlemen, make him your prisoner. He is a most dangerous foe of the King."

Musgrave shook Worthington off, saying, with
a cheery oath, " Peace, Saddle-bags. We will attend you anon."

Worthington straightened his shoulders.

" Attend me now, or it will be too late to save your Captain."

Shipton turned in astonishment. Captain Niggard put his hand on his sword, and came further into the room. Major Greyson's small eyes glittered.

" Gentlemen," exclaimed Worthington, vehemently, " I demand your protection from this rebel here. He holds me prisoner because I have been serving your King. See! Your Lieutenant is in Howe's confidence. He knows well my true position. 'Tis useless to conceal it longer. It must be known that I have been a secret servant of the King. He knows how well I have served the King. I must be saved. You will save me. Howe were right glad. Lieutenant, answer me! Is this not true?"

There was a moment of silence; then Shipton bowed gravely.

" You are safe with us, Doctor Worthington, though Mr. Murray will grant explanation. 'Tis his right."

" Colonel Musgrave, why came you hither?" asked Worthington, with emphasis, turning quickly before Henry Murray could speak.

" You are as curious as a wench, Saddle-bags," answered Musgrave, rudely.

Worthington frowned.

" Put up your frowns, good physician. You will need them on other occasions."

Musgrave's stomach was full of the good farmer's ale, and his head was full of pleasantries.

" Egad! Worthington, hast any physics in yon saddle-bags that will cure the grief that comes from parting? . . . We come, Saddle-bags, to escort our young Captain to camp. We are damnably late, eh, Greyson? But we lost our way in the storm. We want our Captain. We have missed him sore, and now we crave his company. His cousin has arrived from England, and wants him in the city, and we must make short work of wresting the Captain from his pretty siren, who keeps him here." Musgrave turned to Annette. " Bid Captain Peyton hither, I pray you."

Worthington spoke quickly.

" Think you he is here? Oh, ye have been nicely fooled by these rebels! They have played their game well. Your brilliant Captain is now a prisoner at Valley Forge; a noose is round his neck. These Murrays have accused him of treachery. He will be hanged as a spy, and that speedily.".

Greyson and Tarleton and De Lancey started forward. Niggard's face grew set and stern.

" Heed him not," cried Henry Murray, breathlessly. " My sister has gone to free Captain Peyton. She will get there in time."

" Zounds! " exclaimed Musgrave. " Captain Peyton not here? He has been made a prisoner? "

" No! no! It cannot be! " said Shipton. " Tell me, madam," and he turned with appeal to Annette, " tell me the meaning of it all? Where is your sister? Where is Arthur? "

But Annette could not answer. She was still sobbing pitifully. Shipton turned to Charles Murray.

" Tell me, sir. Know you aught of truth in this? "

But Charles Murray's answer was overborne by Worthington's loud and vehement voice. He would have Shipton's attention. He would have the attention of all these Englishmen. And he gained his wish. All eyes were fixed upon him. His eyes glowed with passion and patriotic zeal.

"That man is a dangerous foe to our cause," he shouted, pointing to Henry Murray. "We have fought. See my wounded arm. We have fought over this very matter. He long ago distrusted your Captain, and wished him to leave this house. And 'tis his own sister who has accused him of treachery."

"'Tis he, he who has put Peyton in this trouble," cried Henry Murray, angrily; but no one paid him heed. He shook his fist at Worthington. "'Tis he! 'tis he who has done it!"

"Tell me, old man," said Musgrave, seizing Charles Murray's arm with sudden passion, "is our Captain a prisoner in the rebel camp?"

"Yes! yes! I fear me 'tis true. But 'tis all a mistake. It will be made right. My daughter has ridden thither to have him set free. She will get there in time. You will have your Captain in safety yet."

With a furious oath, Colonel Musgrave rushed to the door and called peremptorily to one of the troopers outside. He came back the next moment, holding a heavy cord. Ere Greyson and the others, who were talking excitedly, could guess his object, he had seized Henry Murray's arms. Shipton started forward, his face pale, his eyes flashing with surprise and indignation. But a significant and threatening look from Musgrave silenced his involuntary protest.

"'Tis well! 'Tis well!" exclaimed Worthington,

hastening to Musgrave's help. " This man is a spy. He it was who carried those letters you were seeking last October. Egad! sir, 'tis meet he have his punishment now."

" Damme, Musgrave! He must be taken to Howe instead," shouted Stoddard.

" Yes, to Howe, to the city!" echoed Niggard.

Worthington looked into Henry Murray's paling face and whispered, with a sneer:

" It is as fair as your threat to take me to Valley Forge. . . . ' As for America, she wants not these loyalists,' quoth you a moment agone. You will find, my dear sir, that she doth not need the precious services of a rebel like you. She will ask in vain. Ha! ha!"

" Shipton, look to the knots, if they be tied well," ordered Musgrave, in a threatening tone. With manifest reluctance, Shipton bent over the knots the Colonel had skilfully and quickly tied. Then he glanced up into Henry Murray's face.

" Your pardon, sir," he whispered, hoarsely. " I will help you when I can."

His eyes spoke still more, and, stepping back, he made an almost imperceptible motion towards the door. But Henry Murray knew it would be useless to make a wild rush to escape. Worthington was watching him closely, and there were troopers outside. He made many efforts to speak, to explain, even to threaten; but his voice was unheard. Musgrave was talking excitedly to De Lancey. De Lancey was talking to Greyson, Niggard, and Tarleton at the same time. There was uproar among the men crowding the big doorway. The candlelight flared on agitated and angry faces.

Charles Murray stood in bewildered amazement. Annette grew faint, and clung to a chair for support. Henry looked at her entreatingly, but could not reach her to render help. It all happened quickly. Ere she could realise the full meaning of her husband's danger, another peremptory order had been given by the angry Colonel. Two burly troopers had seized Henry Murray in their arms, and roughly carried him out. Chairs were overturned in the general confusion, as Worthington and the others rushed after. Shipton went the last of all.

With strained ears, Annette and her father listened. They heard an order given for two troopers to stay behind that the prisoner and the Doctor might have mounts without delay. Then came the sounds of hoarse oaths and peremptory commands, of jingling spurs and swords, of stamping hoofs.

The sounds grew fainter, as one by one the horsemen galloped along the sodden garden road.

Then came silence.

CHAPTER L.

"We will trust to our quick wits and to the help of the Fates."

THE wind and rain had surged and tossed around the old tavern on the " Ridge," till it seemed as if every door and shutter and window-frame were crazy with unrest. The trees moaned and sighed in the adjacent forest. The roads were desolate and storm-swept.

'Twas a night for ghosts to walk, for witches to ride fast and furiously; a night to cause dread and uncanny thoughts; for good and guiltless people to gather around warm firesides and tell cheerful tales.

The soldiers, who since last eve had swarmed around the old tavern, departed as soon as night fell. A messenger had brought their leader word that the rebel General, for whom they had been waiting, would not pass that way now. He had been warned. They galloped to the city, and were already in garrison when Musgrave and his friends turned into School House Lane.

Since the departure of these soldiers, the tavern had been empty of guests. Mr. Kelper, too, had gone, and had not returned. He had paid his score, as was his wont, each morning, because, as he said, he was a man of whims, and vagrancy was in his

421

blood. He might come back that night about ten, and he might not. The hostess took his money, and, with a smile into his genial face, assured him he would be welcome when he came.

The good dame gave no thought to Doctor Worthington, for he was often absent, — late, very late into the night.

Mr. Kelper had gone to the meeting-place on the Wissahickon, but, instead of Henry Murray, he found a piece of paper tied to a stone: —

" Keep yourself safe, and at ten to-night be at the place where you can see the light shining in the window. If you see me there in the room, I may need your help."

The hour of ten came and passed. Then eleven, twelve. 'Twas near one, and the hostess was about to go to rest, when, to her delight, she descried a large party of horsemen up the road. Her delight changed to chagrin, however, when she saw the party upon nearer view. She had scant patronage from men such as they. They had no money to spend, and they were exceeding covetous of property of an edible nature, which might fall in their way.

These foragers from Valley Forge were rough, common fellows, to be sure; but they were honest and brave, and they were serving their country well and loyally. The hardships of the winter had been terrible, and these men, with others like them, had oft kept grim Death from the camp of Washington.

The violent storms had much delayed them; but now, heavily laden with screaming chickens and other satisfactory spoils, they were betaking themselves to the ferry, on their way back to camp. Arrived near the tavern, temptation sore assailed them. For a hasty raid they had no warrant, because they could carry nothing more, — panniers, bags, cloaks, were crammed full. But the grog! They were of mind to halt a mere moment. Their leader did not dismount, but called to Hans from the road, and bade him bring a mug apiece, or he would learn the taste of something far sharper, — something that would burn and sting. This argument was potent. Hans dared not disobey.

They were still busy with the grog, when, dashing along the road, there came a troop of British horse. 'Twas an opportunity Colonel Musgrave had been seeking; a brush with the rebels was what he craved.

Quick shots were fired. There were sword-thrusts in the darkness. The foragers defended themselves vigorously, and in numbers they were greater than their foe. In the confusion and fury of the contest, it was scarce noticed that Doctor Worthington suddenly wheeled his horse, and galloped back along the road he had come, — lost the next instant in the gloom of the trees that skirted the road.

Colonel Musgrave was no coward or braggart, but he soon found that his escort was no match in numbers or in prowess with these sturdy sons of the soil; he, therefore, gave a hasty order; spurs were put to smoking flanks, and the next moment he and his friends were dashing along the road in the direction of Philadelphia. But ere they went, it so chanced that a man broke from among them and hurled himself into the midst of the Americans.

Little injury had been done by the brief, fierce fight. The darkness had been a protection, and many sword-thrusts and pistol-shots had been at random. Streaks of red had flowed over brilliant uniforms and faded homespun coats, and the red seemed of about equal quality. One stout British trooper bore the mark of American steel across his cheek. Another's arm hung useless. One poor Continental cursed his luck and swore savagely under his breath, because of the stings of many wounds. Lieutenant Shipton had suddenly reeled in his saddle, but had been kept from falling by Greyson, who threw his strong arm around him. Then the two friends galloped off side by side, and the way they took was up the Ridge Road, further from the city.

Blood and anger, strife and hate. And a peaceful moon overhead doing its best to shine.

Such a useless, pitiful fight!

Burdened as they were with provender, which was sorely needed in a hungry camp, the Americans had no thought of pursuit. They fired some random shots. Then gathered themselves into a pretence of order, and betook themselves down to the ferry.

And with them went the man who had joined them in such friendly fashion.

CHAPTER LI.

" A mean, cowardly, contemptible blow."

MARGARET and her faithful Jake did not take the way to Valley Forge they had chosen earlier in the day. The darkness made that way perilous. It would have led them across country, through fields and tangled thickets, over rocks and holes. Now they had to keep to the plain road.

As it chanced, they were later in starting from Cliveden than the troopers under Musgrave; thus, when they came to the beginning of the dense wood which skirted both sides of the road, they were startled by the first shots of the attack at the Crossroads Tavern. They drew rein suddenly.

" Missy," Jake said, hurriedly, " we cawn't go pas' dare. T'ink we hab to go back an' strike cross de fields, an' den get back to de Ridge Road furder up, beyon' all dis trubbul. Den go to Swedes Ford 'stead o' de ferry here."

" We lose so much time, Jake."

" I know, I know, missy."

Just then the moon struggled once more from out behind the drifting storm-cloud, and by its pale, spectral light, they saw how near they were to the source of danger. A few bullets fell almost at their feet. Prince reared. For a moment Margaret had all she could do to get him in control. Then Jake continued, in his soft voice:

"Missy, dear, we'll hab to try anudder way."

Just then a bullet whizzed near Tempest's head. He gave one mad plunge, then stood trembling.

Margaret's face grew stern and set.

"Jake, we can go past them. They are so busied with themselves, they will pay no heed to us. We will make a dash for it. The other way means a loss of a full hour."

But Tempest, who had been the most reasonable of horses, showing a sane and wholesome humour oft most comforting to his mistress, now proved how unreliable, at critical moments, horses as well as men can be. He seemed beside himself with unreasoning terror. He refused to go back, he refused to advance. Jake could do nothing.

And as he struggled with the refractory creature, he paid no heed to a bullet that came past him; nor did he note that his mistress caught her breath in a quick sob, and then grasped her left wrist and held it tight.

Time was passing swiftly.

"There is no help for it, Jake," said Margaret. "I will make a dash past those soldiers. Follow me quickly, when your horse learns sense once more." And with the shadow of her old, whimsical smile, she added, "Would I had taught him to be used to petticoats, Jake. Then you could take Prince and leave me behind."

"Ride on now, missy. Dare's a lull in de fight. See, de British are drawin' off. If dare's no moah ob dose bullets, I'll get a chance to follow you an' take care ob you."

Poor Jake cursed his powerlessness. In spite of coaxing or imperative voice, of whip or spur or gentle caresses, Tempest considered it to be his mission to show that he was complete master.

On through the wood rode Margaret, till suddenly, right before her, emerging from the dark shadow of the trees, there appeared a solitary horseman. She gave her horse a sharp cut with the whip; but the next instant her bridle was seized in a strong, rough grasp, and a familiar voice exclaimed:

"Ah! I knew you could not be far behind us. Come! Enough of this wild scheme of yours to ride to Valley Forge."

CHAPTER LII.

"We shall fight against bitter, cruel, overwhelming odds"

IN her surprise at thus meeting the man whom she supposed to be her brother's prisoner, Margaret felt dazed and bewildered. But she soon recovered her self-control. She was too intrepid to yield without resistance. She must ride on. She must get to Valley Forge!

Every nerve was on tension. Everything must bend to this desperate purpose. Doctor Worthington was at her left. She had been holding both whip and reins in her right hand; but now, grasping her whip in her left hand, she raised it to cut it across his face, when there came again that horrible, stinging pain in her wrist. The whip fell from her grasp. Then suddenly the road, the moonlight, the horses' forms, the dark shadows of the trees, blended together in a dim haze.

When she came to herself, she found that she was in a large room with low-hanging rafters. The room was dark, save for the fitful gleams of two sputtering candles upon a common pine table in the centre.

Margaret struggled to her feet, and looked about her in bewildered surprise. At first she thought herself alone; then some one stirred in the shadowy corner. Her eyes met those of Dame Van Slycke.

" Where am I? " she asked, breathlessly.

" There! there! " the dame said, soothingly, as if speaking to a child.

" I asked you to tell me where I am," repeated Margaret, haughtily.

There was a note of authority in her tone which made the woman alter hers.

" You are at the Cross-roads Tavern," she answered, with an awkward curtsy.

" I fainted, methinks, and Doctor Worthington brought me here? "

" Ay, mistress. He seemed much concerned."

" Has Doctor Worthington gone? "

" No, mistress. He lives here. This is one of his private rooms. He will return within the moment. He has but gone to tell the hostler to have your horse baited well, for you tarry, quoth he, till the morning."

" O madam! Help me! I must ride on at once. 'Tis a matter of life and death. Get my horse for me. Help me! I must ride on. You will be well rewarded."

But the dame shook her head. The Doctor, with a significant touch of his forehead, had told her that Mistress Murray would doubtless speak in this fashion. She had, of late, been troubled with a delusion that he was her enemy; whereas they had been dear friends, and he had been at her home near every day. He had found her on the road alone. She had evidently escaped from the custody of her servant. The hostess must pay no heed to aught wild or distraught which she might say. In the morning he would return her to her friends. But she was far too faint and tired to be taken home to-night. Besides, the good dame knew the fat reward if she always regarded his commands.

Margaret went to the door. It gave her little surprise to find it locked.

"Madam," she said, with gentle dignity, "I am quite recovered from my strange attack of faintness, and must go. Unlock this door."

The hostess shook her head.

"That I cannot do," she said; "'tis locked from the other side. But Doctor Worthington will soon return."

Margaret seized one of the candles, and went over to the narrow windows on the south. The shutters were tightly fastened. She went to the east window, and it was also closed. But the shutters were open. She peered out. All she could see were the branches of dark trees swaying in the wind. A high wall enclosed a narrow court.

She was a prisoner. For a moment she was almost in despair. Then she turned fiercely to her companion.

"Madam, you little know the sin you are committing to keep me here. You little know the facts of this matter."

What was happening in the camp now? Could Jake get there in time? How late was it? Was it near morning? Oh! this torture of suspense, how could she bear it? Easier was it riding in that storm, in the wind and the rain.

"Oh! to wait and not know!" she thought, bitterly. "To be quiet and wait! If I could but be on Selim again. Then I could bear it!"

She kept repeating to herself all her father's arguments. In truth, they would delay. They would not show such cruel, reckless haste. Her judgment told her that Mr. Murray was right. A man of Captain Peyton's dignity of character would be treated with respect. He would defend himself. They would listen. He would not be, he could not be, hanged at dawn! And yet the poison of Doctor Worthington's words was having its effect. She was desperately anxious and afraid.

" How slowly the time goes when the heart is on fire with grief and with pain," she thought. " But when one is happy, then the minutes fly. Their wings are gold. The clock never strikes."

She went to the window and looked out upon the swaying, restless trees.

" The happy days can never come back! He said only this morning, he said that he had been so happy all these blessed days with me. And I said I could not bear to think of the time when he would leave me. . . . O God! he left me, and I — I drove him away. My words hurt and stung him. I told him I had never loved him, and he believed me. I saw it in his face. . . . He believed me always. And I could not even trust him. Oh! will I ever be able to rest again? Oh! could I but be on Selim again. . . . Then I could bear it. But to wait here. . . . To wait, and not know."

She looked searchingly at the woman's face while these unquiet thoughts ran riot in her brain. 'Twas a somewhat hard, rough face, one made hard by years of fighting with the world and bearing many heavy sorrows; but there was something soft and tender shining in the eyes. Margaret felt all at once that could a bond of common interest but be formed between them, there might be help and sympathy for her.

"Madam," she said, and her voice had that strange thrill in it which always won people, which made them glad to serve her. "Madam! Listen. There is a British soldier, a man high in favour with men in England. But he was wounded in the great battle here, and has been in retirement. He is now a prisoner in the American camp, put there by treachery. He may be hanged as a spy. Doctor Worthington says at dawn — soon — soon. But he is innocent, innocent. Doctor Worthington himself is guilty. He confessed this to me. He wishes to destroy this Englishman because — because — And you keep me here when I was on the way to get him freed. In truth, Doctor Worthington wishes me not to go. Madam, you little know what you are doing."

A dark flush came into Dame Van Slycke's face. "'Tis different from what the doctor said."

There was a compelling charm about Margaret Murray. No one could be with her long without feeling it. But there was an earnestness, a tender solemnity about her manner now which made even a stronger appeal.

There was some hidden mystery in this matter. And the pathetic sincerity, the sorrowful grace of this lonely midnight guest, stirred emotions in the hostess's heart which she had not felt for years. Margaret felt that she had won the woman to her side.

"Madam, you will help me, that I know. We

will say naught of reward just now. But you will help me?"

"You love this Englishman, mistress?"

Margaret simply bowed her head. The woman's insight scarce made her feel surprise. But afterwards she marvelled at it.

"I love the British," said the hostess, fervently. "I am from England myself. Years ago, 'tis true; but I have never forgot. I lived in Holland, where I married, but I have never forgot the primroses, the hedges, the daisies — "

The woman's eyes filled with unwonted tears.

Margaret felt that the bond of common sympathy had been found.

"You will help me? You will get my horse and let me go? Or you will send a message to Valley Forge?"

"Hush!" the dame whispered. "I will do all possible, but I fear me it will be little. My servants are in that man's pay."

They heard a heavy footstep outside the door.

"You will not leave me?" whispered Margaret, and, in spite of her great self-control, her voice trembled.

"No, mistress, I will not leave you if I can help it."

"Can I not send a message?"

"Hush!" the dame answered.

The door opened softly, and Doctor Worthington came in. He looked at Margaret sharply.

"Quite well again, I hope; but we must have more light. 'Tis dark as midnight here. And we need air."

After he had lit the row of candles on a small

table in the corner, he threw up the window. The
cool wind blew in. Then he came nearer to Margaret; but she stood in chilling silence. As he got
still nearer, she drew back haughtily. He smiled
with full comprehension.

"Bear me no grudge, Margaret. I brought you
where you would have the best of care. 'Tis no
night for you to be out alone. By my troth, you
should be by your own fireside after the hard gallop
you and I had together this morning. You must
be worn out. Believe me, I had no thought of aught
but your best interests when I brought you here.
Our hostess will give you the best of care."

That soft, insinuating voice! How it rasped
every nerve!

How blind they all had been that they could ever
have seen in this man a friend!

He shrugged his shoulders at her continued
silence.

The hostess had withdrawn into the remote corner of the room. Worthington glanced at her, and
then continued, in a low tone:

"You know now that I am not to be foiled or
thwarted. I could not let you go to Valley Forge
again. It would have spoiled my plan."

In her indignation and in her pride, Margaret
would have wished to hide from him all signs of
suffering, but almost against her will she said,
huskily:

"Oh, it was cruel, cruel to stop me in my ride!"

His eyes gleamed.

"And every moment you tarry here lessens his
chance."

"But my brother will get there. Jake may be there now."

He smiled again. How little she knew of what had happened since she had left the hall at Cliveden.

At the sight of that smile, her heart sank.

"Now, Margaret," he said, "this is fate. 'Tis as it should be. 'Twas not willed that you and I should be apart; else why should I have escaped from that troublesome brother of yours who sought to ruin me; why should he now be on his way to Philadelphia?"

"To Philadelphia?"

She looked at him with strained eyes.

"Yes," he answered; and the satisfaction in his tone was not concealed. "Yes, a prisoner of Musgrave."

"A prisoner! And why?"

"Because Musgrave knows now that your brother sought to foil him last October; and he knows now that the Murrays have been the cause of Captain Peyton being accused of treachery, and taken to Valley Forge to be hanged as a spy."

Doctor Worthington had played a desperate game. He had played it cleverly, with a devil's patience. But he had lost. He knew that well. He had lost the part of the game he valued most. He could crush his rival; ruin the man who had exposed his duplicity; but he had now slight hope that he could ever win this maiden. Despite his egotism, he had clear perceptions. He knew now that he could never break down her distrust of him. He knew human nature well enough to realise that Margaret's love would never be given without her trust.

Despite his narrowness of soul, his weakness of character, Doctor Worthington had a measure of the saving gift of humour. He was not like the " villain of the play," who is willing to force or buy or bribe a woman. She must come to him of her own will. He knew now that Margaret would never come to him. He had indeed hoped that, in her despair at her lover's perfidy, she would turn to him for comfort. He would have tried so hard to comfort her, been so kind, so kind. But now! What a fool he had been to give her brother chances to make these discoveries! How had he made them? How was it possible? It was all a baffling mystery.

Despite his disappointment and chagrin, Fate had played into his hands an opportunity for revenge, and he was too small a soul not to take advantage of what Fate offered. He not only longed to destroy the men he hated; he also wanted to be witness of the suffering their ruin would cause.

And yet this man was a strange and puzzling mixture of passion, of inflexible purpose, and of worldly prudence. With all his cruelty to her whom he fancied he loved, but loved hopelessly, — cruelty which sprang from the ignoble wish to display his power and to keep himself in her thoughts, to make himself an unforgettable part of her life, — he was not so cruel as to subject her to the humiliation of being there with him in that lonely inn, alone.

He allowed the hostess to remain; her presence need be no restriction upon his speech; and her presence here would prevent her sending messages to Valley Forge or doing aught to frustrate his plan that Margaret should not have the joy of saving her lover. Doctor Worthington felt that there were certain compensations for his own suffering.

"Margaret," he said, softly, "listen to me. Your lover is lost to you. Even were his life to be saved, and you must know how little chance there is of that, he will never forgive you for your part in this affair. You believed him guilty; you denounced him to Washington; you gave testimony to Hamilton which will make him hasten to condemn him; which will make him merciless in his haste. This very testimony of yours hastens your lover's fate. Why? Because Washington and Hamilton trust you. They trust your integrity. This testimony from you will save them wearisome investigation. It removes any doubts they might have. You were very, very sure, you remember, that those letters were his. You expressed no doubts whatever. Ah! you little dreamed that I had planned that you should give this testimony; and give it as you did. How emphatic you were! How confident!"

His brutality won from her no expression of suffering, except that in her sad and tired eyes. Their expression she could not control.

"You need not trust the reasons for delay given by your father. You little know of the indignation in every patriot's heart because of the haste the British showed in the case of Nathan Hale. Every patriot is thirsting for revenge. An opportunity for it has now been granted. Your part in this tragic affair has been most dramatic, Margaret. I give you congratulation for your skill."

"O madam, help me! Help me! Send a message for me. Go! I beg you. I implore you."

But Worthington lifted his hand authoritatively.

"She cannot go. The doors are locked. And Hans has orders to allow no one to pass."

Margaret's lips tightened. She caught her arm convulsively. Worthington sprang towards her.

"Margaret! Tell me, are you hurt?"

"No! 'tis nothing," she answered, faintly. Then she turned wistful eyes upon him. "I beg you, implore you to leave me."

He smiled and shook his head.

"Leave you? No! I cannot."

"Doctor Worthington," she said, solemnly. "In your inmost heart you *must* know that I can never love you. You have made me suffer. You *know* I suffer. You know there is gloom and horror in my heart because of my failure. Be content and go! Why torture me by your presence here?"

She pointed to the door authoritatively. Then her breath came in a quick, convulsive sob. His practised eye saw that she was growing faint.

He caught her in his arms. She struggled a moment, and indignation gave her strength; then turned her head away and covered her face with her hand.

"It is nothing, nothing. I implore you to go."

He pulled open her sleeve.

"Ah! you are hurt. Come nearer the lights. I cannot see well here."

He led her nearer the candles, and as they passed before the window they could be seen distinctly. But there was naught outside there in the forest but those lonely, swaying trees!

"There! I can see better now. You *are* hurt. And in the darkness I made no discovery of it.

Fool! I might have known 'twas something like this to make *you* faint. Ah! that bullet struck your wrist. 'Twas aimed for Jake's horse, and did good service, too; but it hit you, you!"

There was genuine contrition in his tone.

Calling to the hostess he bade her lend assistance.

Margaret found it useless to struggle against him. The genuine physician's instinct to relieve physical suffering controlled him now. He lost himself in his task. He was tender and kind; and despite his own wounded arm he showed a deft and facile skill.

Suddenly, before she knew that he was through, she felt a passionate kiss upon her hand. She drew back. But he held her a moment longer. Then she broke away and stood with flashing, indignant eyes.

CHAPTER LIII.

"We shall fight and we shall win."

RODNEY BINGHAM was sore put to it to know what to do.

At the first firing near the tavern, Hans Bleeker and his under servants had extinguished all the lights, and then rushed to doors and windows and carefully closed and barred them. The whole place had taken on a grim, unfriendly look, with its dark walls and deserted courtyard. The front door of the left wing had opened once to admit Doctor Worthington and his companion. Then it had closed again.

Thus when Bingham stole around the wall and entered the courtyard, the two houses of the inn seemed to him equally hopeless and forbidding. He doubted much if even he could gain admittance. Anyway, 'twould be useless to ask for Doctor Worthington. He had probably given orders to Hans that no one would be admitted to him during the night. That would be an easy and an obvious method to carry out his scheme.

What that scheme was, Rodney Bingham had no means of knowing. He knew nothing of Henry Murray's discoveries last night. Why had he not arrived? What was the meaning of this long delay? He might come at any moment now, and stand in need of help. Rodney knew nothing of the treachery against Washington. He knew nothing of the misfortune that had befallen his friend in being captured by Musgrave. He was equally in the dark in regard to the danger threatening Captain Peyton. Why was Margaret Murray here in this lonely inn, at this late hour? He had been too far away to see the expression of her face. He could not tell if she were there of her own will, or if she were held prisoner. It was all a sad tangle to Rodney. One thing only comforted him. The hostess was with her. He had seen her through the window. Dame Van Slycke was a good woman. While she was with Margaret, all was well.

If Rodney had but known more! How gladly would he have taken that message for poor Margaret! He would have gone through fire and flood to serve her.

And Rodney's expectations were realised. To his repeated knockings there was no response. Every window opening upon the courtyard and upon the road was dark. Every door was shut. He wandered around, and waited and watched. Then knocked again. Finally a light appeared at an upper window, and a harsh voice called out into the darkness that whoever was seeking shelter at this unseemly hour must begone. The inn was closed for the night; and no guests would be admitted. Rodney called back and asked if a word could not be taken to Doctor Worthington; that there was urgent need. The same harsh voice bade him go elsewhere. Doctor Worthington was in bed, and would not be disturbed. The light disappeared, and the darkness and the silence came once more.

Rodney Bingham knew well the secrets of this house. He knew that Hans and the other serving-folk were in Doctor Worthington's pay; that were he to attempt force or even use threats he would be overpowered. Nothing would be gained. Everything might be lost.

Meanwhile he must await with patience the arrival of Henry Murray. And the obvious task for him just now was to keep as near as possible to Margaret. If she called for help, he would surely hear her. If the hostess left her, he would soon know it.

He looked well to the priming of his pistol; and then stole quietly back into the sheltering darkness of the trees.

CHAPTER LIV.

"We came, Saddle-bags, to escort our young Captain to camp. We have missed him sore — and now we crave his company."

MUSGRAVE and his men galloped madly; then he suddenly called a halt. To his surprise, neither Major Greyson nor the young Lieutenant were in his troop.

"Egad! we must turn back," he said to De Lancey. "They may have taken shelter in that tavern where we fought."

"The dawn will come soon," De Lancey answered. "We'll get Greyson and Shipton; and then perchance may have the luck at some breakfast from the landlord. I have no stomach for a long ride to the city in this chill air."

"'Tis a beastly climate," said Tarleton.

"Changeable as a wench."

"Yes, my bones are shivering," said Stoddard.

They turned their horses and rode slowly back.

"What became of Saddle-bags, Tarleton?"

"Methinks he went back the road we came — School House Lane, they call it? At least I lost sight of him just when we turned into the Ridge Road. It irked him to leave the comfort of Cliveden's warm fires, perchance."

Five minutes of silent riding; then the Colonel spoke again.

"Would I had a thousand men. I'd soon get Peyton free. 'Tis a hard dose we have to swallow."

"Would we could rescue him," said De Lancey, sadly.

"But we have made those miscreants smart."

"But not one prisoner, egad!"

"And we have lost the one we had. How came it, Tarleton, that Murray got away?"

"He and Shipton were riding close, their horses neck to neck, when we came suddenly upon this foraging party. Your order was to attack. During the fight in the darkness, Murray must have joined the rebels; for of a truth, when we got near that scrub of a tavern, Murray was not among us."

"Damned careless of Bob," exclaimed Musgrave, with an angry oath.

Tarleton and De Lancey looked at each other in consternation.

Arrived at the "Ridge," the tavern looked grimmer and more unfriendly than ever. 'Twas still dark and silent,—and the chill of the early morn was already in the air.

Colonel Musgrave motioned to a trooper. He dismounted and beat loudly with his sword-hilt on the door. There was no response. The trooper struck the oak again—this time impatiently. Then a light appeared at an upper window.

"Ho! ho! landlord, open to us, open to us!" shouted De Lancey. "We are King's men, of a surety. Open to us."

The light disappeared. The trooper struck the

oak until the echoes rang again. Then they saw the door open a little way. Hans Bleeker stood there, holding his candle above his head.

"Open to us, landlord," called Musgrave. "Thought you we were beggarly rebels bent on forage?"

"Ay, 'tis an unseemly hour, but the need is urgent," said De Lancey. "We seek two of our number who must have sought shelter with you after our skirmish down the road."

Hans opened the door wide and bowed obsequiously.

"No one is here, sir, already. No one."

"Art sure, sirrah? Have no officers quartered themselves upon you?"

"Not since last night, sir, already. Zis afternoon gone zey all avay."

"Has no one passed? Tell me, rode two officers past the shadows of those trees? Bethink yourself well, now. 'Tis worth your while."

But the burly German shook his head.

"Ven I heard ze muskets cracking already, I hurried in ze doors. I saw no one."

"The beggarly rebels must have left behind a goodly array of geese and chicks which they had gathered for their starving camp. Gad! 'twould be bliss to know if they surrendered aught of their hard-won spoils."

Niggard snapped out the words as if he wished revenge for the disappearance of his two friends.

"The chicks and geese can furnish banquet for this worthy landlord," said Tarleton.

Hans stood with a puzzled look on his keen, shrewd face. Then he bowed again obsequiously.

" There are chicks on the road yonder, good landlord. They will supply you with eggs."

" Ha, ha! There are geese yonder, landlord; get eggs from them, too."

" And a pig or two, landlord, which the cowards would have dropped in their flight. If their legs be not broken, raise them up, sirrah, to supply your guests in the years to come."

" No, no, my man," said Tarleton to the sergeant, who had just spoken. " We need the pigs to-day — a rasher of bacon and eggs, landlord, as soon as occasion serves."

" Be a loyal raiser of chickens, good landlord," said the sergeant, laughing, " and when King George has broken the stubborn pride of these rebels — "

" The chickens will be fat and comely hens."

" Hast any pretty wenches in thy parlours, landlord?"

" Peace," said Musgrave, authoritatively. " Landlord, see to these men. Bait their horses well, and let them have refreshment. We shall be in no haste to go."

He threw himself from his horse and came to the door. As he slipped a piece of gold into Hans's willing hand, De Lancey and Tarleton also dismounted.

" Grog, sirrah, grog, if ye have to tap every barrel in your cellars. Our bones are shivering."

'Twas Tarleton who spoke.

" Grog and your fireside, sirrah," said Captain Niggard. " Abundance of fire within and without. The morn is raw, and we return not to the city till our needs grow less urgent."

"Yes, yes, landlord — a good breakfast as soon as you can bestir your household."

And Musgrave and his friends entered the tavern.

The swift-coming hoofs along the road had been a relief to Rodney Bingham's strained nerves. The silence, the darkness, the suspense, had in truth been painful. Now the quiet tavern was in an up-roar; there were hurrying footsteps, jingling spurs, loud voices.

Rodney moved along in the shadow of the wall and looked out.

By the flaring light of torches and lanterns he saw that the courtyard was filling with troopers and their steeds. The creaking of damp saddles mingled with the jingling of spurs and swords. Then broad bars of light began to stretch across the courtyard as the shutters were thrown open and lights were lit in the lower windows opposite. Soon Rodney could see the faces of the officers entering. He started back into the shadows as he recognised Colonel Tarleton. 'Twas he who had discovered him in the bell-tower of Christ Church. Those piercing black eyes haunted Bingham's im-agination. No disguise, in truth, would deceive Colonel Tarleton. It behooved Bingham to be most prudent, most cautious, and run no risk of meeting that man face to face, else it would be all up with him. Then he could no longer serve his friends; and the work for his beloved General which lay so near his heart would be unfinished.

He watched anxiously till the horses were led to the stables, and the troopers began to settle them-selves in the comfortable rooms opposite. He could hear an occasional loud laugh, then some of the men broke forth into singing. Musgrave and his companions were however strangely quiet. Had Bingham known that their hearts were heavy because of Peyton's danger, and the uncertainty in regard to Greyson's and Shipton's fate, he would have felt a thrill of sympathy.

He had taken a great liking to the warm-hearted, genial lad whom he had helped that terrible October morning, when the gallant Captain had fallen in the midst of the fog and the smoke and the sharp bayonet-thrusts.

CHAPTER LV.

"The blood of the intrepid Murrays and the peace-loving Trents."

THE night fires of the camp were already fading in the light of the morning sun when a horseman dashed along the street bordered on each side by rude huts; past the outer posts and on — on into the open country. He dug the spurs into his steed, and the creature responded with splendid vim and spirit. Stones flew from behind its hoofs. It breathed the breath of its own speed as well as the fresh, invigorating breath of the morning.

Arrived at Swedes Ford, the horseman slackened speed and looked back. Away in the distance on the crest of a hill he saw the outlines of two figures against the sky.

"Dey'll soon be 'long after me," he said to himself.

The river ran gray and sullen, because of the recent storms. And the shadows from the hills and bluffs still rested upon it. The sun would need to climb much higher ere those slopes would be touched with gold.

The rider paid little heed to the fresh beauty around him. As soon as he had crossed the ford, he gathered speed once more. At every inn on the way, he had halted a moment to make inquiry for his mistress. He had intention now to stop at the Cross-roads Tavern; and if no one there had seen her or heard of her, he would gallop to Cliveden as fast as breath and feet could take him.

He rode up to the left wing of the Cross-roads Tavern with a measure of decorum to compensate for the previous wildness of his ride. Through the open windows of the right wing there came the sound of voices and the rattle of dishes. The windows of the left wing were all closed. In the morning light the place looked scarcely less grim and unfriendly than it had looked to Musgrave's impatient eyes an hour before.

Jake flung his bridle over the nearest post and strode to the front door. Failing to open it, he rapped softly — then more loudly. Then he went to the window nearest him, wrenched open one of the shutters, and looked in. The room was empty, save for a man who lay asleep on a rough bench before a dying fire. He was stirring uneasily in his sleep as if the noise of the rapping on the door had begun to force an entrance into the cavities of his dulled brain. Jake struck the window a lusty blow. The man started and looked up. Jake motioned towards the front. The man was seen to stumble across the floor and come to the door. Jake met him on the threshold. The man muttered an incoherent curse in a strange tongue. Then stretc.ied his arms and yawned hungrily.

Jake began to question him. But to every inquiry he shook his head obstinately. He knew nothing.

"Whar' de lan'lord? He help me fin' her."

Jan pointed to the adjoining house.

"Busy. No come," he said, laconically.

Jake turned away from the door and had just taken hold of his horse's bridle when around the other side of the house came a man who seemed to him most familiar.

In Philadelphia, that day, Margaret had told Jake that should they meet Rodney unexpectedly, or recognise him in any disguise, they must not show recognition or surprise. The warning had remained in Jake's memory. He therefore paid this man no special heed. The curious Jan might see or hear.

But Rodney knew that Jan could not hear at that distance. And Jan knew Mr. Kelper quite well. There was no mischief in Mr. Kelper.

"Jake! You come for your mistress?"

"Yes, Massa Rodney," Jake whispered.

"She is in this side of the house. In the back room. Doctor Worthington is with her."

"De debbel!"

"Yes. Now tell me, Jake. Know you anything of Henry Murray? Where is he? Where is he?"

"He comin' 'long berry soon, now. Be heah soon."

"Which road? By the ferry here, or from Cliveden?"

"Needer way, massa. He come from Valley Forge, 'cross Swedes Ford."

"Then I will walk up the road and meet him and tell him where your mistress is. Take good care of her, Jake. And be sure not to let Doctor Worthington go to the city with these British. Keep him here till we come."

"Yes, massa."

Bingham waited no longer, but hurried up the road. This time Jake entered the tavern without the ceremony of knocking. Jan was in the tap-room, opening the shutters. A maid servant was seen at the head of the stairs. She also was yawning in right vehement fashion.

"Doctah Worthington lib' heah?" asked Jake.

Jan nodded.

"Whar is he?"

The Dutchman shook his head.

"You fin' him for me quick."

Jan shook his head again.

"Whar is his office?"

The maid servant had come to the bottom of the stairs. She pointed to a room at the end of a long passageway. Jake rushed past her down the passage and into the surgery. It was dark and silent. Then he turned back to Jan who had closely followed him.

"You fin' Doctah Worthington for me quick, or you fin' dis bullet in your skull," he exclaimed.

The intruder's huge size and the murderous-looking weapon in his hand were potent arguments. The frightened Dutchman forgot all instructions. He pointed with trembling finger at the closed door at the further end of the room.

"Open de doah quick."

The Dutchman shrugged his broad shoulders.

Jake tapped smartly on the door. Then he bent down to listen at the keyhole. He gave the knob a vigorous, unfriendly shake. He could hear a chair move within, then a step cross the room.

"Who is there?" called an impatient voice.

"Open de doah."

"Who is there?" called Worthington a second time.

"Open de doah or I fire in de lock, an' den 'twill open."

Jan motioned eagerly. The key was creaking in the rusty lock. The door opened a little way. Before it could be closed, as closed it might soon be were Worthington to see the intruder plainly — Jake, quick as a flash, with a sweep of his mighty arm, thrust Worthington aside and darted through the space of light. But once inside, he looked around in vain for whom he sought. There was no one in the room but Worthington.

"Whar is my missy?" he said, hoarsely, and his fist doubled up as if he would strike. In his other hand he held the pistol.

"She is not here."

"She mus' be. You gib her to me mighty quick, Massa Doctah."

Jake's voice trembled with passion.

Doctor Worthington smiled.

"You rave, you black rascal; go home and sleep it off — sleep it off."

But Jake's keen eyes had been searching through the gloom of the shadowy room. At its farthest end was another door. In it was a key. He was quick. Ere Worthington could guess his purpose, he had made a dash to the door and flung it open. Then had closed it even more quickly, and locked it on the inside.

In the centre of the room stood Margaret, leaning against the table. The morning sun came behind her through the narrow panes of the window and fell in little chequers across the floor.

Jake flung himself on his knees at Margaret's feet.

"T'ank de Lord, missy; you safe heah. You tole me to ride on, missy. I did right to leab you? You tole me to ride on."

Margaret put her hand tenderly on his head.

"You did right, Jake, my Jake. You are always right. But — but — "

She stopped in fear and dread.

"Yes, missy, I got dare in time — in time. My dear Cappin's safe. T'ank de Lord for dat."

Margaret swayed. Jake sprang up and caught her in his arms. But she recovered herself quickly, and sank in the chair. The next moment she had buried her face in her hands on the table.

Her sobs distressed Jake sorely.

"Dare, missy, doan' do dat. Doan' do dat, missy, dear."

Then he turned in helpless appeal to Dame Van Slycke. She had been standing near the window. She looked pale and haggard in the searching morning light, and her thin gray hair was in disorder.

She walked slowly and feebly over to Margaret and placed her hand on her shoulder as if with the wish to help her.

"Tell her all," said the hostess. "She has the wish to know, though she cannot speak just now. Tell her where her brother is."

"Massa Henry comin' 'long soon heah. I leff him in de camp talkin' to de Gen'ral."

"Then he was not made prisoner. Doctor Worthington spoke not the truth!"

"I doan' know. I doan' know. When I seen

Massa Henry dare wid de Gen'ral I knowed all was right. An' I had to hurry away to fin' my missy."

Chloe had often said that Jake lacked an eloquent tongue. But his simple dignity now; his unconsciousness of self; his absorption in his mistress made both face and voice eloquent.

"I got dare fust. Eben ef de sentries had stopped me, I'd 'a' dashed froo. Tempest, good, true hoss, after he once ober his fright. I got to de Gen'ral. 'You wait proceedin's,' I says to de Gen'ral. 'You do nothin' to my Cappin till Massa Henry or Missy Margaret come. They tell you he doan' mean no harm to you' gov'ment. He good man an' hones' British sojer; an' it break my missy's heart ef he doan' come back to her.'. . . I knowed I could trus' dat Gen'ral. I tole him I mus' ride back an' fin' my missy; an' he gib me promise dat he tell Massa Henry when he come, an' dat he make it all right for my dear Cappin."

Jake paused for breath; then as Margaret was still silent, he continued:

"Gen'ral Washington mighty kin' man, missy. Dese ole eyes like to look at him. Wish he'd come an' lib at Clibeden all de time an' let dis ole war manage on its own legs. Eber seen Blueskin, missy? I'd like to take care ob dat hoss. Mos' as good a hoss as my dear Cappin's Brown Bess."

Jake could think of nothing more to comfort his mistress. He ventured to touch her arm furtively. His honest eyes were full of trouble.

"Dare, dare, missy, dear. Doan' do dat. You pow'ful tired. Cawn't take you home till you hab some res'. You pow'ful tired."

" Let us go home, Jake. Now, now."

And Margaret started to her feet. But Dame Van Slycke interposed.

" I will get some coffee for you if you can spare me."

Margaret nodded.

" I thank you, yes."

" Yes, dat's de berry t'ing for you, missy. Gib you strength. We had some pow'ful hard rides yesterday, missy."

Margaret smiled up into his face. The smile was a faint one, and it was sad. But it made Jake's heart glow.

He went to the door with the hostess. He had just turned the key, when the door was flung violently open.

Doctor Worthington stood on the threshold.

" You lie, you black rascal," he shouted, vehemently. " Henry Murray is Musgrave's prisoner."

Jake's soft eyes flashed.

" I doan' lie, massa. I leff Massa Henry talkin' to Gen'ral Washington. He be 'long berry soon now."

Worthington looked from Jake to Margaret. Their faces told him of the ruin of his hopes. For a moment agitation and fear looked out from his own face. Then the mask came over it once more.

He turned to the door. His hand was on the key. But Jake was too quick for him. His hand was thrust aside and the key was wrenched out from the lock. Then Jake went through the other rooms and took the keys from all the doors.

Doctor Worthington laughed.

" If you interfere with me much more, you black rascal, you will repent it."

And his hand went to his belt. Margaret saw that in the belt were knife and pistol.

" And Henry Murray, if he dare venture to this inn, will get into a hornet's nest. He escaped by foul means from their hands. They like not the disgrace of losing their prisoner. For see, Musgrave, Tarleton, and the others have returned for him. They are in the adjoining house. See! "

Worthington went to one of the south windows and threw open the shutters. Jake followed him and looked out. The courtyard was already filling with noisy troopers. There were gleams of scarlet coats passing the windows opposite.

" That captain just within the window is Oliver De Lancey, — John André's friend. They both are friends of Arthur Peyton. De Lancey's ire is stirred against Henry Murray, for he believes that 'tis he who has been the cause of Peyton's capture and disgrace. . . . See! There is Musgrave. There is Stoddard, — Stoddard, the man of learning and of gentle manners. Henry Murray will have a sorry time with these friends of Peyton's when he arrives."

Worthington turned and looked at Margaret with a strange, hard smile. He could not forbear this one more thrust to make her suffer. Why had he not spoken of the young Lieutenant? Had he not noticed that the friend of Peyton, — the friend of all friends, was not there?

Jake quickly interposed to relieve his mistress's fears.

" Nebber you min', missy. Massa Rod— "

Jake caught himself in time. "A man done gone to meet Massa Henry an' tell him all 'bout dese British. No harm come to Massa Henry. Nebber you feah."

But in his heart, Jake feared disaster. Worthington's words had set him thinking. Would Massa Rodney warn his master? Would he make it clear to him about the presence of these British here?

Jake's thoughts made him restless; and he became all the more restless as he noted the look on Worthington's face.

He turned and watched the swiftly moving redcoats for a moment or two. Then he went towards the door.

"I be back soon, missy. I jus' go to a front window to see if Massa Henry comin' 'long de road."

The next moment Margaret was alone with Doctor Worthington. Why did he not go? Why did he persist in remaining?

"Why will you not go while you have time?" she asked. "Of a truth, there is need for haste."

His face darkened. He shook his head.

"You know that you are lost if you meet my brother. I cannot have you meet him. He will soon make everything clear to these Englishmen. In truth, you know that he will tell them of all your treachery to their friend. Think you, they would have patience with you? Go! I implore you."

"You fear for your brother," he sneered. "You have cause to fear."

Margaret saw that his hand still rested on his belt, in which were knife and pistol. She saw, also, the grim determination in his face.

As by a flash of intuition she knew his plan. Even at his own peril he had intention to remain until her brother came. He would fire upon him as he entered that door. He would take Henry Murray by surprise. And Jake himself might suffer harm.

She was in desperate case, and she made a quick resolve.

With a rush she was upon him. His hand was seized by the firm, nervous grasp of her right one. She would have had no advantage whatever had he not been taken so completely by surprise. Ere he could draw out the pistol it was in her hand and she had sprung back. He started towards her; but she held it out. He stopped irresolutely. He saw firm determination in her eyes; and her hand was as steady as his own would have been.

" Doctor Worthington, you come one step nearer and I fire. . . . Put your knife on that table."

He hesitated, but she compelled him. He went and laid the knife on the table.

" Now your sword."

He hesitated. But her face had the same look her brother's had when he had fought the night before, and his blade had been like a beam of light.

" Doctor Worthington," she said, " you *must* obey. Be assured that I am brought to a desperate case. Your sword *must* be put beside that knife."

He held his head high; but with dark and scowling face he laid his sword on the table.

" Doctor Worthington, you must go."

" Without defence," he said, bitterly. " I am a desperate man, Margaret. Beware! "

" You move towards me and I fire. Now go —
while you have time. You know that you are lost
if you meet my brother. . . . I have no reason to
depend upon your honour or your truth. But I feel
that you will do as I wish. You will take your
horse, ride to the city, and never come again."

She compelled him by the authority and the
solemnity of her look.

He gazed at her as if fascinated. Then his head
bent as if in shame. His fingers twitched nervously.

He turned towards the door; then went swiftly
from the room.

CHAPTER LVI.

"Love, not hate; forgiveness, not revenge, is what we all need."

COLONEL MUSGRAVE had eaten nothing; and he had been most silent and morose. Even the feeble attempts at cheerful talk made by Major Stoddard and Captain De Lancey met with scant response. A feeling of coming disaster haunted the Colonel's heart. The suspense in regard to Greyson and the Lieutenant was fretting to one of his impatient temperament. If ill had befallen them; or if those rebels had taken them, too, prisoner, he felt he could scarce bear the disgrace. As for Peyton's danger — the pain of that was beyond words.

He had given orders that they should ride on; and the troopers were already bringing out the horses, when he chanced to look out the window that commanded a view of the road in front. He started from his chair excitedly.

"Boys! Look, look! Our prisoner!"

And in truth there was Henry Murray just appearing on the top of the hill. He was alone.

"Leave him to me," Musgrave cried. "Put up your sword, Tarleton. Niggard, lower that pistol." And the Colonel raised a warning hand.

461

"No fear of his escaping us. We have him sure."

The next moment the Colonel had sprung through the window and was running across the courtyard. Just as Murray rode up to the left wing of the house he came face to face with the angry Englishman.

The other officers crowded around the window and watched and waited.

"Egad! Murray shows no fear," said Tarleton. "He seems rather to wish to speak with Musgrave than to avoid him. See! he goes to meet him and he acts as if he wished to talk to him."

They waited in silence; then Niggard spoke.

"There is no anger in Musgrave's face now. What on earth has happened?"

"Egad!" said Tarleton again. "I believe the old man was right. His daughter, he said, had ridden to Valley Forge to get Peyton freed. 'Twas all a mistake, and we would have our Captain yet."

"Mere guesswork, Tarleton," said Niggard, laughing.

"We were so angry we would listen to no explanations," said Stoddard. "We hurried out and seized Murray as if he were a common thief. But Tarleton, why think you that Peyton is safe? Methinks you jump to swift conclusions."

"What reason have you to think that?" asked De Lancey.

But Tarleton did not answer. His far-seeing eyes were busied with the two men in the distance.

"Look, look! Murray is moved over something, as if he had brought bad news. See, he has covered his eyes with his hand a moment. . . . A man does that not often. . . . Tom, too, seems to be troubled."

Again a moment of silence, then Tarleton spoke again:

"They are talking of it still. See, Murray is pointing up the road. Musgrave is saying he will go. He is nodding assent."

"The anger is coming again into Tom's face."

"But 'tis not with Murray that he is angry."

"No; for see, Murray has put his hand on Tom's shoulder as if in friendly protest."

"There! Musgrave seems satisfied. He is nodding his head again."

De Lancey laughed.

"Well, boys, we are like children. In good truth, we know little and we are guessing at random and idly watching. If we could hear their voices, and understand an iota of what they are saying, we might know something. As it is, we know nothing to give their actions meaning. I, for one, can make little out of the matter. 'Tis better that we leave conjectures alone. . . . Let us be men, not children."

"Yes, let us not be consumed with curiosity," said Niggard. "Let us be philosophers like Stoddard."

But neither Niggard nor De Lancey took the good advice they gave. They continued to look out the window and watch the two men across the yard. And it must be confessed that De Lancey longed to join them and take his own share in the talk.

Then he saw that Murray was dismounting, and wonder of wonders, he was grasping Musgrave's hand as if in friendly farewell. Then Musgrave must have bethought himself of something else to say, for he began talking once more.

Finally the conference seemed ended. Henry Murray went into the adjoining house; and the Colonel with bent head came slowly back across the courtyard. When he got near enough for them to see his face, a strange and sudden hush fell upon the group of waiting officers. Arrived at the door, Musgrave whispered something to Tarleton, and then turned away to hide his emotion.

A few moments after that, officers and men had mounted and were riding up the road, their scarlet coats against the tender green of the trees making a bright and brilliant dash of colour.

Then they disappeared, and the green alone remained. But the sunshine fell upon it and touched it with beauty.

CHAPTER LVII.

"And blended with this love for you has been this tenderness for her."

SHE was alone, and she felt she could for a few moments give way to the pain that was becoming almost unbearable. . . . Last night, it had seemed that if she could but know that he was safe, she would be content. But now she wanted something more.

"If I could but see him once again just to ask for his forgiveness! Then he might go. I might be able to bear it then! But he will not come. I shall never see him again."

She paid no heed to the hurrying footsteps in the courtyard, the stamping of hoofs, the creaking of the still damp saddles, the jingling of the spurs and swords. The tavern grew hushed and quiet; and still she was fighting this battle with herself, fighting this pain, this desperate longing. . . . She had been so cruel, so hard, so blind. She would never be able to win from herself forgiveness. He might forgive her; but she could — never. This deep humiliation, this regret, this heartache, were punishment in truth.

"Oh! that my heart should suffer so much and not break!"

465

Through the adjoining room came swift foot-steps. They were her brother's.

She listened in vain for other footsteps. Her back was to the door when Henry Murray entered, for she felt strangely loath that he should see how deeply moved she was.

His dress was in disorder, his coat was torn, and there was a slash across his forehead.

" Margaret! " he exclaimed, as he came up behind her. " Oh! I have suffered for fear of you."

" But he — he is safe," she answered, huskily.

" Ay. 'Twas Jake got there first. I was not far behind. In truth, 'twas not too soon. Not that he was in immediate danger of his life, — they would have waited a fitting time; but the proofs were so overwhelming that they would have thought further investigation scarce necessary. And your testimony, Margaret, had great weight. . . . And yet they were kind to him, Margaret. Well I know you like to hear that."

" But to be brought before Hamilton, to have his hands bound, to suffer the humiliation of Lee's scorn. Oh! the shame of it! The shame of it! "

Henry laid his hand soothingly on her shoulder.

" Peyton was closeted with Hamilton and the General when I got there. They both were rejoicing over the news that Jake brought, but they understood not the whole matter till I told of Worthington. It seems that the General and Hamilton distrusted him from the first, yet could never find aught to justify their thought. And it seems that Captain Peyton has known all the time that there was a spy near us, but his honour as a British soldier forbade his betraying the secret. In truth, it has been a pretty tangle, Margaret."

" He can never forgive me," said Margaret, in a low tone. " It is useless to hope."

" What are you saying, dear ? "

" Nothing," she answered, faintly.

" Margaret, the more I think of it, the more of a tangle seems it, and the more foolish and — and blind seems our trust in this Worthington. And our trust in ourselves, Margaret! It seems as if I could never trust myself again. I have been so weak, so self-confident, so proud of my own judgment, so proud of my own pride. I have been ungrateful, blind to the beauty and the sweetness of a service which was godlike in its kindness. I have made so many mistakes."

She turned and looked up at him as he paused. Then she started from her chair impulsively.

" A mischance has happened to you, Harry? "

" Ay, I escaped, but 'twas with difficulty."

" Escaped! Then those redcoats molested you! Doctor Worthington spoke truth!"

" They bound me and dragged me to their horses. Lieutenant Shipton kept close beside me. When Musgrave turned to give some order, he whispered in my ear: 'I will cut your cords as soon as possible. In the darkness it will not be seen. Seize your first chance.' Then he turned away. Soon afterwards he whispered again, 'Should we never meet more, remember.' Then his voice grew husky."

Henry Murray paused a moment. He was evidently deeply moved.

" 'Remember,' said he, 'my love for you all. Arthur Peyton loves her, and you are her brother.

I cannot bear that she suffer. It makes me forget my duty.' Then he turned away. The next moment we saw on the road before us a troop of rebels, — a foraging party as it chanced. Musgrave's ire had been flaming all the way. In faith, he had not ceased to curse us all from the moment that Worthington had told him 'twas I, 'twas you, who had put Peyton into this danger."

Henry Murray began walking up and down the room restlessly.

"Musgrave ordered a rash attack. With the others I was carried in a mad rush upon the party from Valley Forge. Quick shots were fired. There were sword-thrusts in the darkness. All at once I felt a quick lunge at the cords around my wrists. See the place where the knife cut the flesh. I turned my horse suddenly and was with the Americans the next moment. Methinks the change was scarce noticed, save that I got this slash from a British trooper as I dashed past him. . . . Ere the British drew off I caught sight of — of — of Shipton's face as he fell across the saddle because of a knife-thrust dealt most treacherously, most damnably."

Henry Murray's voice choked. He turned away, and his hand went up to his eyes.

Margaret's face grew white.

"And he perished?" she asked, faintly.

Henry Murray was silent. He walked to the window, then back, ere he had conquered his emotion enough to speak.

"There is a little farmhouse up the road, not far from Rittenhouse's. You can see its red roof from the front windows. . . . He is there, Margaret."

A great wave of grief swept over her. Then her head went down on the table. She could not feel even the relief of tears.

" We were riding hither, past the house, when a boy ran out and hailed us. He had been twice to this tavern, but could make no one hear. Rodney has told me how this could have happened. The hostess was shut in here with you. A British officer was dying at the farmhouse. Another officer who was with him begged our aid, as his troop had swept on into the city, and might not return in time. We halted at the house. Judge of our surprise when 'twas Greyson who met us at the door. We were too late. 'Twas all over, Margaret. I can never tell him how I thank him for what he did for me last October. And I have wanted so to tell him. . . . The dear lad had — had — had — "

But Henry Murray could speak no more.

" You will go and bring him home — home — to — us ? " asked Margaret, huskily.

" Yes."

There was a long pause, then Henry said, softly:

" We will put him with those other heroes in the garden beside the wall."

" Yes, yes."

Another pause, then Henry Murray said:

" In truth, I shall not feel content till we have taken Worthington to Valley Forge."

" Worthington ! "

" Ay, 'twas his knife that did it. I saw it plainly. I saw him do it. I saw his devil's face. Then he wheeled his horse and galloped back the road he had come. Methinks he bore the lad some grudge, or Shipton knew too many of his dark secrets. . . .

Washington *must* have opportunity to have a reckoning with him, which will compensate us for our sorrow."

"No, Henry, nothing can do that. No revenge can compensate for sorrow. Love, not hate, forgiveness, not revenge, is what we all need. And our sins, our errors, nothing can undo them."

And Margaret was again thinking sadly of her own mistakes and lack of trust. And her heart was very sore because of the words of scorn that had hurt the man who loved her.

If she might see him once more, to ask for his forgiveness. But he would not come. She would never see him again!

"If I could but spare him this fresh sorrow," she thought. "If I could but bear it for him. O that I could!"

She rose restlessly from her seat by the table.

"There are Doctor Worthington's sword and pistol," she said. "If he is caught, he can do none of you harm, for he is unarmed."

Henry looked at her in surprise.

"Worthington is safely in our hands, Margaret. Rodney and Jake have him in charge."

"Rodney!"

"Ay, to him owe we the discovery of the mischief which has well-nigh been our ruin. . . . I have much to tell you when I have time. . . . Musgrave wanted Worthington. But he yielded him to me. Methinks he would have shorter shrift with Musgrave than with me."

"O Henry, let us try to have pity for him."

"This from you!"

"By our own mistakes and sorrows," she said, solemnly, "let us learn to have pity."

Henry walked to the window, then back once more.

"'Tis utterly impossible to forgive this man, Margaret. I shall not try. He deserves nothing from us."

"I know it, Henry, I know it."

"And till he has sorrow for his own misdeeds, we are not required to think of him with aught but righteous anger."

"For hours, Henry, I have been fighting my anger against this man."

"Well, fight no more, Margaret."

"Henry, I have suffered more these past few hours than I had thought I could suffer, and I have had much humiliation, because of my own mistakes. . . . Henry, I am not one to talk of my feelings. You know that. I cannot do it now. But by my own suffering, I have begun to catch one little glimpse of what love and pity and forgiveness are."

"That man deserves punishment," said Henry Murray, fiercely.

"I know it, Henry, and he must have it. 'Tis not that I mean."

There was a moment of silence between them, then Henry spoke.

"'Twas pitiful to see the grief of Shipton's friend, Margaret. It cut me to the heart. I left Peyton in the farmhouse."

Margaret's breath came in a low sob. She put out her hand blindly and caught the edge of the table. Her brother hastened to her, and put her gently in the chair. She bowed her head on the table and he leaned over her.

"Margaret," he said, tenderly. "We will try and forget Worthington, and we will try to bear this fresh sorrow. Peyton's friends are with him now. Their sympathy will help him. They all loved the lad. They all loved him.

"And now, dear, I want to tell you what the General said of you. . . . I told him of your love, dear. He would have been pleased, he said, to see you wed one of your own countrymen; but love, he added, is a gift sent down from Heaven itself, to bless this sad, distracted world. These injustices, this fighting of brother against brother, belong to earth. They are not of Heaven. He fights against Heaven who takes not love into his soul. And, therefore, he was glad, dear Margaret, that you have had the courage to look love in the face, and feel its power and its glory. From what I told him, he said he knows this man is worthy."

Henry Murray laid his hand on Margaret's bowed head. His voice trembled as he continued:

"When this war is over, and, please God, we meet again, he hoped, dear Margaret, to see you happy. And then in almost a whisper I caught the words: 'She deserves to be happy. I would I had such a daughter. My friend is rich.'"

Margaret put out her hand to her brother with a quick, passionate impulse. He bent to kiss it.

Margaret did not hear the quiet step in the adjoining room.

But Henry Murray saw Peyton at the door.

He raised his hand to him in caution. Then
motioned to the bowed figure at the table. . . .

Peyton stood there in silence, looking at Margaret.
Then he went over to her and laid his hand on her
head. . . . She looked up and saw that it was he.
She sprang to her feet — uncertainty, hope, joy,
and contrition struggled for mastery in her face.

" Margaret! " he said.

She put her hand on his shoulder and held him
off, searching his face, tenderness, sorrow, exquisite
pleading in her eyes.

" Arthur! Love! Can you forgive me? "

He opened his arms and she threw herself sobbing
on his breast.

THE END.